OPEN SKIES

OPEN SKIES

MY LIFE AS AFGHANISTAN'S
FIRST FEMALE PILOT

NILOOFAR
RAHMANI
WITH ADAM SIKES

CHICAGO
REVIEW
PRESS

Published by Chicago Review Press Incorporated
814 North Franklin Street
Chicago, Illinois 60610
ISBN 978-1-64160-334-8

Library of Congress Control Number: 2021934716

Typesetting: Nord Compo

Printed in the United States of America
5 4 3 2 1

For all the women of Afghanistan who dream

CONTENTS

Author's Note   ix

Preface xi
1   My Father 1
2   The Soviets 9
3   Courtship 16
4   Civil War 22
5   Escape 31
6   The Refugee Camp 39
7   Karachi 47
8   Our Return 53
9   Life Under the Taliban 62
10   September 11, 2001 70
11   Invasion and Freedom 76
12   School 85
13   Not Everything Changes 94
14   Dreams Form 98
15   University 104
16   A Commercial 107

17 Recruitment 111

18 Basic Training 115

19 Friends, Reflection, and Graduation 121

20 Joining the Air Force 127

21 Medical Test and More Tests 134

22 English Is a Requirement .138

23 Move West 143

24 Flight Training 150

25 First Flight 157

26 Things Change. 168

27 Up Where I Belong. 174

28 Outed. 181

29 Graduation 191

30 The Squadron. 194

31 Flying Operations. 200

32 The Threats Come. 207

33 India and AWOL. 213

34 Back in the Air 222

35 Contacts 229

36 The United States 236

37 My Return 240

38 Everything Crumbles. 244

39 Opportunity. 250

40 Back in Training. 255

41 Asylum 262

42 What's Next 267

Afterword. 269

Acknowledgments 271

AUTHOR'S NOTE

EVERYTHING IN THIS BOOK is true to the best of the author's recollection. Some conversations have been re-created from memory, and certain names have been changed for privacy and/or security reasons. All fictional names are indicated by the use of SMALL CAPS on first mention. Any similarity between the fictionalized names and the names of real people is strictly coincidental.

PREFACE

I WAS FIVE YEARS OLD the first time my father told me about our homeland. We were living in Karachi, Pakistan, having recently left one of the refugee camps that lined the border. It was 1996, and my family had escaped from Afghanistan and the rise of the Taliban just a few years before.

My father used to say he grew up in Paris. Not Paris, France, of course, but Kabul—the "Paris of Central Asia"—during Afghanistan's golden era that lasted from 1919 to 1979.

I wish I could have experienced this period in Afghanistan's history—the culture, the energy, the freedom—but I was born long after *that* Afghanistan had been wiped from the face of the earth. The Soviets and the Taliban, with all their brutality, made sure of that.

Still, when my father talks about his childhood and what it was like growing up in Kabul in the 1960s and '70s, I can see it all, like I'm right there beside him—touching, hearing, smelling, tasting, and feeling. I'm in the bazaar sipping green tea mixed with cinnamon, cardamom, saffron, and sugar, with the heavy scent of incense wafting out from the cafés. Men in suits and women in skirts are discussing Greek philosophy and business, sharing a plate of spiced kebab. A university student taps his thumb on the steering wheel while a Beatles tune blares out of the car radio. When I close my eyes and listen to my father tell these stories, nothing is more real.

This land was and still is my home, my country, and a place I was willing to die for.

Ironically, it's also a place I would eventually flee because the very people I'd sworn to defend and fight alongside would come to threaten my life and those closest to me. They hated me, my family, and everything we represented.

As an Afghan woman, I dared to dream, and there were some who believed I should be punished for it, perhaps even killed. But I didn't let them stop me. I became Afghanistan's first female fixed-wing pilot and a captain in the Afghan Air Force.

My name is Niloofar Rahmani, and this is the story of my father, my family, and me.

My first memories of having a roof over my head are from Karachi. We lived in a modest apartment with a single room for the five of us—my parents, my older brother and sister, and me; my two younger siblings hadn't been born yet.

The place wasn't much to speak of, but it had four walls, two windows with real glass, a door with a lock, electricity sometimes, shelter from the wind, and a bed that wasn't on the sandy, gritty earth. Compared to the camps where we'd lived for the past four years, crowded among hundreds of thousands of other refugees, with only a tent on the hard ground, this place was luxurious. It was a whole new world for me, with all new sights and sounds and people—and there was a playground outside.

The day we arrived in Karachi, I bubbled up inside when I saw the swings and the other children playing. They had huge grins on their faces, some with missing front teeth, and they were shouting with joy and laughing. I don't think anyone can help but smile when they hear children giggling or see them with smiles stretched from ear to ear or watch them running in circles chasing the wind and each other. I could barely contain myself and began hopping up and down and squirming—everything you'd expect from a typical five-year-old with too much energy.

Once my mother had had enough and finally released me, I charged outside, laughing and yelling, with my older brother and sister in tow. We wove in and around the other children, over the rocks and across the sandy lot, racing toward a big, beautiful, amazing swing that we knew would take us soaring into the sky. The sun was shining, there was a cool breeze, and laughter echoed against the surrounding apartment buildings. We were safe and free here.

I reached the swing first and flashed a big smile at my brother and sister, delighted at my victory. Even at a young age, I was very fast, and I'd beaten them once again. I jumped onto the swing and started pumping my legs forward and backward. I strained and leaned as hard as I could, but I was only five, and my expectations of instantly launching up toward the clouds with great speed didn't exactly pan out as I'd hoped. There was a lot of struggling and kicking with very little actual swinging. Still, I was determined.

Then a boy who was about seven years old approached me. I didn't know him, but I smiled anyway. This was a wonderful place and a beautiful day, and I thought he wanted to play with me.

There were lots of children playing together; at the time, I thought there must have been over a hundred boys and girls on the playground, though in reality there were probably only twenty or so. The playground wasn't all that big, just a small scrap of earth wedged between windbeaten brown and gray concrete buildings with the usual amount of trash, standing water, and broken glass common in Karachi's poorer neighborhoods. When you're just a child and you've only ever seen a playground once or twice before, even the simplest of play areas is a glorious sight.

This boy who came up to me, however, didn't want to play. Instead, he started yelling at me. I didn't understand what he was saying, perhaps because he was shouting or maybe because I didn't know the language he was speaking. I don't know and it doesn't matter; the look he gave me said it all. His eyes were full of spite, and he had a scowl on his face that frightened me. I remember wondering if I'd done something wrong.

Without warning, the boy pushed me off the swing. His bony hands hit my shoulders and back, and I fell. My hands and knees scraped the rocky ground, and I started bleeding. I began to cry, shocked at what this boy had done—a boy with so much anger and malice in his eyes.

While still on the ground, I heard my brother's voice. Through my tears, I looked up and watched him confront the boy. They were both yelling, their arms waving in the air and in each other's faces. I still didn't understand what the boy was saying, until the end when I heard him spit, "Go away, dirty Afghans. This is not your place."

At five years old, I didn't know what he meant by that, but I absolutely understood something was terribly wrong and we were not wanted here. The boy was jabbing his finger at the air and telling us to go away, over and over again.

This hurt more than the cuts on my hands and knees. This place where I thought we'd have so much fun struck me now as foreign and strange, and it scared me. My chest tightened and I wanted to run—I wanted my father.

I felt my brother's and my sister's hands pick me up, and they walked me off the playground toward our apartment, but as we neared our building I pushed them off and ran. I scampered up the stairs and burst through the front door, tears streaming down my face, with dirt and blood smeared on my skin and clothes. My father was standing on the other side of the room, and I rushed into his arms.

Through my sobs I kept repeating, "Baba Jan, Baba Jan," which means "my dear father." I asked him: Where do we come from? Why are we here? Where is our country and our home? Why are these people mean to us? I was just a little girl and too young to know what hate and xenophobia really were and what it meant to be a refugee, but the scowl on that boy's face haunted me. I wanted answers.

Then, finally succumbing to the warmth of my father's embrace, I looked up at him as he wiped my tears. I've always considered my father a handsome man, with his brown eyes and brown hair, rectangular face and square jaw, and keen stare. Wrapped in the strength of his arms and calloused hands, I always felt truly safe. When he saw the hurt in my eyes, he held me tight against his chest. I could feel his presence protecting every part of me, like a shield behind which nothing could hurt me, including that boy.

He sat me down, took my tiny hands in his, and asked what happened. I told him what the boy had said, and I repeated my questions. Why did he say that? Where is our home? I knew we had just moved, but there had to be more to why that boy said we didn't belong here.

My father looked at me with hurt in his eyes, though it wasn't just the hurt that a parent feels when their child cries over a skinned knee; it was something deeper. I saw intense pain and loss, and a sense of helplessness in his face that I'd never seen before. But instead of revealing this deep sense to me, he forced a smile.

He told me to forget that boy—he was a bully, my father said—and that we came from a beautiful country. Our home was Afghanistan, a place full of culture and life. It had learning, music, movies, football, kites, food, fashion, a history dating back thousands of years, and freedom.

He dazzled me with descriptions of a bustling city where men and women from around the world would meet, work, sit, smoke, and drink tea. There were bazaars and markets where you could haggle over the price of fresh fruits and vegetables, fabric for clothing, handmade carpets, or meticulously crafted ornaments. He told me about a place where all children—boys *and* girls—went to school, and where the women were as free as the men. It was a place for family, a place where we had cousins, aunts, uncles, and grandparents. Spread across the region were homes filled with warm laughter and enough food for everyone to eat their fill.

When I heard my father describe these things, I imagined a magical place and wanted to know more, and I wanted to know why we had left. It sounded perfect.

My ears were too young to hear the full story of what had happened to our country with the wars and the Taliban regime, so my father simply smiled. The pain that I'd seen in his eyes was gone, replaced by joyful memories. Still, I pressed him until he told me about his life and our home.

I didn't know it at the time, but I think this was the moment when my dreams of flying, serving my country, and fighting for the rights and freedom of others took root.

1

MY FATHER

MY FATHER WAS BORN MARCH 8, 1965, to my grandfather Abdul Jamil Rahmani and my grandmother Bebe Gol at Rabia Balkhi Hospital in Kabul. They named their son Abdolwakil, but from the beginning they called him Nooragha, meaning "bright man."

Allegedly, my father was the perfect little boy. I say "allegedly" because I suspect most parents think they have a perfect child when he or she spends time awake smiling and cooing, and sleeps peacefully. Nevertheless, having personally observed my father's disposition over the decades, I'm not surprised they described him that way. He's a gentle soul, yet stronger than anyone I know.

My father was the firstborn of seven children, five boys and two girls, and they lived in a humble family dwelling with two rooms in the Dih Qalander area of Kabul. Although Kabul was a thriving city with free education and a developing economy, many people were destitute. Most families had between four and seven children (family planning in the Western sense was nonexistent), and as the families grew in numbers, food and basic necessities often became scarce.

My father's early years were no different. My grandparents weren't rich. They were uneducated and barely middle class, and they struggled for everything they had. If the house needed a repair, my grandfather and his sons would do it, often cobbling together the fix from whatever they could scrounge. If clothes ripped or wore through, my grandmother would mend them. The little amount of food they had was strictly portioned, and there were many nights my father and his siblings went to bed hungry.

Being the eldest, my father was keenly aware of the pain and discomfort his younger brothers and sisters felt. A child's cries from an empty stomach are some of the most heart-wrenching sounds one can hear, and in situations where there isn't anything more to eat, the cries don't stop.

My father couldn't resign himself to watching his siblings start the day on empty stomachs. When he was ten he began working to bring in whatever additional money he could. It still amazes me that as a ten-year-old he considered it his responsibility to go out and work. He didn't ask others to work harder; he took the burden upon himself and chose to better his family's situation through his own labors. Rather than coming home after school to play football—soccer—or fly kites, my father walked three miles to my grandfather's woodshop and worked into the evening. It was hard, physical work laboring next to grown men, but he did it well for many years.

At the end of each day, father and son would walk home together, but instead of going to bed for a good night's rest to be ready for school the next day, my father would venture out into the kiln yards on the city's edge to make bricks by hand. He'd knead the clay and water with his tiny fingers, packing the gritty mix into wooden molds, which he'd carry over to the drying beds to bake in the next day's sun. My ten-year-old father toiled hunched over or on his hands and knees, while the previous day's bricks were fired in massive kilns that sent black soot into the air, soot that filled his every breath. He'd do this every night until he reached his quota of more than one hundred bricks.

Afghan nights can be bitterly cold, and for anyone subjected to these conditions, it's hard, skin-cracking work. Sometimes my father would fall asleep standing up or kneeling at his work station, and one of his friends, another boy about his age, would slap him to wake him up. A hard whack to the shoulder or back of the head usually sufficed, and my father was grateful for these jolts. He had a family to help provide for, and he couldn't waste time or get fired for laziness.

This was not a carefree childhood, but my father worked hard, earned a small amount of money to help the family, and felt proud to do it. And despite these challenges, my father grew up in a loving household and had lofty dreams. During this period of Afghanistan's history, men and women—even the poorest among them—had many opportunities. Kabul truly was the Paris of Central Asia.

Between 1933 and 1973, the country was united under a king, Mohammed Zahir Shah. He was nineteen years old when he took the throne after his father, Mohammed Nadir Shah, was assassinated in 1933. Afghanistan had been a sovereign and independent state since 1919, after the conclusion of the Third Anglo-Afghan War, and the various rulers who preceded Zahir Shah had set the country on a course for modernization that he dutifully continued.

Afghanistan established diplomatic relations with the world powers, joined the League of Nations, and encouraged foreign investment and tourism. The government made elementary education compulsory for all children, and the authorities abolished the medieval burka. Women were seen as equal to men in many ways, and even were able to vote a year before women in the United States.

The various ethnic groups that composed Afghanistan's dispersed population—Pashtuns, Hazaras, Tajiks, Uzbeks, and others—also began to assume a national identity.

Of course, there were growing pains. Some tribal leaders were less than enthusiastic about the changes emanating from the capital, but no one could deny that this landlocked country, which had a wild and proud history dating all the way back to the ancient Greeks and Alexander the Great, was moving steadily and confidently through the twentieth century.

By the mid-1970s, my father had grown into a tall, broad-shouldered boy who liked wearing blue jeans and T-shirts, and who on occasion took his mother and siblings to the cinema to see the latest flick out of Bombay (now Mumbai). He'd also scraped and saved to buy himself notebooks for school and dresses for his mother and sisters.

My father looked to his future, and with his inclination toward math and his experience working as a carpenter with my grandfather, he aspired to attend Kabul Polytechnic University and earn a degree in construction engineering. He also wanted a family of his own, a wife and children.

Of the many stories my father told me over the years, there was one in particular that I believe had a tremendous impact on him and that served as preparation for overcoming the great hardships he would face later in life.

For my father's eleventh birthday, my grandfather surprised him with a cross-country trip to Mazar-e-Sharif in northwest Afghanistan, which is roughly 264 miles from Kabul. While not that far by today's standards, it was a multiday journey in 1970s Afghanistan, on a crowded bus along dirt roads—there were no interstate highways—up perilous hills, and across vast plains. It would no doubt be an arduous trip, but also an adventure.

When my grandfather told my father about the trip and that it would be just the two of them, my father was overjoyed. Not only would he have a special time and experience with his father—a man he loved and admired—but he would also get to see more of his beloved country. He'd heard about the provinces outside of Kabul, seen foreigners coming from as far away as Europe and America, and gazed at pictures of cities like New York and Islamabad, but he himself had never ventured beyond the city limits. It would be a once-in-a-lifetime experience, he thought.

When the day finally came, father and son climbed aboard a diesel-belching bus and sat crammed among roughly forty other passengers. The occupants quickly opened the windows to allow in a breeze, hoping the stifling air inside, which was filled with the smells of sweaty bodies, animals, and other unwelcome odors, would dissipate.

My father wore his blue jeans, and my grandfather had on his white dishdasha and black turban. Between them, they carried a small bag with a change of clothes and a loaf of bread and two onions to share on the two-and-a-half-day trek. It wasn't much, but their provisions would last if they rationed them smartly.

When there's only a limited amount of food, the key is never to eat your fill in one sitting, because the food will be gone and in a few hours you'll be hungry again. It's better to eat small amounts throughout the day, and if the trip is unexpectedly extended (perhaps because the bus breaks down), you can stretch the remaining crumbs even further.

Their route to Mazar-e-Sharif cut across a breathtaking and unforgiving landscape. Kabul is surrounded by mountains, so they first drove the winding roads west out of the city, at times passing through groves of trees and fields, and soon thereafter jostling along rocky paths with sheer drops on one side and walls of rock on the other. As they got farther along, off in the distance they beheld the snowcapped peaks of the Hindu Kush, followed by the expansive western desert that led into Iran. The views were spectacular, my father recalled; the diversity of Afghanistan's geography was both treacherous and magnificent, and something only nature could create.

When my father described these things to me, he took my hand in his and told me that he'd held my grandfather's hand the same way, sitting up against him like I was to him now. At home my father and grandfather worked tirelessly doing backbreaking work, and he wanted to savor these moments with his father's strong arm around him. As my father held my hand, whether on this day after the playground incident or later in life walking the hills outside Kabul together, I could relate.

When they finally reached Mazar-e-Sharif, the first place they visited was the Shrine of Hazrat Ali, more commonly known in English as the Blue Mosque. It's a spectacular site dating back to the fifteenth century, with blue and gold tiles gracing the walls and domes both inside and out. On the vast apron surrounding the ancient structure, there are usually hundreds of white pigeons that you can feed and pet with your hands. Some people believe Ali ibn Abi Talib, the cousin and son-in-law of the Prophet Mohammed, is buried here, making it an exceptionally sacred site. As a pious Muslim, my father was awed by the beauty and grandeur of this holy place, just as millions of other visitors, Muslims and non-Muslims alike, have been.

Later that day, my father and grandfather went to stay the night with relatives. It had been decades since my grandfather had seen these members of the extended family, and it was my father's first introduction to them. He was nervous but also excited to meet the cousins, aunts, and uncles he'd only heard about. He also knew that the tradition of Afghan hospitality was genuine, and the arrival of guests—particularly family, even distant cousins—is an opportunity for the hosts to spare no expense to welcome people into their home, even if they have little food to share and only a floor to sleep on.

A wave of embraces, kisses, and heartfelt tears welcomed my father and grandfather when they arrived. Everyone jostled to hug and shake hands with the visitors, all of them asking repeatedly how their journey was, for news about relatives and friends in Kabul, how things were in the capital, and more. The greetings went on and on, until finally the women beckoned everyone to come and eat. They all raised their voices in merriment and grasped each other's arms and shoulders to walk into the next room, where a feast awaited them.

Having eaten next to nothing over the previous two and a half days, my father wasted no time stuffing himself on a sweet and savory traditional Afghan dish of Kabuli pulao. It's made with rice, lamb, raisins, carrots, and a host of spices, and is served on a large metal platter. Everyone crowds around to reach in with their right hand to scoop up chunks of meat and rice.

With each mouthful, my father listened to tales going back generations. The men regaled each other with stories about the early days of Afghan independence, the years when the British and Russians were vying for dominion across the region, and how our ancestors lived during the era of the great Central Asian empires. My father knew family was important, but this night he saw how far those roots extended and how rich our family was in culture and Afghanistan's legacy.

The night finally came to a close when the neighbors returned to their own homes, the hosts retired to their rooms, and my father curled up on a mat in the corner of the main room and closed his eyes.

My grandfather woke my father early the next morning, before the sun was up, and asked him if he knew why they had traveled all this way. After he wiped the sleep from his eyes, my father thought for a moment and realized he didn't know why, nor had he thought to ask.

My grandfather had one more surprise for his son—the experience of *buzkashi*.

Buzkashi is a centuries-old sport of the Afghan people that was brought to this region by the Mongols of days past. It involves hundreds of horsemen on a massive field—whipping their horses and slamming into one another—as they do battle to carry or drag a headless animal carcass (usually a calf) to the scoring circle at one side of the field or the other.

Many riders get thrown off their mounts, and some of the unlucky ones get trampled. It's not uncommon for one or two men to die from their injuries. The spectators who stand too close to the field are sure to get peppered with rocks and dirt as the horses gallop past, and it's their fault if they get in the way of a charging horse.

It's a rough and violent competition, but it's an exciting staple of traditional Afghan culture, and my father loved it. He cheered and jumped with the rest of the crowd, watching Afghanistan's hardy men clash on the field. For a few hours, my father forgot about the daily hardships that he and his family endured, and reveled in being a proud Afghan in a strong nation with a vibrant culture and promising future.

My father didn't want the trip to end, and as he retold this tale to me, I didn't want the story to end either. The natural spectacles, the sights and sounds, the journey, the people, the comfort he felt with his father—all these things not only brought joy to my Baba Jan but also helped mold his view of life.

Seeing for the first time other Afghan peoples like the Kuchi—an ethnic group that migrates seasonally across the region—my father felt so lucky to have a loving family, a place to work, a place to eat and sleep, and a place to laugh. This trip and these moments helped my father see what he wanted for himself, what sort of man he wanted to be, and what he wanted for his own family. He knew how to persevere and he knew how to survive, and he'd seen firsthand the greatness of his homeland.

Unfortunately, my father had no idea about the tragedy that would befall Afghanistan a few years later—no one did—but I have no doubt this experience helped prepare him to lead his future family through some of Afghanistan's darkest days.

For my father, all that began on December 24, 1979, when the Soviets invaded.

2

THE SOVIETS

I N LATE DECEMBER 1979, CBS News aired footage of Russian tanks, troop carriers, and formations of fighter jets and helicopter gunships streaming into Afghanistan. The images of the Russians, in brown and olive-drab uniforms topped with steel helmets or fur hats, set against the backdrop of the barren hills and snowcapped peaks, seemed to show a cold and harsh faceless horde flowing across the border. It was a lonely, barren, and merciless scene, where men, women, children, soldiers, and rebels would violently clash. Even now, as an Afghan and a survivor of the Taliban regime, remembering these pictures gives me a chill.

This move by Moscow was supposedly in response to the growing unrest against the People's Democratic Party of Afghanistan (PDPA), a Communist regime that had come to power in a military coup the year before. According to statements by the Kremlin, Soviet troops had been deployed to Afghanistan to quell the turmoil brewing in the countryside, where rebels, warlords, and religious fanatics were opposing the Soviets' reforms and modernizations, many of which were deemed anti-Islamic.

Moscow called its involvement an intervention. The West put it more plainly, calling it what it was—an invasion.

For my father, who was just fourteen at the time, the diplomatic back-and-forth between the Soviets and the West, and the countless debates occurring in national security and academic circles about how to describe what was happening to Afghanistan, meant nothing. He, along with the rest of the Afghan people, had to deal with these life-shattering changes merely to survive from one day to the next.

Once my father felt I was mature enough to hear the truth about what he went through during those dark days, I was surprised to learn how slowly everything had happened. Within hours of the first tanks and planes crossing the border, Russian units moved quickly into the capital's streets. But the change on the ground, from an era of prosperity to what would become a horrific spiral into bloody chaos, took time.

When I think of the word *invasion*, my thoughts naturally turn to my own experiences when the United States and NATO came to Afghanistan in 2001. It was sudden and clear to all Afghans what lay ahead of us. The US-led coalition had come by force to hunt down Osama bin Laden and al-Qaeda and to topple the Taliban regime, and the transformation of the country from relative peace to that of violent war was practically instantaneous. The entire American war machine had mobilized—aircraft, rockets, missiles, tanks, infantry—and it hit the enemy with a shock that rattled the world. There was no question about what was happening, even if the outcome was unclear.

In 1979, however, reactions were mixed. My father told me that on December 24 he remembered looking up to see Russian aircraft circling overhead. At first, people on the ground didn't know whose planes they were. Afghanistan had an air force that was fully equipped and trained by the Soviets, but these jets in the sky seemed faster and the pilots more skilled. There were also Mi-24 helicopter gun-ships, which were new to Afghanistan, and there was gunfire. It hadn't reached the city yet, but the rattle of heavy machine guns and the deep booms from artillery could be heard in the distance.

I thought he would have been scared, but my father was more in awe at the strength of the great superpower, Russia. He used to lie in the backyard of his parents' home and watch the planes screech across the sky. The power and speed of these aircraft amazed him, and he told himself that one day he would be a pilot up there, soaring above his beautiful Afghanistan. He wanted to feel it—the tonnage of a huge machine, the controls in his hands, and the sensation of flying over the highest mountains while looking down upon the earth.

In the coming months, my father became increasingly enamored with the idea of becoming a pilot. He'd learned to fly kites from his father, and he became the best flyer in the neighborhood. Every Friday, my father and his friend Zolmai would buy a kite. They would go to the neighborhood lot with the rest of the boys and compete in the skies, making their kites dive, veer, and cut. My father imagined chasing the Russian planes with his kite, dreaming that soon it'd be him strapped into the cockpit, weaving through the clouds.

Unfortunately, the path for my father to become a pilot was practically impossible. Afghanistan did not have any civilian flight schools, and my father didn't have the economic means to go abroad. His only option was to try to join the Afghan Air Force to undergo training as a military pilot.

In 1980, when he was fifteen, my father and Zolmai went to the recruiting office to apply for pilot training, but back then most things were based on personal connections. It's much the same today. Afghanistan is a collection of tribes and familial groups, and the belief is that you can trust only your own people. Everyone else is suspect, especially in the government where power is concentrated. It all boils down to connections. My father had none, and very quickly he realized that his dream to fly would never come to fruition.

When he told me this story I was six, old enough to see the disappointment in his face, even after the passage of nearly twenty years. I saw a man who was smart, hardworking, and willing to sacrifice anything for those around him. He'd already given so much to his family, but he realized that the one thing he wanted for himself would never happen.

––––––––––

After accepting that he'd never fly a plane, my father dove back into his studies at school. He graduated a year early and entered Kabul Polytechnic University, where he earned a degree in civil engineering.

Given that my father started life going to bed hungry and making bricks in the dead of night to help support the family, this was a tremendous achievement. He'd risen from the role of brickmaker, one of the lowest occupations in Afghan life and now classified by many humanitarian groups as akin to modern-day slavery, and he earned a university degree.

My grandfather attended the graduation, which was the first graduation he'd ever been to. He hadn't finished school himself, and he'd never had a reason until then to go watch other people receive a diploma, but he wasn't going to miss seeing his son receive his. When the ceremony was over and he found my father in the crowd, he reached forward and grasped my father's hand with both of his. He gripped it steadily while he looked into his son's eyes and said with a slight quiver in his voice, "You make me so proud."

My father said he cried and hugged his father, just like he had years ago on their trip to Mazar-e-Sharif. It was one of the proudest moments of his life.

My grandfather was illiterate, and he'd worked tirelessly to provide for his family over the years. He'd done the best he could with what he had, and my father was a product of that effort. My father hadn't wasted his gifts or opportunities, and he became the first in the family to receive a university education.

When I heard this story, I was still young and felt like I had my entire life ahead of me. Although at the time the Taliban controlled Afghanistan and oppressed women as if they were animals, I told myself that I, too, would do the best with my life, just like my father had. I wanted to make him proud.

Youthful dreams of happiness were short lived in the early years of the Soviet-Afghan War, and in later years there were no dreams or youth at all, only tragedy. The insurgency in Afghanistan had started to simmer in 1978 under the PDPA regime and prior to the arrival of the Russian tanks. But by 1984 battle raged across the country.

Moscow wasn't willing to have its soldiers do all the fighting. They'd sent troops to "intervene," not die on nameless hillsides at the hands of primitive villagers. The puppet Afghan government needed to do its share, raise an army, and send troops to the field. My father was one of the thousands of young men conscripted and sent to the front.

I think the method of his conscription is indicative of the hardship imposed on my country by the Russians. My father was on his way home from work when he, along with thousands of other teenage boys and young men in Kabul, was taken off the street and pressed into service. The operation was brutal, swift, and total. Kabul's young men were rounded up and forced into trucks at gunpoint and driven away. They were all gone within hours. Many would never return, and countless others would be forever scarred both physically and psychologically.

The families of the conscripted boys and men had no idea what had happened. Their loved ones had simply vanished; no one had been allowed to return home to tell their families of their fate. The fear felt by these mothers, fathers, brothers, and sisters must have been unimaginable. A dear family member ripped from his life without warning or reason, just gone. The ache felt in so many hearts, including those of my grandparents, had to have been unbearable—a void in the soul.

In the coming weeks, news spread about what happened. The PDPA had conscripted thousands of Afghan men and boys from around the country into the army to support the fight against the various rebel groups. I won't analyze the geopolitical situation, except to say that Afghanistan was now split unto multiple factions and embroiled in a brutal civil war. There were multiple sides: the Soviets; the various warlords and their insurgent fighters; the mujahideen from across the border, being aided by Pakistan; and the United States, picking and choosing whom to finance and provide training and weaponry to.

The Afghan people were being slaughtered, and the country was being torn to pieces. The Paris of Central Asia had been wiped from the face of the earth.

———————

To this day, my father won't talk much about his time in the military. He is proud of his service and believes it made him stronger, but he didn't want to fight. Moreover, he hated the Soviets and Russian occupiers. They devastated his country, indiscriminately killing innocent Afghans who were mostly women, children, and old men, and he wanted no part of it. Yet he had to wear the uniform and follow orders.

They trained him as an infantryman and a driver and sent him to fight his countrymen in the mountains, on the plains, and in the valleys. His Afghan commanders and the Russian advisors were cruel, but in the field my father also witnessed the brutality of the rebels. No one wins in war, he learned, and all sides are victims. The innocent and the kind are the ones who suffer most; the young boys carrying the guns are often blown to bits by rockets and land mines.

My father admitted to me that every day he feared he might be killed, and he was scared he'd never be able to go home and see his family again. The military didn't allow him to go on leave to Kabul while he was in service; he was away for four long years. Even after my own service in the Afghan Air Force, it's difficult to imagine being cut off like that, totally isolated from one's family.

I don't press my father to tell me about these things. I think for him it's like a bad dream. My father is a happy and gentle man, but the nightmares visit him on occasion. When they do, I can see the weight press down on him. Some things are better left alone.

3

COURTSHIP

MY FATHER FINALLY CAME HOME IN 1987, but a lot had changed in three years. Hundreds of thousands of people had been killed, mostly civilians, and millions of Afghans had fled the country as refugees. A generation of children were coming of age who knew nothing but war, and for those who stayed in Afghanistan, the economic situation was dire. Every family suffered.

Yet there was hope, because my father would soon meet my mother, Tahera.

When my parents describe their courtship, it sounds like a love story out of a romance novel. A boy spots a beautiful girl at a party, but he can't go talk to her. The boy tells his parents about the girl, and they find a way to approach the girl's parents. The two families debate whether the two young people should be introduced, if one or the other is good enough, and whether he or she is suitable. Agreements between households are eventually made and chaperones are designated. The girl is anxious about meeting the boy for the first time, perhaps not knowing what he looks like. And the boy is nervous too, having only ever seen her from afar. Questions about whether she will accept him fill his mind, and questions about whether she will like him fill hers. But once they finally meet, both boy and girl marvel at each other. Then . . .

My father was twenty-three when he fell in love with Tahera. He said she was the prettiest girl he'd ever seen, and he sensed that she was a pure and honest woman. He first saw her at an Eid al-Adha family ceremony, and as he told me in his own words, "She caught my breath and heart." She stood five feet, seven inches tall, with long, dark, wavy hair; big, round eyes; and an alluring face, with gentle olive skin. That night she wore a red dress with black high heels, and my father knew she was *the one* right then.

But according to Afghan culture, he couldn't just walk up to her and say hello. He couldn't go near her. It would have been very disrespectful. Therefore, after the party he asked a friend who was a relative of hers, "Who is this beautiful girl?" My father found out that her name was Tahera and that she lived with her family in the Kart-e-Say section of Kabul, not too far from my grandfather's home.

As soon as my father came home from the party, he told his parents about her and that she was the most beautiful girl he'd ever seen. He'd never been around anyone like her before, and only in his dreams had he hoped to find such a wife one day. Just by looking at her and watching the way she moved and spoke with other people, he could tell that she was smart and passionate. It showed in her face, in her expressions and gestures, and in the intelligence in her eyes. She was perfect, and he knew it.

My grandmother, however, did not approve of my father's interest in this girl Tahera. She did not know her or the family, and would have preferred my father marry a girl from her own village. She wanted him to wed an extended family member, someone she knew and whose parents and relatives she knew. It was better if his bride was illiterate and uneducated, she thought. My grandmother wanted someone traditional whom she could control.

My father didn't want that. He didn't want an arranged marriage to a girl he'd never seen before, or a relationship of convenience for the parents. He was not that type of person. He had too much will and too big of a heart.

It took time and many conversations, but my father gradually convinced my grandmother to visit Tahera's family home to discuss courtship. She was reluctant and expressed her reservations vigorously, but she finally agreed, giving in to the earnest pleas of her cherished son.

Tahera's family treated my grandmother with great respect on this first visit, and the family was amenable to future discussions about the potential union of Tahera and Nooragha. However, Tahera's parents had one condition: Tahera must be allowed to finish high school before getting married. She had one year left.

My grandmother, still hesitant about the union, nearly told my father that this was unacceptable. Although my grandmother had grown up during Afghanistan's golden era, when girls were expected to go to school just like boys, she was still a very conservative woman and did not see the point of her son's future wife graduating high school. It wasn't as if Tahera would be working; her duty would be in the home, raising a family. And my grandmother certainly didn't know that Tahera desperately wanted to be a journalist.

My mother likes to say that since her first day of school, she dreamed of becoming a reporter, perhaps with an international news organization like the BBC, the Associated Press, or Reuters. She wanted to travel, meet people, experience the world, and then write about it. She'd been working hard at her studies to make this dream a reality, consistently being first in her class year after year. I suspect if my grandmother had known about my mother's ambition, her opposition to the marriage would have been even stronger. There'd be no controlling a woman like this.

Fortunately for me and all my siblings, my father persuaded my grandmother that he was deeply in love with Tahera and that she was his one desire. The courtship discussions continued, with each side learning more about the other, until a date was set for the two to meet.

As a daughter, I was naturally curious what my mother thought and felt during the back-and-forth between the families and the time before she actually met my father. I knew I might very well find myself in a situation similar to what my mother went through. Although the dream of flying had been with me since I was a little girl, it was still just a dream. I grew up in the 1990s under Taliban rule, and the prospect of becoming a pilot was a mere fantasy. I knew that, like my mother, I might be married at a young age—and I wanted to know what it had been like.

When I was old enough, about nine or ten, to finally ask the right questions, the first thing my mother told me was that she had been scared—terrified, actually, which surprised me. I'd expected her to say she was nervous or hesitant, but not scared. But as she told me the story, I came to realize that my mother is also exceptional and brave.

Unlike my father, who had seen my mother at a party from a distance, my mother had no idea who Nooragha was. She didn't know what he looked like, what kind of personality he had, what his temperament was—nothing at all. She was completely in the dark, knowing only what her parents had told her, which they had only learned from my grandmother.

Furthermore, my mother was deeply worried that if she married she would not be allowed to finish school or become a journalist. In Afghanistan, if a husband says no, that's the end of it, and she was terrified my father might say no. Most Afghan men would.

My parents were set to meet on a Friday. The year was 1988, and the war was still raging, but the sun was shining and life in the city was relatively normal. My mother and her mother took a taxi to the Cinema Pamir section of Kabul. It was busy with traffic up and down Maiwand Road, with throngs of people walking across the courtyards, in and out of buildings, and through the alleys.

Standing on the sidewalk, my mother searched the many faces in the crowd, a collision of curiosity and nervousness bubbling inside her. She'd never seen Nooragha, and she only knew what he might look like from her parents' description, but her eyes eventually settled on a young man just a few feet away who was staring at her. My mother said that he was tall, with dark hair, and that he wore a black suit and carried a small handbag. She said she felt a tingle in her stomach and took hold of her mother's hand and asked if that was him. Her mother responded gently, "Yes, that is him."

Looking upon Nooragha for the first time, my mother felt a sense of calm. Her heart stopped pounding, the butterflies in her stomach went away, and the fear tugging at the base of her mind disappeared. Something inside my mother's heart told her that Nooragha was a good person.

The introduction was brief, with my father and mother speaking to each other for the first time, exchanging anxious pleasantries. Then the three of them went to a nearby restaurant for lunch. My mother told me that she instantly felt at ease around my father and that he seemed honest, genuine, and kind. He also treated her own mother with great respect, and she knew right then that he was right for her.

Within days of that first meeting, my mother's family sent a letter to Nooragha's family informing them that they approved of the courtship. A week later, Nooragha and Tahera were engaged. Over the next two months, my father spent every weekend with my mother's family at their home, each time bringing gifts not just for my mother but for her parents and siblings as well.

For many Afghan women, falling in love before the wedding doesn't always happen. Sometimes love develops over time after the wedding ceremony, and sometimes it never happens. But my mother fell in love with my father during the two months they dated. She knew he was unique, not like other Afghan men, and she was lucky. She wasn't afraid anymore, and she knew my father would support, love, and respect her. It was evident by the way he talked and how he treated others.

On February 5, 1988, my parents were married at my father's house. Two hundred people attended, with the neighbors opening up their homes to help accommodate all the guests. It was a wonderful celebration, and after ten years of war, it was a bright moment for my parents.

Unfortunately, Afghanistan's greatest troubles were yet to come.

4

CIVIL WAR

————————

I **LIKE TO THINK** that my parents had a happy first year of marriage. My father found a job after the army, and just as he promised, he encouraged my mother—who was only sixteen at the time—to finish high school. He knew about her dream to become a journalist and recognized she was an excellent student, and he meant to support her. Two days after the wedding, he took her to the bazaar to buy school supplies and new clothes.

But my mother soon got pregnant. My grandmother was a very traditional woman and pushed my parents to start a family right away. My mother didn't want to; she knew a baby would change everything, but she had no choice since birth control was never an option.

Still, even with the pregnancy and the social expectation that new wives should focus on the home, my father wanted my mother to graduate. He helped her make arrangements to continue going to school, and when it became too hard to attend class, she studied at home.

In January 1989, seven months pregnant, my mother graduated high school and ranked second in her class. Initially she was disappointed because she was no longer number one, but my father helped her see past that. Number two was nothing to be ashamed of, and she needed to turn her attention to the Kabul University entrance exam that was in two weeks. Even with a child on the way, he told her they'd figure it out.

On March 25 my mother delivered their first child—a baby girl they named Afsoon, which means "magic." My father was overjoyed, and with tears in his eyes he thanked God for giving him a healthy daughter. My mother, though exhausted and overwhelmed, was also filled with love when she held Afsoon for the first time. She said it was amazing to hold something so tiny and so fragile, and to know that this tiny life had grown inside her.

But there was also a tinge of disappointment in my mother, because the baby was a girl. Afghan culture does not celebrate the birth of girls, and the in-laws will often chastise a new mother for not producing a boy. My grandmother was like this, and she immediately treated my mother with disgust, even refusing to hold her new granddaughter.

My father didn't let this faze him. He, his wife, and their baby girl were making a life together. They still lived at his parents' home, and during the day he worked as a grocer; the war had made engineering and construction jobs nonexistent. At night, my mother and father worked to build a small room in the backyard to have just for themselves. In July 1990 my brother was born, and they named him Mohammad Omar, which is a strong, traditional Afghan name.

This birth marked the end of the joy for quite some time.

The Russians left Afghanistan in February 1989, and a bad situation got worse. During the war, the Soviets controlled the population centers, which remained relatively secure. Although food was scarce and the economy had ground to a halt, people still attended school, got married, built houses, had families, and eked out an existence. The real danger was in the countryside and the border provinces, where the US-backed mujahideen operated. They shot helicopters out of the sky, executed brutal ambushes against military convoys, and murdered their fellow Afghans who supported the central government or who were from rival tribes.

With the Russian army heading north back across the border and their Afghan puppets crumbling, a power vacuum ensued, and Kabul was the prize.

Numerous mujahideen factions descended on Kabul, a two-thousand-year-old city. Rockets, gunfire, mines, snipers, poisoned food, and other hardships made life virtually impossible. The city became a war zone, and my parents were caught in the middle with two young children and a third on the way—me.

One night in the summer of 1991, when my sister was two and my brother was one and my mother was seven months pregnant with me, a neighbor came rushing over to my parents' house. She banged on the door and woke everyone up.

My father ran outside to see what the commotion was, and she told him that Gulbuddin Hekmatyar, the leader of the Hezb-e-Islami mujahideen, had just seized control of this area of the city. It was no longer safe to stay here. The rockets and bombings would start soon.

My father, trying not to scare his wife or their children, had them pack a small bag with extra clothes and what little food they could find. My beautiful mother then put on a burka for the first time in her life.

For those who have never been forced to wear a burka, it is oppressively stifling and degrading. It forces the wearer to breathe stale air that carries one's own body odor, which is hot and sweaty from being shrouded under a head-to-toe canopy of coarse fabric.

The mesh window you look out of severely restricts your vision and blurs what little you can see. Coupled with how the bottom edge of the burka falls around and underneath your feet, it's easy to trip.

My mother suffered through all these things and more. It was dark and she could barely see anything out of the mesh window. She said she felt like her hands and arms were tangled in a blanket, and she struggled to hold her infant son and also manage her pregnant belly. With every step she worried she'd stumble and hurt the baby or herself.

Rather than being seen as a strong, intelligent, beautiful woman, my mother was now relegated to a faceless figure and stripped of her dignity. She wore this garment so the religious fanatics, the ones destroying our country, would allow her to pass unmolested. She put it on for pure survival.

My family first went to a relative's house on the north side of the city and stayed in the basement, somewhat safe from the bombs, but they could not live there indefinitely. There wasn't enough room or food to last long, and my father expected the fighting to only get worse. The warring factions might very well come there next.

With two small children and a pregnant wife, my father decided to leave Kabul and head north to Pol-e-Khomri, which was 140 miles away. They left in the middle of the night on foot, walking through a city that had once been vibrant with music, light, and happiness but was now marred by crumbling buildings, debris, and the dead. Severed hands, legs, and feet, along with entire bodies, littered the streets, and my parents did what they could to shield my brother and sister from these sights.

The Russians had come first, sowing death and destruction with their tanks and helicopters, and then they left. Now the mujahideen and warlords were coming, not with aircraft but with equally lethal ground firepower that they'd just used to expel the Soviets. They would kill each other and anyone who got in their way, all of them trying to assert control over the capital and destroy their adversaries. It was a total civil war.

At the edge of the city, my father hailed a truck that was going north and begged the driver to allow his family to ride in the back. Exposed to the cold air and wind, the dust and grime off the road, and the many mujahideen checkpoints along the way, my family made the seven-hour journey through the dead of night.

With the dawn cresting Afghanistan's northern hills, they arrived in Pol-e-Khomri the next day. The truck driver dropped my family in the city. My father didn't know anyone, but the driver told him there was an abandoned apartment a few miles away in a deserted area on the edge of town. He thought they might find shelter there.

My parents, with two children in tow, walked until they reached a decrepit one-room shack with no doors or windowpanes that was overrun by stray dogs and cats. They cleaned the place as best they could and found some sheets of plastic to cover the open windows and doors. They fed the kids the few scraps of food they had left and then got them ready for bed.

My mother remembers wrapping their dirty shoes in the extra clothes they'd brought and putting these "pillows" under my siblings' heads. She couldn't believe this was happening and what had become of their life. They'd been part of the middle class in Kabul. They hadn't had much, but they'd had shelter, clothes, food, and a few basic comforts. They'd had a garden with beautiful flowers, red poppies and yellow tulips, and sometimes birds would land in their courtyard and sing. That was all gone.

My mother and father stayed awake all night, watching over my brother and sister, praying they wouldn't remember any of this.

My family stayed in Pol-e-Khomri for two months. Each day my father would work at the truck stop unloading cargo, and by late afternoon he'd usually have earned enough money to buy a few scraps of bread and some milk to bring home.

They were squatting in a shack without windows or doors, and it was getting cold. There was no electricity and no wood to burn, just a small gas capsule they used to cook with and briefly warm themselves. Each night the wind howled through the breaks in the plastic, and the next morning they would all wake up with a film of sandy dust on their faces and clothes.

The lack of food and the filthy living conditions caused both my sister and brother to get sick with heavy chest colds and fevers. My mother, who was now eight months pregnant with me, fell ill as well. My father knew they couldn't stay here through the winter—they would never survive. They had to go back to Kabul and hope that the worst of the fighting was over.

───────────

My parents left Pol-e-Khomri with the same small bag they'd brought with them. They reached Kabul the next day and went back to my father's parents' home. The small room that my father and mother had built had been damaged by gunfire, but they had nowhere else to go. They collected the broken bricks and patched the walls with the few construction materials they had left.

A few days later, while my mother, brother, and sister were in the cellar, a rocket struck what remained of the main house, completely destroying it. The roof crumbled, as did most of the walls. They were lucky they survived, but now the place was uninhabitable.

My father moved my siblings and my very pregnant mother to my aunt's house across the city. Aunt Mari lived in a Soviet-style apartment building, a big, monolithic, barren concrete structure. When they arrived, they found the door locked and no one home. With my brother and sister crying from hunger, my father was so distressed that he broke the lock to get them inside and something to eat.

Aunt Mari came home later and found my family. After getting over the initial fear of finding her home broken into, she was glad to see them. Times were desperate, and she said they could stay for a little while until they figured out what to do next, but they couldn't stay forever. She had her own husband and children to care for.

A month later, bombs destroyed the adjacent apartment building. Things like this were becoming commonplace. Rockets and artillery would shower down on an area, sometimes because there were known fighters positioned nearby, and sometimes for no reason at all. Buildings would collapse and civilians would die, be maimed, or become homeless. No one bothered to rebuild, because it was quite possible that another attack would happen and cause a similar amount of damage. For the survivors, it was better to find somewhere else to go.

On December 4, 1991, my mother went into labor with me. It should have been routine. My mother was healthy, and the pregnancy had gone relatively smoothly, all things considered. This was also my mother's third child, and her body knew what was coming. She expected to labor for a few hours as she had with Afsoon and Omar, and that would be the end of it.

But as the contractions started, rockets hit a nearby building. The explosions shook my aunt's building, and dust and smoke filled the air. Toxic fumes seeped in through the window and caused both my mother and aunt to choke and cough. They quickly ushered my sister and brother into the back room to shelter them if another barrage struck.

Then came the screams from outside. Families had been in the building that got hit, and scores of women and children had been killed or severely injured. The ones who could walk came stumbling out of the rubble, while others sat stranded on the upper floors, staring blankly at where the walls and floors had been just moments before. Boys and girls were crying, and mothers were hysterical with fear.

My father wasn't home, and my mother and aunt decided it was too dangerous to go to the hospital. There were no cars or taxis around, and my mother would need help walking. A doctor wouldn't come to the house, either. More rockets might hit the area, and no doctor was going to risk his life for some nameless woman giving birth. The few doctors who still remained in the city had enough to do with all the sick and dying in the hospitals.

The contractions were getting closer together, and my mother realized she would deliver any minute. It was going to happen right here, in a dilapidated apartment building, with a war raging on the doorstep.

My mother later told me that she was terrified, crying and screaming, and afraid she might die. Her two children were in the back, both in shock from the rocket attack, and she was in immense pain. She felt she had no control over anything, which was compounded by the chaos outside. She didn't know what to do or what to tell my aunt. She'd never had to manage her own childbirth; there'd always been a midwife present and a doctor nearby.

My aunt didn't know what to do either, so she ran outside and found an old woman who was from a village up north. My aunt assumed this woman might possess the traditional skills of a midwife, and the old woman said she did.

When they returned and the old woman started working on my mother, however, it became apparent she had no idea what she was doing. The woman was probably a bit crazy, and she was determined to push on my mother's stomach and in other places, which caused my mother immense pain. The old woman muttered unintelligibly and kept poking and prodding. If she had continued, she likely would have killed my mother and me.

My aunt realized what was happening and yanked the old woman off my mother. She screamed at her and pushed her out of the house, slamming the door. My aunt then rushed back to my mother's side, held her hand, and assured her everything would be all right.

My aunt told my mother to breathe and to push. She kept her eyes locked on my mother's and spoke to her gently, encouraging her to keep breathing and pushing. At this point that's all she could do. The baby was coming and they just needed to let it happen.

This went on for a time, my mother breathing and pushing, mothers wailing and children crying outside, and the toxic stench of explosives lingering in the air, until eventually my aunt helped deliver me.

Miraculously, my mother and I were healthy. We survived when dozens outside had just perished. It was all unbelievable.

Despite the relief that came after the ordeal was over, my mother was devastated and so was my aunt, because I was a girl. My mother had one son already, but it didn't matter. Giving birth to a girl was shameful. Even amid all this madness, the cultural stigma of having a baby girl plagued my mother.

My mother knew my father was different and not like other Afghan men, but she was still afraid to look him in the eye when he got home. It took her a while to shake this feeling, because it was something that had been etched into her, but she eventually did. She told herself that Nooragha would be grateful and happy to have another baby girl.

My father arrived home later that night, and my two-and-a-half-year-old sister met him at the door, bursting with excitement. My father rushed into the bedroom, overcome with joy, and lifted his second daughter into his arms to welcome her into the world.

They named me Niloofar, which is a Persian name that means "water lily." It also signifies peace, purity, and spiritual enlightenment. I couldn't have asked for a better name.

5

ESCAPE

————

I **WAS SEVEN THE FIRST TIME** I heard the story about how we got to Pakistan. We were living in Karachi, and it was 1998. My sister Afsoon was about to turn nine, and we'd never celebrated her birthday before. None of us had celebrated a birthday before.

That night after work, my father came home to surprise Afsoon with a cake, a beautiful dress, and a set of hairclips. Both my mother and father tried to make every moment of that evening special. They wanted her to experience what most children did on their birthday—to be doted on and made to feel loved and celebrated.

My sister was of course overwhelmed, never having been the sole focus of attention for an entire evening of celebration, but it was more than that. We were all emotional, thankful, and happy to be a family and to have finally found a degree of safety and stability. Our life in Karachi was better than it had ever been since the wars started.

I already knew our home was Afghanistan, having learned that on the playground three years earlier, but I didn't know how we'd come to Pakistan. I asked, and in the midst of the celebration, my parents told the three of us what had happened.

I was six months old in May 1992, and the violence in Afghanistan was spiraling out of control. President Mohammad Najibullah and the remnants of his Communist government had been holding on by a thread since the Soviet Union's collapse in December 1991, but without that support he had nothing left. He resigned from the presidency in March 1992. The United Nations tried to broker a peace plan between the warring mujahideen parties, but five armies sat perched outside Kabul with tens of thousands of troops. Major fighting erupted in and around the city and lasted into the summer, forcing half a million civilians to flee Kabul, while thousands of others died in the fighting.

My father saw his country falling apart, and he knew it wouldn't end soon. If we stayed in Kabul, the chances were very high that we would be killed, starve, or die of some disease. He had to make one of the hardest decisions of his life: we would leave Afghanistan, perhaps never to return.

At midnight on May 24, 1992, we were ready to go. My parents and siblings each had a small bag. My father wore traditional Afghan attire, and my mother donned her burka. We weren't able to say goodbye to anyone, including our family; it was too dangerous to venture across the city, and the phone lines had been cut long ago.

My father said he saw my mother crying, but there was no time to ask her what she was upset about. He suspected he knew, and years later my mother admitted she feared she'd never see her family again. She wanted to stay in Kabul. It was her home, and she wished there was some way she could protect her family and remain, but it was too dangerous. The civil war had brought Afghanistan to its knees, and death and violent oppression were the norm. They had no choice but to leave.

My father, my siblings, and my mother, with me in her arms, walked ten miles through Kabul's darkened streets to the bus station on the east side of the city. Tired and hungry, with blistered feet and aching legs, we arrived just before dawn. My father found a taxi driver willing to drive us to Khost Province, which was the best place to cross into Pakistan.

Khost Province is located on the eastern edge of Afghanistan and shares a border with Pakistan's Federally Administered Tribal Areas (FATA). The Pakistani government exercised limited control over this region. It's where the Americans trained and supplied their mujahideen allies in the war against the Soviets in the 1980s and where, fifteen years later, after 9/11, numerous insurgent networks would find a safe haven in their fight against NATO and the newly installed Afghan government.

The actual border—the Durand Line—is just a scribble on a map rather than a physical marker on the ground, and my father knew we could cross over using the centuries-old smuggling routes.

The 145-mile taxi ride from Kabul to Khost took six hours. There were no rest stops; it was too dangerous to stay in one place for too long, what with all the bandits and warring factions. My father told us he thought we might be ambushed or robbed at any point along the way. My mother said she felt like a prisoner under her burka, barely able to see out and crammed in the back of the car, breathing dusty air that reeked of diesel.

We arrived in Khost in the afternoon on May 25, and the taxi driver dropped us on the edge of the city near a small mosque. At least ten other families were waiting there, over thirty people, and we were all in a similar situation. Everyone was trying to escape the war with hopes of making it across the border into neighboring Pakistan.

There weren't any inns for us to spend the night, and there wasn't a camp with humanitarian services to help. No aid organizations could get into Afghanistan, and there weren't any international peacekeeping forces present to establish safe zones. The situation was completely lawless.

We were strangers here, with no relatives nearby, so our only option was to seek refuge in the mosque's courtyard. At the very least we'd be safe there, because even the most ruthless of bandits wouldn't dare rob and murder women and children hiding in a mosque.

That night was cold, and all my parents could do was hold us tight to keep us from freezing. We were hungry too; food was scarce, and those who had some kept it for themselves.

I don't remember any of this, but my family does. They remember the tears and the fear, mostly. They can recall the fear they felt from having escaped the only place they'd ever called home, walking for hours at night in a bombed-out city, and convincing a stranger to drive them over a hundred miles away.

And there was the fear from arriving in an unfamiliar place and finding clusters of other families and groups who were just as exhausted, desperate, and frightened. The cold, the hunger, the dusty wind coming out of the surrounding highlands—the emptiness they felt must have been staggering. Thinking about it saddens me to this day.

The next morning, three smugglers approached what had become our larger group. These men wore long, black perahan tunbans with black-and-white scarves around their heads. They told us to wait until nightfall in a deserted area near the border that was far outside the city. With piercing eyes and long, scraggly beards, they barked out these instructions.

We went into the desert to wait, as we'd been told to, but my father was suspicious of the smugglers. He'd heard rumors about other refugees who had tried to flee the country, and he feared the smugglers might rob and kill everyone. Such atrocities had occurred before in this now lawless frontier. Anything could happen, and no one could be trusted.

My father knew we were helpless if the smugglers came back with guns to murder us. But if they only wanted to rob us, he had an idea. He carefully gathered all of our valuables—our money, my mother's jewelry, his watch—taking care not to let anyone see what he was doing. I can picture my mother flicking her eyes this way and that, doing her best to keep calm while the terror roiled inside her.

Once my father had collected everything, he looked at me, his baby girl. He then gazed at my sister and my brother, and then at his wife. He stared at their smudged faces and dirt-stained clothes and saw the exhausted vacantness in their eyes and felt the hunger in their bellies. He then looked back at me and told himself that he had to do this.

He asked my mother to change my diaper. She gave him a confused look, but he insisted, and she began to change me. My father then wrapped our valuables inside the removed diaper. He walked away from the group as if to relieve himself and buried the package. When he returned, he secured a knife in his boot.

This moment cemented the perilous destitution that had become our reality. My father armed himself with a knife in his boot and buried the only valuables we had in his daughter's diaper. He sat and waited, keeping watch over his three children and wife, anxious for the return of the men who would either murder us or smuggle us across the border.

One of the smugglers appeared just before the sun went down. He had a long red beard and a booming voice. He ordered everyone to take out anything of value and then went from family to family, confiscating their possessions and yelling at them to hurry up and be quiet. He didn't care what people had—he took everything.

When he got to us, my father said we had nothing, that we were poor. The smuggler didn't believe him and ordered all of us to stand up so he could search us. The man had fiery eyes and a mouth that curled, the face of a murderer, but no one said anything or resisted. We allowed him to rifle through what few possessions we had before he gave up and moved on to the next family.

When the smuggler had finished with the last family, he told us no one could leave. They would come back to take us across the border at four the next morning. With the smuggler gone, the tension that had hung over our group seemed to relax, but it didn't go away.

My father chatted with the other fathers and husbands, and many of them worried that when the smugglers returned later that night they would kill everyone and that this was all just a ploy. My father agonized over this possibility, too, and contemplated whether we should leave and try to make the crossing on our own.

He decided against this, not knowing where we could cross, and also because if something were to happen, there was safety in numbers. If it was just the five of us, bandits could easily slaughter our family and none of us would ever be seen or heard from again.

At four the next morning, the three smugglers returned and told everyone to get ready. It was pitch black, but they instructed us to start walking east toward the border. My parents had retrieved the diaper a few hours prior without the smugglers suspecting anything, but we were still hungry, cold, and whipped raw from the dusty wind. Still, my family stood up and walked.

After a few hours and with the sun rising, our group reached an isolated border checkpoint. The smuggler with the red beard, the one who'd stolen from everyone, bribed one of the Pakistani guards, who waved all the families across. The exchange was simple, like a menial transaction in a downtown market. Our lives were at risk, but this was everyday business for them.

Wearing their light-green camouflage uniforms, the Pakistani guards told us to get away from the border quickly, that it was not safe to remain here. Heeding their warning, our large group split into smaller groups, each family moving at their own pace depending on the number of children and the strength of the elderly and sick.

People were tired and thirsty as we left our homeland behind, but we were also happy. We'd made it to Pakistan, where there was no war, where it was safe, and where we'd find shelter, food, and work—another chance at life. We didn't know where to go or what it would be like when we arrived, but it didn't matter. We'd survived.

Most families wanted to find the refugee camps they'd heard about, which were run by various international aid organizations. These were places where we could get food and shelter before making our next move.

This last leg of the journey proved the hardest physically. We were hungry and tired, and most people were dehydrated. The region was abnormally dry, and with summer coming, the heat and dust made every breath feel like chewing chalk.

My family's group eventually found a muddy lake, but no one seemed to care about the muck. The other families scooped up the stagnant brown water, brought it to their parched lips, and drank. But my father wouldn't let my mother, my siblings, and me drink straight from the lake. He put the dirty water in bottles and waited for the mud to settle at the bottom. Then he let us drink. It was a small amount, but it was enough to keep us going.

A few hours later, we encountered someone who directed us to a nearby refugee camp. My earliest memories are from this camp; I didn't know anything better or different. It was where I grew up.

But I can only imagine what my parents felt the first time they looked upon it. It was barren land framed by barbed wire, masses of people huddled together, others waiting in endless lines, a sea of tents as far as the eye could see, and dusty earth that swirled up into the sky at the slightest breeze. It was the kind of place they'd only heard about or seen pictures of on the news. This camp would supposedly allow us a chance to survive and take time to figure out where we would go next; yet, living in the camps is one of the lowest forms of human existence.

Once we registered with the camp authorities, the aid workers issued my family a tent, a few blankets and pillows, and some rations of water and food. We found our assigned plot of ground, a ten-by-ten-foot square, and my father raised the tent. My sister and brother then asked my parents where they were going to sleep, and that's when my mother explained that this tent was our new home.

My siblings were still too young to fully grasp the tragedy of the situation, and they were unaware of the uncertainty that clouded the future. Nevertheless, they were awed by the curiosities of the refugee camp and happy to see so many children in one place. They went out to play, and like children across the world, they laughed and smiled and brought joy to those around them.

6

THE REFUGEE CAMP

WE ENTERED THE REFUGEE CAMP ON MAY 27, 1992, and we
lived there for three years. From the beginning, my parents
knew they needed to work tirelessly to get us out.

The day after we arrived, my father woke up before everyone else
and ventured outside the camp fence to find work. The food provided
by the aid workers wouldn't be enough, and he didn't want us to stay
in this wretched place a moment longer than we had to. He needed
to immediately earn money so we could survive.

There were dozens of other men from the camp looking for work,
and jobs were scarce. Everyone would gather to wait at a place known
as the worker's circle, and employers looking for cheap labor would
come by and pick up as many men as they needed. The workers would
load and unload trucks, clean yards or bathrooms, dig ditches, haul
timber—the lowest forms of unskilled work.

For an educated and talented man like my father, the situation was painful. He'd been trained to design buildings and facto-
ries, to allocate funding and organize men and materials, and to
execute complex construction projects. He'd earned a degree from

Kabul's top technical university and worked for a brief time as a civil engineer.

Yet here in the camp it was as if he were back making bricks in the dead of night. He was an expendable, insignificant face without a name, scrambling for any job that would pay him.

As my father waited at the worker's circle, the sun climbed higher into the sky and the heat intensified, rising to 50 degrees Celsius (122 degrees Fahrenheit). There wasn't any shade, so my father soaked his shirt and scarf in water to stay cool. He couldn't leave the circle to refresh himself, because if he did, he might miss his one opportunity for work.

After truck upon truck passed by and picked up loads of men, a shop owner selected my father to unload cargo of big, heavy bags of rice and other staples. After that, he went to clean someone's house. For eight hours of work, he earned the equivalent of five US dollars.

That night when my father returned to our tent, he carried a bag of fruit and a long red dress for my mother, which he'd bought with his day's earnings. It wasn't much, but considering everything my family had been through, my father's gifts were a grand surprise that brought smiles to all our faces.

God had protected my family, and we were safe across the border.

My father worked two shifts a day. He'd get what jobs he could at the worker's circle, toiling for eight or nine hours; then he'd work another eight hours either polishing shoes or carrying groceries in a wheelbarrow to people's houses.

The money he earned allowed us to eat decently—vegetables, bread, and sometimes meat. He eventually bought a small propane burner so my mother could cook our meals inside the tent. In time, he saved enough money to buy notebooks and pencils with the expectation that Afsoon and Omar would start school. Both my parents believed an education was crucial to our future.

As Afghan refugees, however, we had no rights or immigration status in Pakistan, and the authorities prevented my parents from registering my siblings for school.

Faced with no other option, my mother designated one small corner of the tent as the classroom, and the next day, my father came home with a board to write on, along with more notebooks and pencils. Every morning, my mother began the day teaching us the alphabet and numbers, and then moved on to other subjects like history, language, and science.

I also attended class, though I was barely a year old. While my sister and brother learned to write their letters and numbers, I tried to imitate them with my own paper and pencil, holding the pencil in my tiny fist and drawing squiggly lines. My mother said I was very curious and that I admired my older sister and brother, aspiring to do the same things they did.

Other families in the camp soon noticed my mother teaching us, and she realized that most of the other mothers weren't educated. She offered to teach some of the children from the nearby tents, and their parents gladly accepted.

Being needed encouraged my mother. If it hadn't been for the war, she would have attended Kabul University. She valued work and education. This kind of interaction with the other parents and children helped my mother get through each day, I think, giving her a purpose beyond just us.

However, the totality of everything—the hardship and the loss of all she'd known and held dear—weighed on my mother. Years later, she admitted that she despaired about what happened to our family and our homeland. She'd lived in a beautiful house in Kabul, waking up every morning to the sounds of birds singing. Our family had had enough food and nice clothing, and they had shelter and the basic necessities of life, along with a few luxuries that they'd acquired through hard work and determination. They had a large family, many friends, and an intimacy with the land. Afghanistan was their home, but the civil war had destroyed it and forced them to leave.

This camp was now our existence; we were refugees in a foreign country where we had no rights, no home, and no future.

When we're young, I think, we assume nothing happened in the world before we were born. We may have seen old pictures of our parents and family and heard stories about events from years past, and we superficially recognize that our parents led complex and interesting lives, but our developing minds haven't made the abstract connections that allow us to understand how big and diverse the world is beyond our little piece of it and what we know about it.

As a little girl in the camp, I didn't know my parents had owned a house in Kabul or that they'd grown up in a cosmopolitan and vibrant city. I didn't know that my mother used to wake to birds singing outside her window, or that my father had a good job where he only had to work a normal day's shift, and that he would often bring home gifts and fine foods. I didn't know that they'd spent special occasions with relatives, feasting, laughing, and playing games, or that at one time my parents believed all of their children would have a chance to go to a real school and pursue a bright future of our choosing.

That was all gone, and had never existed for me.

The camp was all I knew. There was a torrent of smells, from burning wood and trash, from the sewage, from the spices coming off the cooking fires, and from the cauldron of thousands of people crammed into a confined plot of land. There were also sounds of

trucks driving by, mothers yelling for their children, the wind causing the tents to whip and flap, and legions of boys and girls playing
and laughing, oblivious to it all. Sand and dirt were everywhere, and
the grime got into everything we owned, into our clothes, and into
the crevices of our bodies. It permeated our daily lives completely.

I remember waking up in the tent and seeing the sun stream
through the canvas. I remember sitting next to my brother and sister as my mother taught them to add and subtract and how to spell
their names. I remember wearing the same faded pink dress every
day and eating the same rice, onions, and beans for every meal. I
remember running through the camp for what seemed like miles but
was probably only fifty feet, and playing with the other children. In
the evening I'd watch the sun go down while my mother or father
held me until I fell asleep. Then I'd wake up with a film of dust on
my face and in my mouth and do it all again.

This was the only life I knew, which was why I was so confused
when my father came home from work one day in 1995 and said we
were leaving.

My father worked himself ragged to provide a better life for his family. He'd promised himself that as long as he was healthy and had
strength, he would do everything in his power to take care of us. He
never complained, he never made us feel like a burden, and he would
often go hungry so we could eat.

He searched tirelessly for better employment and eventually
secured an interview with a construction company. They weren't
interested in him as an engineer, only as a laborer, but it was good
work, and my father didn't want to lose the opportunity. He told the
bosses that he'd work without a salary or compensation for the first
three months. At the end of the three months, if they were satisfied

with his work, they could decide if he should stay with the company and get paid.

My father did this without complaint, never backing down from a task. He'd work a full day with the construction company, and then he'd go back to his other jobs to earn money so we could eat. We never knew any of this, only that he was working every day so we could survive.

After three months, the company hired my father full time and started paying him a working wage. In six months, they promoted him to supervisor, and he started earning decent money. He'd show up at the job site an hour before everyone else and stay an hour later to demonstrate his dedication and work ethic.

Then, one day in April, he rented a car and parked it outside the camp. He came to our tent and told us to gather our belongings because we were leaving.

At three years old, I didn't understand and started peppering him with questions. "Where are we going? Will we ever come back here? What about our tent?"

My father smiled and hugged me, and told me to get my things because I'd find out soon enough.

My family had arrived at the camp with four bags. In our time there, we'd acquired three pans and a propane stove, and that's all we had when we left the camp. The drive from the camp to our destination took seven hours. I had no idea where we were going because my understanding of the world was confined to the perimeter of the camp, but I heard my father say we were going to a place called Karachi.

That evening, we found ourselves in an urban area filled with apartment buildings and small, run-down shops with metal siding that was propped up as awnings. Other buildings had an odd construction where the second floor jutted out above the first floor, like a mushroom, which effectively blocked the sunlight in the narrow streets. The alleys had broken pavement, and the ground was coated with a layer of brown dust and grit, most of which was damp from seeping drainage pipes. All the ground-floor windows had bars covering them, and cows were tied to buildings or being walked by their owners in the street.

This was Baldia Town on the western edge of Karachi, not far from the Hub River to the north and the border of Baluchistan.

My father announced we had arrived at our destination, and told us to follow him. With our few belongings in hand, we entered a building and walked up one flight of stairs. We came to a door, which he opened with a key he removed from his pocket, and he said this was our new apartment.

We were speechless, and it took us a moment to take it all in. There were two rooms, a kitchen, a balcony, and a bathroom. I'd never seen anything like it, and years later my mother told me I ran all through the apartment laughing and giggling with wonder. So did my siblings, and between laps we'd stop and hug and kiss our father and mother, then take off running again, our little feet pattering on the floor.

The sight of the apartment delighted my mother. Her precious children would now sleep in real beds, have electricity, use a bathroom, have running water, and at night she could lock the doors and feel safe. It'd been so bad, so destitute and hopeless for so long, but life was getting better.

My father brought home food from a local restaurant for dinner that night. I hadn't seen this kind of food before; my father told me it was chapli kebab made from marinated lamb, which was then flattened and cooked as a patty. We also had samosas, with chicken and onions and potato fried in a pastry shell. There was naan bread, and plenty of it. It was a true feast as we all sat on the floor in a circle, eating and talking.

While everyone was still together and satisfied from our beautiful meal, I leaned over and rested my head on my Baba Jan's leg. I fell asleep happy, listening to my family's voices, feeling warm and safe inside our apartment protected from the wind. It was like a dream, a magical dream. We were so blessed.

My father picked me up and carried me into the bedroom. He laid a blanket over me and placed my head on a pillow. It was a real pillow, not a bag filled with dirty clothes and dusty shoes, and he swore to himself he'd never let us suffer like that again.

7

KARACHI

COMPARED TO OUR PREVIOUS SITUATION, life was good in Karachi. My mother continued to homeschool us because we weren't permitted to attend the Pakistani schools. I was just three years old, so I didn't fully appreciate the problems we would have if we lacked a formal education as adults, but I truly enjoyed spending time with my family in our new apartment.

We played together outside and with some of the neighborhood children. Aside from the one incident with the playground bully when we first arrived, having a playground and friends to play with was marvelous compared to the refugee camp.

My mother also started teaching us how to cook. The first dish she taught us was rice. It was a very simple dish and something we ate at almost every meal, but it was the time spent alongside my mother and sister in the kitchen that was most special to me. I began to understand how much love and care my parents put into the basic elements of our lives, which up until then I'd taken for granted. I became keenly aware of how much they did for us throughout each and every day, from the cleaning to the laundry to the cooking to the teaching to the attention they gave us whenever we asked for it.

But my fondest memories are of the trips we took into the nearby mountains. After a few months working for the construction company, my father had saved enough money to buy a scooter. It was a tan 1979 Vespa with a sidecar. It was a bit run-down since it was close to twenty years old, but it looked like a grand chariot to me. In the city, I'd seen hundreds, perhaps thousands, of Karachi's citizens riding motorcycles and scooters just like this one, and now we had our own.

The first time I got to ride it, my Baba Jan picked me up off the ground and set me on the seat in front of him. He hit the throttle and sent us down the street with the hum of the engine buzzing in my ears, and I found the experience exhilarating. With the speed, the wind against my face, and the scenery passing by in a blur, I felt free and alive. My father said I was fearless, always wanting to go faster. I fell in love with this sensation; it was like I was soaring.

On the weekends, we would all climb aboard the scooter and ride into the Kirthar Mountains north of the city. The range runs through the provinces of Baluchistan and Sind, serving as a natural border and marking the transition from the western ranges and valleys of Baluchistan to the lower Indus River plain to the east. The Kirthar Mountains are also home to Ranikot Fort, which dates from the ninth century and is often compared to the Great Wall of China with its thirty-foot-high walls and its sixteen-mile circumference.

None of this was of much interest to me. For me, the mountains were something much simpler—a magnificent place where we could run, climb, hike, cook, have campfires, and enjoy wondrous picnics. We were a happy family living a peaceful life.

My father took me on walks during these trips, a tradition we continued for years to come. He and I would wander off into the hills, my hand in his, and we'd talk. We'd chat about the rocks and the trees, and we'd look up to watch the birds fly across the sky.

As I got older, my father would talk to me about my dreams and encourage me. He'd tell me I could do anything I wanted if I worked hard enough. His steadfast and unwavering support has been a pillar in my life for as long as I can remember.

Yet, amid the happiness we'd found in Karachi, there were also struggles that, unbeknownst to me, would compel my father to make another fateful decision that would change the course of our lives forever.

———

On December 25, 1998, my mother went into labor with her fourth child. My father rushed her to the hospital, leaving the rest of us at home. He was present for the delivery, and my mother had another baby girl, whom they named Maryam.

Unlike at my and my older sister's births, when my grandmother had shamed her for not producing a boy, this time my mother was happy and did not despair. My father was again elated, saying that this baby girl would bring another light into our family.

Now we were six: my mother and father with four children. My oldest sister, Afsoon, was nine; my brother, Omar, was eight; I was seven; and my youngest sister, Maryam, had just taken a breath.

Most days we stayed around the house helping my mother with chores. We washed our clothes by hand and hung them to dry both inside the apartment and on the balcony. We helped cook and clean, and also played with our new baby sister. Moreover, my mother continued to homeschool us; she never missed a day.

But some days my mother suffered from severe back pain so acute she could barely walk. My heart went out to her, seeing her like this. There were other days when she would get terribly sick and be so weak she couldn't get out of bed. I remember sitting by her side, stroking her hand, praying she'd feel better. My mother was so dear to me, and she did so much for us; it pained me to see her hurting.

Many years later I came to realize one of the reasons she got sick was because she carried so much stress and worry inside her. She loved and cared for our family with all her heart and soul, and sometimes the uncertainty and fear overcame her. She would hide it from us and persevere, always delivering our lessons and making sure we had enough to eat and clean clothes to wear, but it took its toll on her body. Her emotional and physical strength amazes me.

As I got older, I began to notice other, subtler things. We kids would get new clothes and new shoes, but in all our time in Karachi I never once saw my parents wear new clothes. They just mended the ones they had, year after year.

I also saw the worry in my parents' faces. I wouldn't find out until many years that they were concerned about our lack of a real education and what the future held. In Pakistan, even though we'd been there for over seven years, we were still refugees with no real immigration or legal status.

There were times when my father wouldn't get paid for months. His employers knew that as a refugee he couldn't protest or go to the authorities, so they took advantage of him. As kids we didn't know this, of course, but I do remember nights when we had less food to eat. There was usually enough for the four children, but often I would hear my parents say they weren't hungry, and they would not eat. A simple excuse that most children might overlook, but I sensed something wasn't right.

I knew my father, and I knew when he was hiding something. He never complained, but I saw it in his eyes. Something troubled him.

Throughout our time in Pakistan, my parents kept an eye toward events in Afghanistan. They would catch bits and pieces from the radio, and I'm sure they heard rumors from the other refugees they encountered in the city. When we could finally afford a television for our apartment, they truly got to see that the Afghanistan they remembered was no more. The Taliban had come to power and a cloud of medieval barbarity had descended upon the country.

My parents didn't share this with us. The first time I asked about our homeland after the incident on the playground, my father regaled me with tales about the greatness of Afghanistan. I believed him and desperately wanted to see our homeland. In time we would go back, he told me, once things were better, but he never fully explained what he meant.

A few years later, there was an instance when my parents were watching the news and told us children to leave the room. Something had come on the TV they didn't want us to see.

Later on, I found out that it was a news broadcast about the last Communist president of Afghanistan, Mohammad Najibullah. On September 26, 1996, the Taliban entered the UN compound in the city of Kabul and escorted him under armed guard to the public square outside the gate of the compound. For all to witness, they castrated him, shot him in the head, tied his body to a truck, and dragged him through the city streets. When they were finished, they hung his battered corpse from a pole and left it there for the crows. This practice of hanging bodies for public display was a signal to the population that a new era had begun.

My mother and father, despite publicized events such as this, could only glean bits and pieces of what was happening in Afghanistan from the news. They didn't really know how bad things were, and my father had faith in his homeland's history of struggle and survival against great odds.

No invader or oppressive regime had ever lasted long in Afghanistan. The Afghans had defeated and pushed out the Greeks, the Mongols, the Persians, the British, and most recently the Soviets. He believed it was only a matter of time before the Taliban fell. They were the remnants of the CIA-backed mujahideen from the Soviet-Afghan War. They wouldn't last long without foreign support, he thought.

After seven years, my father was tired of being a refugee. He was at the mercy of his employer, and he feared his children were falling behind in their education and social development. Everything we had—our apartment, our belongings, the scooter—could be taken away for no reason at all. We had no future in Pakistan, and my parents missed their homeland. It might not be the same place they remembered, but it was still home.

In 1999 my parents made the second-hardest decision of their lives: we would leave our apartment in Karachi and move back to Kabul. My father knew his daughters would not be able to attend school in Afghanistan, but at least his son could. He knew his wife and daughters would have much less freedom under the Taliban, but he was optimistic things would change in time. The Taliban regime couldn't last forever. And once back in Afghanistan, he could work, and the economy would pick back up eventually. He could be an engineer again.

The reality of what life would be like in Kabul, however, was something none of us could have imagined.

8

OUR RETURN

———

MY MOST VIVID CHILDHOOD MEMORIES start at about eight
years old. Yes, I remember moments from when I was younger
during our time in the refugee camp and in Karachi—the playground,
the mountains, the food, the apartment—but the year I turned eight
proved seminal for me on multiple levels.

It was 1999, and I can recall the smells, the textures, the hot,
the cold, the dryness, the sights, the emotions, the uncertainty, and
the excitement. We started off the year in Karachi, and I like to think
that I was growing up into a young woman who was becoming aware
of the world around me and my place in it. My memories have such
clarity that, even when I close my eyes today, I can transport myself
back to those days in our apartment, on the scooter, and walking in
the mountains with my father.

There are some events I hope never to forget no matter how much
time passes, but there are others I wish I could eradicate from my con-
sciousness. Our journey from Karachi back to Afghanistan, however,
is a memory I'm unsure whether I want to keep or forget entirely.

———

In July 1999 my parents told us we were moving back to Afghanistan. They'd gathered us together in the main room of our apartment and stood before us as we children sat on the rug. We'd just finished dinner, and the aromas of savory rice and roasted lamb still lingered in the air. The weather was warm outside, and the windows were open to catch the summer breeze, along with the sounds of Karachi's streets.

Instead of this gathering being a moment for celebration because we were going back to our homeland, to a place our parents had told us about so longingly and with such joy, the mood was unmistakably somber. Despite our parents' efforts to sound excited, the tone of their voices, the look in their eyes, even the way they stood so stiff and unmoving, made me think things were not right. They seemed to be hiding something, or at least they weren't telling us the whole truth.

My father said we would leave in a few days' time and that we couldn't take much with us, just a small bag to carry some clothes, a few snacks, and some water. Everything else that we'd collected from our time in Pakistan—our pots and pans, the gas stove, our blankets and mattresses—had to stay. We gave these items to the other Afghan families we knew in the neighborhood, who wished us luck and said goodbye.

When the day came to start our journey home, we woke early. The sun had just started peeking over the tops of the buildings and in through my bedroom window, and I remember feeling the summer heat on my face and breathing the dusty air. Outside, the wind kicked up scraps of plastic and trash that littered the nearby streets and alleys, swirling them around.

As we packed, my mother shared with me that I had been about the same age as Maryam was now when we left Afghanistan all those years ago. She said she'd held me in her arms the entire journey, making sure I was safe and warm and secure.

Normally this kind of comment would have touched my heart, showing me once again how much our parents loved and cherished us. But this time, my mother's words fell on me with a gravity I wasn't sure I understood. She then told me that during this journey, I would have to hold and care for Maryam like she had for me.

I felt special that she trusted me with such an important responsibility, caring for my baby sister, but I was nervous. My little sister was so small and delicate, and I didn't know what to expect on the journey. I'd been a baby myself the only time I'd ever traveled so far.

Then I watched my mother pull out a long blue burka. I'd seen this piece of clothing in my mother's things before, but I'd never seen her wear it. I asked her why she was putting it on; it looked hot and cumbersome, covering her entire body like a sheet and draping heavily over her head, hiding her face. She said she hadn't worn it since she left Afghanistan in 1992, but now was probably the right time to put it on again. Her reasoning escaped me, except for her final comment about wanting us to have a safe journey.

I didn't ask anything more, but her words about a safe journey made me pause. I knew about the typical hazards associated with long journeys, but the site of the burka and my mother's words made me think something dangerous awaited us. I sensed we would need to hide and not draw attention to ourselves, that there were people who would do us harm if we weren't careful, though I didn't know why I felt this way.

When my mother finally took the clumsy garment off, she handed me and my sister each a long scarf called a chador. She told us that we were now grown and that we'd need to cover our heads whenever we were outside. It was very important we do this, she said, clasping my tiny hands in hers.

I didn't know what to say. I always trusted my parents and everything they told me, but I knew something was different about this trip. It was like everything I'd ever known and found comfortable was slowly and quietly disintegrating with each passing moment. I wanted to understand and I wanted to know why, but I didn't have the words to ask the right questions. There was just a feeling in my gut.

When we were all packed and ready to leave, my father gave the apartment key to the landlord, who embraced my father and wished us luck. The driver was already waiting for us downstairs; the plan was for him to take us to Quetta, Pakistan.

The seven of us crammed into a tiny Suzuki Alto, with the driver, my father, and my brother in the front and the four women, with me holding Maryam, in the back. It was oppressively hot, and at times the road was rough. There was little comfort to any part of this trip, and there were long stretches where I thought it would never end.

After ten hours of driving, with very few stops, we reached the city of Quetta. The sun was already going down, and my father had planned for us to stay the night in a hotel. However, our driver, Ahmed, said it was not safe. Ahmed did not elaborate, but my father said his young family couldn't continue on like this and we needed rest.

Ahmed offered to take us to his brother's house and said we could spend the night there. My father thanked him for his kindness. When we pulled into the drive and crawled out of the cramped vehicle, his brother's family came out to welcome us with open arms. They offered us tea and cookies and sweets as soon as we got inside. We ate Afghan shorba for dinner, which is a soup made with beef, potatoes, and tomatoes. Even now I can still taste the delicious, savory broth, tender meat, and vegetables.

We'd spent most of that day on the road and had barely eaten anything. We'd left our home in Karachi and everything that was familiar and comfortable, and now we were in a strange city. We didn't know this family at all, and they had no warning we were coming.

Nonetheless, they opened their home to shelter us for the night and fed us. For me, that soup and the family's generosity illustrate the hospitality of the people of this region.

The following morning, another driver drove us the fifteen hours to Peshawar, Pakistan. Along the way, we listened to music by Ahmad Zahir, a traditional Afghan musician. I drifted in and out of sleep, with the music and sounds of the car humming in my dreams.

We arrived in Peshawar at about five that evening, but my father decided to wait until the following morning to cross the border into Afghanistan. He knew neither what awaited us on the other side nor where we might find shelter, and I could tell he was nervous. The driver stayed with us in the motel that night, and the next day we woke before sunrise.

As we drove the remaining miles to Torkham Gate, which is the busiest official border crossing between Pakistan and Afghanistan, excitement bubbled inside me. The exhaustion from the past few days had vanished, and I recalled all the stories my parents had told me about our homeland. I pictured the house my parents had built, what it would be like meeting my grandparents for the first time, experiencing the sights and sounds of Kabul with all the cafés and people and bazaars, and beholding the beautiful landscape of the Afghan mountains. We were going *home*.

But upon reaching Torkham Gate, we were greeted by a scene I did not expect. The border crossing was a simple metal drop arm guarded by a handful of Pakistani soldiers in long black uniforms. There were numerous jinga trucks, which are large flatbed and container trucks lavishly decorated with bright colors and designs, as well as chains and other decorations that jingle when they drive. They were parked in a rocky lot waiting to transport foodstuffs into Afghanistan. Just over the border, I could see the majestic Spin Ghar mountain range, which would become famous after 2001 and the battles in Tora Bora.

However, what struck me was how desolate everything looked. Although there were people and cars and trucks around, and I could see small houses scattered on the hillsides in the distance, the entire landscape looked barren. The sky was gray and the weather was cool, and I could practically see the wind rushing across the plains and through the hills. More ominously, the far side of the border along the eastern edge of Afghanistan had a sharp and dangerous appearance, as though it were another world, harsh and unwelcoming.

When it was our turn to cross the border, we passed through the checkpoint without incident. Our Pakistani driver dropped us near a lot where other cars were waiting for passengers. My father soon found an old man from Jalalabad who agreed to take us to Kabul.

As we started off toward Kabul, I admit that at first I squealed with excitement. We were finally home. But my mood quickly changed.

Right away the driver advised my father about life under the Taliban. He said if we get stopped, don't talk too much. Only speak when spoken to and keep answers short and simple. Speak Pashto. No one else in the family should talk, and no one should get out of the car unless ordered to. Women, especially, should not open their mouths or look at anything. The old man also told my father not to reveal that we were coming from Pakistan. We were coming from Jalalabad to visit family in Kabul; that was the story. Last, if the Taliban tried to take anything, let them have it and don't argue.

My father listened intently as the man spoke, as did the rest of us. No one made a sound. The old man's instructions raised our anxiety level from wariness to genuine fear.

We encountered a Taliban checkpoint twenty minutes later. The driver told my father to remember what he'd said. If my father did as he'd advised, everything would be OK.

Three men carrying rifles and wearing long black clothing stood in the middle of the road, directing all vehicles off to the side, where other men with more guns were searching and questioning travelers. Their beards hung down to their chests, some pitch black and others dyed a rusty red. Their hair was either wild or tucked under a turban, and several of the men seemed to have smudged soot around their eyes.

These were the scariest people I'd ever seen, and my heart raced. I saw them pointing their guns at cars and trucks and yelling at people to get out. They hit some people indiscriminately and grabbed and shoved others. They also took bags of flour and rice and anything else they wanted from the travelers. I heard the driver whisper that if anyone resisted, the Taliban would shoot and kill them. I was so scared I buried my head in my lap and closed my eyes.

There was a loud crash, and I looked up just enough to see two Taliban militants standing in front of our car smashing their rifle butts against the bumper. I felt my chest tighten and my throat constrict. I nearly stopped breathing. I wanted to cry, but I was frozen with fear.

The men were yelling, and both our driver and my father opened their car doors and got out. My brother followed; out of the corner of my eye I could see him shaking.

The Taliban questioned them. What's your name? Where are you from? Where are you going? Why? Why's your beard so short? Their voices were hard, like grinding stones, and their eyes were angry. They looked at everyone and everything with disgust and hatred.

The questioning lasted about ten minutes before they sent us on our way, apparently satisfied with the answers our driver, my father, and my brother had given them. I thanked God they didn't speak to me or my mother and sister. They didn't even look at us, actually.

We encountered three more checkpoints just like this before we finally reached Kabul, and I admit, each time I was terrified. All I could think was that these men were evil and that they would kill us for no reason and over nothing.

We arrived in Kabul around noon and, as before at the Torkham Gate, a sense of desolation crept over me. This was not the city of warmth and vibrancy my father had told us about. There was no music, there were no colorful kites in the air, there were no bustling bazaars, and there were no travelers who'd come from faraway places.

Instead, Kabul was full of fear and decay, almost entirely deserted by its former inhabitants. The crumbling buildings, marked by the scars of war and neglect, appeared abandoned. Everything was gray and brown and coarse looking. The few men who were out had hollow looks in their eyes. There was not a woman to be seen.

I asked my father if this was the city he remembered, the Paris of Central Asia. After taking a deep breath, he said, "No, not even close." I looked at my mother, and through the mesh window of the horrid burka that covered her face, I saw her weeping.

We eventually arrived at my grandparents' house, but it was locked and no one was inside. A neighbor came out from next door and at first thought we were thieves, but then he recognized my father. There was a warm exchange, and he invited us inside his home. We learned that my grandparents had fled to Iran a year ago and were now safe. The neighbor had no news other than that, and regretted that he didn't know the fate of my mother's parents.

The neighbor let us into my grandparents' house. Bombs had hit it during the civil war, and much of the house had been damaged or completely destroyed. The room that my parents had built had been reduced to rubble. The courtyard was hard and dusty; there was no garden, no birds, and no life. There was only a well and a bucket, which we used to clean a section of my grandparents' basement floor to sleep on. The sun had already set, and it was getting cold.

That night, as soon as I closed my eyes, images of the city and our drive through its deserted streets plagued me. No people. Abandoned and bombed-out buildings. Hollow faces. The Taliban and their guns. I could hear their shouts and see the hate in their eyes.

I remembered the warnings from the old man who drove us to Kabul and the ones from our neighbor. During prayer time no one could be outside. The Taliban would whip anyone who did not comply. If they saw someone stealing, they would cut off the person's hand. If a woman was seen alone outside her home or if any bit of her skin was exposed, they would whip her until she bled.

Violence. Anger. Hate. That was Kabul. That's what the Paris of Central Asia had become, and there was no place for women here except as modern-day slaves who were treated worse than animals.

For the first time in my life, I wished I were a boy.

9

LIFE UNDER
THE TALIBAN

———

WE'D BEEN IN KABUL no more than a week before my father's handsome face began to disappear behind a growing beard and mustache. He looked different to me, somewhat foreign; the change in his appearance seemed to represent the upheaval happening in our lives.

In Karachi we'd been happy and we'd been free. We'd laughed, smiled, played, dreamed, loved, and so much more. But now we were in Afghanistan, where there was no joy, no hope, and no life. My father couldn't find work as an engineer, because educated people were not needed in Afghanistan. There was no need for infrastructure and modern buildings; the only thing that mattered was the Taliban's corrupt view of Islam. My father eventually found a job as a laborer on a farm.

My brother started going to school, which was good, but no girls or women were allowed anywhere near the schools. The schools were only for boys, and religious education was paramount. The schools taught some academic subjects—writing, reading, and arithmetic—but the Koran and the history of Islam dominated everything. The religious leaders declared that memorizing the Koran and strictly adhering to Sharia law were more important than all other subjects.

Each day when my brother came home from school, he'd share with us what he could, which we were grateful for, but the fact that he had to sneak us the information made it all seem poisoned. Everything here was wrong.

During these first few months, I remember looking at myself in the mirror. I was just eight years old, a little girl with curly, dark hair and big, brown eyes, and I felt ashamed. Women were nothing and were not important.

A few months after we arrived in Kabul in the fall of 1999, something happened I will never forget. The day had started like any other. My father had gone to work at the farm, and I had stayed home with my siblings. My mother was teaching us math.

That afternoon, we heard an eruption of gunfire coming from our neighbor's house next door. We knew these neighbors; the father was a carpenter, the mother was an older woman, and there were two daughters, Samira, who was eighteen, and Nargis, who was thirteen. They were our friends.

After a few more shots, we heard screams. I heard the mother wailing and Samira and Nargis crying.

The gunshots and the screams shocked me, and I started shaking. I had no idea what was happening. The noise echoed throughout our house. The sound of a truck driving away was followed by more screams. I was terrified.

I saw my brother jump up and run out the front door toward their house. My mother threw on her burka and followed him. After a moment's hesitation, Afsoon and I followed. To this day, I cannot forget what I saw and heard.

As I trailed my sister into our neighbor's courtyard, I heard the mother screaming, "Please, God, help. They took my husband. They took my daughter from me. Take me! Take me! Take me!" She kept shrieking over and over again, and her cries of anguish pierced my ears.

She was crumpled on her knees by the front door, flailing her arms against the wall and beating the ground. I saw Nargis standing there, frozen like a statue, with tears streaming down her blazing cheeks. She was screaming with each breath, her eyes wide and staring at nothing.

Then I saw the body on the step by the front door. I could tell it was the father. One of his sandals had come off, and his tan shalwar kameez was rumpled, exposing his stomach and calves. A pool of blood had formed around his head and shoulders, and dark-red droplets had splattered his clothing. There were splashes of blood on the wall beside him.

The Taliban had shot him in the head. A group of Taliban had come to take Samira, but her father had tried to stop them. They shot him while his wife and children looked on. They took Samira, my friend, and they drove off. No one knew where they took her or what they did to her. She was gone.

I kept asking my mother what happened and where Samira was. I just kept asking and asking, staring at the mother, staring at my friend Nargis, but my eyes always returned to the blood on the ground and the broken skull that had been shattered by a Taliban bullet.

My mother yelled at Afsoon and me to go home. She told us to go inside and lock the door and not to open it for anyone. My sister took my hand and led me away. I started shaking, and as soon as we got inside our house, I ran into our bedroom and hid inside the closet. I shut the door and curled up in the corner, hugging my knees to my chest, crying. I was crying so hard I couldn't control myself, my body quivering. I lost all sense of time, and at some point I fell asleep, my entire body exhausted from fear and trauma.

Sometime later, I awoke to my father's voice. He was standing over me in the door of the closet, his warm hand on my shoulder. He encouraged me come out, but I wouldn't move. I asked him what had happened to Samira. I told him to tell me the truth. "What happened to my friend?"

My Baba Jan stayed silent. All he could do was hug me.

For the next two days, I couldn't eat. I was sick, I barely talked, and I didn't want to do anything. I wouldn't play with my sisters and I wouldn't study. I wouldn't go outside. I wanted to be alone.

At night, when I closed my eyes to go to sleep, I could hear the screams of my friend and her mother, and I could see her father dead in the doorway. In truth, I can still hear the screams and picture the body lying in a pool of blood. It's seared into me.

––––––––––

A year later, one day in the fall of 2000, my siblings and I were at our house in Kabul with our mother, as usual. Our father was working at his job on the farm on the outskirts of the city.

That morning, Afsoon had come down with a severe fever. Her temperature was so high my mother feared for her life, so she sent my brother, Omar, to the fields to find my father. My father had to be the one to take my sister to the clinic because, as a woman, my mother was not permitted outside the house without a male escort. If the Taliban caught her, they would punish and shame her.

But when Omar returned, he said he couldn't find our father. Omar then told my mother that he could escort her and Afsoon to the clinic. Though just ten years old, he was a man, and as long as he was the escort the Taliban couldn't challenge them. He stated this as confidently as he could, and my mother agreed.

She told my brother to find a taxi or a cart to transport his sick sister while she got ready to go. She hurriedly put on her burka and told me that I needed to watch my younger sister, Maryam. If Baba Jan came home, I was to tell him where they'd gone.

They left and the house fell silent. Three hours passed. I was playing with Maryam in the backyard when someone started pounding on the front door. The bangs against the metal door were so loud I jumped, fearing it might be the Taliban. Thoughts of my friend and her murdered father flooded my mind.

My heart raced, and I told my little sister to be quiet and to stay in the backyard, out of sight. I took off my flip-flops and tiptoed barefoot through the house to within a few feet of the front door. I planned to get on my stomach and look through the crack underneath to see who it was.

Then I heard my brother's voice. He was yelling, calling my name, telling me to open up. He kept pounding on the door, the booms echoing through the house. Without thinking, I jumped up, undid the bolt, and yanked the door open. I didn't know what to expect, but I found myself short of breath and scared.

Looking out into the front courtyard, I saw my sister crying and my brother by her side, his face flushed. They were on their knees in the dirt. My mother stood beside them, having just come through the gate, but she moved haltingly.

I immediately knew something was wrong. Standing in the doorway, I pleaded with them to tell me what had happened. My mother didn't look at me; she yanked off her heavy burka and threw it into the dirt. My heart stopped when I saw her bleeding feet.

She fell down. I started crying and kept pleading for someone to please tell me what had happened. Then, sensing something behind me, I turned and saw my little sister's face at the back door. She was also crying.

My mother asked for a cup of water, so I rushed into the kitchen to fetch her one. When I returned, she was holding her bloody feet. Afsoon was sitting on the ground and crying. She kept saying, "It was all because of me! It was all because of me!"

Then the story came out. My brother, mother, and sister made it to the clinic and were seen by a nurse. After they left the clinic, a Taliban truck drove past. A Taliban fighter with a long red beard and a bald head, wearing a long, black shalwar kameez, jumped out of the truck and advanced toward them. He was yelling at my mother for exposing her feet.

In her rush to get out of the house, my mother had forgotten to trade her flip-flops for shoes that covered the skin of her ankles and feet. Women were not allowed to show even an inch of skin in public. She had broken the law.

The Taliban fighter with the red beard started whipping my mother. My brother and sister rushed to her side, but she told them to stay back. The fighter yelled wildly at everyone. My mother dropped to the ground, pleading for him to stop hitting her and not to hurt the children. She'd only taken her daughter to the clinic, she'd forgotten to change shoes, she was sorry, it was a mistake—please have mercy. But he kept beating her until her feet were bloody and bruised, and then he left.

When I heard this story, I couldn't stop my tears, and I hugged my Mother Jan as tightly as I could. I asked her to please let me help her inside. We could clean her feet inside the house, where she could rest and get better.

As I tried to help my mother up, I heard the courtyard gate open again. Fear coursed through me, but when I turned to see who it was, I saw my father. He was carrying groceries, but upon taking in the scene before him, he dropped the bag and rushed to my mother's side.

While my brother tried to explain what had happened, my father picked my mother up out of the dirt and carried her inside the house. My mother clutched his neck, and her cries turned into sobs. My father

told me to bring him some clean towels and bandages, and he eased
my mother down onto the couch. I brought what he asked for, then
watched as he tended to my mother's injuries, wiping the dirt and
smudges from her face as he did so.

That night I fell asleep silently crying to myself. I had nightmares
about something terrible pressing down on my chest, making it hard
to breathe, but I couldn't remember specifically what it was. It just kept
getting heavier and heavier, and I couldn't get away. I couldn't move.

The next morning, I woke up and found my mother making
breakfast: eggs, tomatoes, and peppers. She was sitting on the floor
cross-legged with white bandages on her feet, stained red from where
the blood had soaked through and smudged black from the traces of
dirt on the floor.

I asked her if her feet still hurt, and she said yes, but that it was
OK. She could sit on the floor and do what she needed to there. I sat
down beside her and offered to help. I took one of the peppers and
worked silently for a time. Eventually I asked my mother if we made
her and Baba Jan's life more difficult.

This question had been festering in the back of my mind for quite
a while, and I needed to know. They gave us so much and took care
of our every need before their own. They'd given up their lives and
their dreams so they could raise us. And if it weren't for us, she would
have not been beaten by the Taliban. Or so I thought.

My mother looked at me with both pain and love and told me
that I should never think such a thing, that she and Baba Jan couldn't
imagine life without us, and that we'd brought so much light and joy
into their lives. She said they were gardeners and that we were their
fruit to be tended to and nurtured. Each one of us was like a tree that
they'd raised from the tiniest beginnings, and what they wanted most
in life was for us to have happiness and health.

I believed her and her words warmed my heart, but I asked her
why we'd left Pakistan. "We were happy there, right? We used to play

outside, have picnics, be free . . . Why did we come here? And why is it bad to be a woman? Why must we be treated this way? What is wrong with us?"

She told me that nothing was wrong with us, and yes, we'd been happy in Karachi. But we had to return to Kabul for our future. Things were bad now, but that was life. Sometimes there is happiness; other times there is sadness. That is how life works.

The Taliban's rule was barbaric and cruel. There was violence all the time, oppressive, sadistic violence. They were worse than mad dogs—they still are. I pray the Taliban, or any regime even remotely like them, never comes to power in any part of the world ever again.

During these first few years back in Afghanistan, the Taliban took everything from me: my innocence, my peace, my right to an education, and my freedom to walk down the street without fear. They took away my childhood.

I will never get those years back, nor will the thousands of other girls who grew up under the Taliban's heel. The Taliban ruined an entire generation of children. And as I write this, the remnants of ISIS's caliphate in Syria are withering, but my heart cries out for the innocents who had to endure that hell: the children, women, and men forced to serve such evil. Make no mistake—the kind of rule meted out by the Taliban and ISIS is truly evil.

Thankfully, my father was right. No oppressor, foreign or domestic, lasts forever in Afghanistan. Their day would come. I knew it would. And when I was old enough, I told myself, I would fight back. I would not live in fear.

10

SEPTEMBER 11, 2001

A T 8:46 AM ON SEPTEMBER 11, 2001, American Airlines Flight 11 crashed into the North Tower of the World Trade Center in New York City. At 9:03 AM, United Airlines Flight 175 struck the South Tower. At 9:37 AM, American Airlines Flight 77 hit the Pentagon in northern Virginia. And at 10:03 AM, United Airlines Flight 93 crashed into a field near Shanksville, Pennsylvania, its intended target likely the US Capitol or the White House.

By the end of the day, 2,977 innocent people were dead, the towers had fallen, the Pentagon was burning, and plane wreckage was strewn across a Pennsylvania field. Nothing would ever be the same.

Most of you have memories of that day. Perhaps you were at work or at school, maybe driving in your car, or at home watching a morning news show. You've likely heard all sorts of reasons and theories about why the attacks took place.

Some of you reading this book may not remember the attacks, either because you were too young or not yet born, but you likely learned about them in school or heard stories about those world-shattering events. Perhaps the stories are more personal, or perhaps they're distant and detached, like an evocative image that you recognize but don't really know.

What I've realized is, each person's knowledge or memory of 9/11 varies. Therefore, here is a very brief explanation of why I think the attacks occurred, which will put into context my personal experience and that of other Afghans as victims of al-Qaeda and its alliance with the Taliban.

———————

The signs of the growing threat from Islamic extremism go back at least to 1979, which was a watershed year in many respects. Most people know about the Islamic Revolution in Iran, as well as the Soviet invasion of Afghanistan. Both events occurred that same year.

But there is an incident people probably don't think about, and which I myself didn't learn about until I was older: the Grand Mosque seizure in Mecca, Saudi Arabia. One could draw a direct line from this incident to the rise of Osama bin Laden and al-Qaeda and the eventual attacks on 9/11.

Although it's hard to believe, prior to 1979 Saudi Arabia was also on the path to becoming a progressive, modern society like Afghanistan. Women were joining the workforce and appearing in the media, and young men were moving away from religion and closer to sports and other distractions. This was in no small part due to the influence of the West on Saudi Arabia's oil sector. Consequently, the push for various freedoms—particularly those for women—were slamming up against traditional Saudi society.

Men like Juhayman al-Utaybi—a deeply religious man, a former soldier, and an antimonarchist—believed these reforms were an affront to Islam and, in response, planned and executed an attack on the Grand Mosque in Mecca. The attack became a siege, with al-Utaybi demanding the overthrow of the House of Saud, the expulsion of all foreign influence, and a return to a stricter rule over society.

The siege lasted from November 20 to December 4, 1979. It involved hundreds of hostages trapped inside the mosque, upward of five hundred Islamic militants holed up inside the compound, and over ten thousand security forces, including French commandos, poised outside locking down the area. Casualties were high on both sides. When it was all over, the Saudi government beheaded sixty-seven militants, including al-Utaybi. After the attack, rather than cracking down on Islamic extremists, the Saudi king allowed the ulema (religious leaders) to institute increasingly stricter forms of Sharia law across the kingdom.

Osama bin Laden was in his early twenties and finishing up his degree at university when the siege occurred. He would have undoubtedly witnessed it on TV. He would also have seen the subsequent storming and burning of the US embassy in Islamabad and the attack on the US embassy in Tripoli, both of which were attributable to rumors that the siege in Mecca had been an American and Zionist plot. Within the year, bin Laden would be in Pakistan with the mujahideen, supporting the fight against the Soviets in Afghanistan.

These events likely cemented bin Laden's visceral hatred of foreigners and their intervention in Islamic lands. To me, it's chilling to know that I lived and traveled in the same areas as bin Laden.

Fast-forwarding to Iraq's invasion of Kuwait in 1990, bin Laden was a hero of the jihad coming out of the Soviet-Afghan War, and he commanded an international network of battle-hardened Islamic fighters. He offered his forces to the Saudi king to help defend against a potential Iraqi incursion, but the king turned him down. Instead, an international coalition led by thousands of American troops came to Saudi Arabia—the land of Islam's two holiest sites. Consequently, empowered by his newly formed international terrorist organization, al-Qaeda, bin Laden set out to strike at the heart of the United States and the West.

On February 26, 1993, al-Qaeda operatives detonated a truck bomb in the garage of the North Tower of the World Trade Center. It killed six people and injured over a thousand but failed to bring down either tower. In Riyadh on November 13, 1995, a car bomb killed five Americans who were training the Saudi military. On August 7, 1998, al-Qaeda executed two simultaneous attacks on US embassies in Nairobi, Kenya, and Dar es Salaam, Tanzania, killing 224 people and injuring more than four thousand. And on October 12, 2000, in the Gulf of Aden, two suicide bombers drove a boat laden with explosives into the USS *Cole*, crippling the US Navy ship and killing seventeen sailors.

In hindsight, the evidence of the gathering storm is unmistakable; the audacity of the 9/11 attacks and their successful execution is still hard to fathom. My family in Kabul was not aware of the combined significance of most of these events. We lacked access to the international media and had our own struggles to contend with, which were often as basic as trying to put food on the table or avoid being shot by the Taliban.

However, there was one event that struck fear into us all.

———————

On September 9, 2001, my father was listening to the radio in his small store. He'd built this shop by himself a few years back, and we'd helped him make the bricks in our backyard. This had become his place of business, and he sold produce from the local farms along with other small items. He always kept a radio there.

The Taliban allowed people to have radios because that's how they spread their propaganda and rallied supporters, and it was how the mullahs broadcast their edicts. My father, though not a believer in anything the Taliban preached, always had the radio on because it was the only source of outside information. On September 9, some particularly disturbing news was broadcast and quickly spread across the city. A suicide bomber had killed Ahmad Shah Massoud, the commander of the Northern Alliance and an adversary of the Taliban.

Massoud had been a renowned fighter and commander of the mujahideen during the war against the Soviets; during the Afghanistan civil war he had fought against the rise of the Taliban. But since the 1990s, he'd held his forces in the northern provinces and prevented the Taliban from occupying more land. His murder sent shock waves through most Afghans.

At the time, none of us knew that bin Laden and al-Qaeda were behind the assassination, but we did know that Massoud's murder would allow the Taliban to extend their control over more territory. My father explained these things to us when he returned from the shop that night. We were all worried, but we didn't know the worst was yet to come.

At three in the afternoon on September 11, my father was again in his shop. That's when he heard about the US attacks over the radio. When he heard this announcement, he said he froze, and everyone else in the shop stopped what they were doing and stood silently and listened. The news was unbelievable.

No one knew that bin Laden and his terrorist organization were behind the attacks, but the gravity of the situation was lost on no one. The Taliban and their supporters were ecstatic and thrilled that someone had launched such a successful attack against the American infidels and the Zionist enemy. But my father, my family, and others like us were shocked and saddened by this unspeakable tragedy. I remember asking my father if the Taliban was in America. He said he didn't think so. I asked who could have done such a thing. He didn't know, but I heard the fear in his voice.

That night, we ate dinner in silence with only candles to light our meal. It wasn't just my family who was eating quietly in the dark. There was an odd stillness over the city that night, as if everyone knew Afghanistan was somehow connected to the attacks in New York and Virginia, and that something ominous was about to overwhelm us.

At one point during our dinner, another news broadcast came on the radio and my father pressed his ear to the speaker so he could hear. Both towers had fallen, the Pentagon was still burning, and thousands of people were believed dead.

The last thing I remember my father saying that night before we went to bed was "No one is safe anymore. God help us all."

11

INVASION AND FREEDOM

———————

DURING THE FIRST WEEK OF OCTOBER 2001, we heard that American troops had invaded Afghanistan. Taliban fighters and their supporters still ruled all aspects of life, and they tried to control the information with their propaganda and sermons and declarations, but people were talking. Our neighbors, my family, laborers in the fields, and people at my father's shop heard rumors that American soldiers were in the north rallying the Northern Alliance to fight the Taliban and take back the rest of the country.

Warplanes appeared in the skies over Kabul. They were hard to see; they were so fast and so high up in the air. I would hear the high-pitched screech of jet engines as they soared over the mountains and through the clouds, but often I couldn't track them. By the time I looked up, they were usually disappearing in the distance or behind a mountain peak.

The sight of the American planes both concerned and fascinated me. I worried because I remembered my mother telling me how a bomb had destroyed our house many years earlier, and I didn't want that to happen again as the Americans fought the Taliban. Yet the aircraft overhead also captivated me, especially their speed and power, and I was elated because of what these planes represented. All of us who had lived in fear for far too long knew these warplanes had come to destroy al-Qaeda and the Taliban.

At our home, we heard the bombs falling and exploding on the outskirts of the city. My father said they were targeting the Taliban training camps, airfields, and supplies. The Americans would remove them from power. He was so happy, and he welcomed the American invasion, telling us not to worry. We would be safe if we stayed in our basement.

We were all amazed at how quickly things changed in the city. It was still October, and one day my father ventured out of the basement to see what was happening. When he came back, he told us that he couldn't see any Taliban on the streets, nor any of their trucks. He'd heard they'd fled the city, either to the south to Kandahar and Helmand, or east to Pakistan.

After that, it was as though a new city emerged out of the ashes. My father allowed us to come up from the basement and venture into our neighborhood. On occasion, we could still hear the planes overhead, but the sounds of bombs were farther off and at times too distant to hear.

Kabul was coming alive again. Somehow it seemed brighter; it was no longer only gray and brown sandstone and bone-cutting cold. Colors appeared in the windows of buildings, on people's clothing, and in shops, and the sun gleamed off these surfaces.

There were more people in the streets than I'd ever seen in the city before, and they were smiling. I could hear the laughter of men, women, and children. I heard the songs of Ahmad Zahir again, as well as new music from India. Many of the same melodies I'd heard on the car radio when we journeyed from Karachi to the Torkham border crossing nearly ten years ago were now playing inside shops in the bazaar. I felt like my eyes and my ears had been opened to a whole new world.

Most spectacularly, I started to see things change for women. They were small changes at first. The Taliban were not walking the streets in packs like before, harassing and beating anyone who dared to have a beard too short or who allowed the skin of an ankle or wrist to show, but all of us feared there might be someone hiding in the shadows. Some men, although they may not have fled with the other fighters, were still believers, and I sometimes feared they would come for me at night.

Gradually, more women went out to the markets to buy food and clothes. Soon I saw women throw away their burkas. Those awful, stifling, oppressive garments that the Taliban had forced us to wear were now being tossed aside by Afghan women.

When I saw my mother do it, a wave of delight flowed over her. She beamed with joy as she threw her burka on the ground in the dirt, and then moved it to the trash barrel.

I saw the happiness in my father too. He'd hated seeing his beautiful wife, our loving mother, humiliated and forced to wear clothing that was intended to oppress and confine. Now she was free, and his girls would never have to wear that horrible garment.

The Americans were coming, and everything would change.

During the first few months of the American-led invasion, it still wasn't safe for women to be out in public without a male chaperone, but that changed in December. We saw American armored vehicles drive through the city and American soldiers patrolling the streets.

Most people, especially children and teenagers, would wave and shout hello to the passing trucks and men.

We were warned never to walk in front of the American vehicles or get too close. They might run us over or, worse, shoot us. They were here to hunt down al-Qaeda and fight the Taliban, not play. For those first few weeks in late November and early December, anytime I saw one of the American trucks I would run and hide. I'd been conditioned by the terror of life under the Taliban to fear trucks with armed men, even those in uniform.

In time I realized the Americans wouldn't shoot me or run me down. Though I'd never met an American, I knew just by looking at them and from what my parents had told me that they were different. They weren't like Afghans, and I knew they were here to help us.

Soon, my mother was able to take her girls to the bazaar. It was just us, no men as escorts, freely out in public. I felt excited and liberated. We were no longer prisoners in our home, no longer slaves in our beloved country. I remember breathing the air and thinking that it actually felt freer.

I saw it in my Mother Jan too. She didn't have that cloud of depression haunting her face anymore. She held her head up and looked people in the eye; she would speak or ask a question if she wanted to, no longer silent with her head down and eyes averted. She had her confidence back, and it was beautiful.

One day in early November of that year, my father came home with amazing news. He gathered Afsoon and me in the main room of the house. We stood together and gazed up at him. Our younger sisters, Maryam and Manizha, who had just been born the year prior, were still too young. My father looked so handsome and happy since he'd shaved his beard after the Americans took control of the city; now his faced blazed with a huge smile.

Earlier, at his shop, he had caught wind of a rumor that schools for girls would soon reopen in Kabul. Afsoon and I would be able to get a formal education from a real school!

This was some of the best news I'd heard in my entire life. Ever since we were in the refugee camp in Pakistan, I'd dreamed about going to a real school. I was grateful for my mother and all she taught us in the camp, in our apartment in Karachi, and here in Kabul, but this would be an actual school.

My imagination ran wild, thinking about the teachers I would meet, the students I would make friends with, and the subjects I would learn. I so wanted to read my textbook, write in my notebook, and answer questions. I was giddy with anticipation.

My father, in the midst of sharing our joy, told us that he still needed to find out more information, to verify that what he'd heard was actually true. He said it might take him a few days to confirm the news, but as soon as he knew something he would tell us.

For the rest of the day and into the evening, I could barely keep still, bouncing around and chattering about what it would be like to finally go to school. At night I'd lie awake dreaming about it, and then in the morning I'd wake up wondering if today was the day my father would find out the rest of the details about where and when we could go to school.

After three agonizing days, my father came home with news from the Ministry of Education. Yes, girls' schools were being built across the city, funded by international donors, and they would be opening soon. But because no girls or women had been permitted to receive an education under the Taliban, everyone would need to take placement tests to determine their grade level. The tests were scheduled to take place at the ministry in a few weeks.

I could see the pride in my father's face, and he told us he knew we would do well because our mother had worked so hard to prepare us over the years. We were his brilliant little girls.

For the next two weeks, our mother and father helped us review our school subjects. We practiced day and night—reading, writing, arithmetic, science, and history. We used the same books we'd been studying for years. We used my brother's books to study more, and he drilled us on the material he'd learned in school.

None of this was work for me. It was my dream to go to school and get an education. Yet part of me wondered if it was actually true. Were they really building schools for girls, and would we truly be allowed to get an education? I knew what my father had told us, and I knew what I'd heard the few times I'd been outside the house, but the possibility that this wasn't real and wouldn't happen still tugged at the back of my mind.

Finally, November 20, 2002, arrived—the day of the test. My sister and I woke up early, and I remember feeling butterflies fluttering in my stomach like never before. Both my sister and I had worked so hard, and I wanted both of us to do well on the exam. I wanted to prove to my parents that everything they'd done for us, all that they'd sacrificed, was going to work out for the best. I wanted to make them proud.

I also wanted to do well for me. My Baba Jan had always told us that an education was one of the most important things in life because it made all other things possible. I believed him and wanted to earn my education so I could follow my dreams. My dreams may have been innocently formed at this point in my life—I was only eleven years old—but I had them and knew I needed an education to achieve them. With an education, opportunities would be open to me that otherwise would be out of reach.

My mother made a hearty breakfast that morning, and we all ate together. It was still dark outside, but at seven, with the daybreak, we all headed to the ministry. Although it was cold and rainy, which added to my nervousness, I was also filled with excitement and joy. So much had changed since the Americans came the year before, and now a dream that I'd had for as long as I could remember was actually coming true. An avalanche of emotions rushed through me, but I was determined to do well.

When we arrived at the ministry, I was shocked at how many girls were there. Since returning to Afghanistan, I'd never seen so many women and girls together at the same time in the same place. There must have been over a hundred of us, all ages, shapes, and sizes, all at the ministry to take the exam with hopes of attending school. I found the scene inspiring.

While my mother and other siblings waited outside, my father took Afsoon and me into the building to get in line for the test. I started talking with the girls around me, asking who they were, where they came from, and what they thought about school. I learned that a lot of girls came from families similar to ours who had fled to Pakistan or Iran during the Soviet-Afghan War or the subsequent civil war and rise of the Taliban. Most families had returned only in the last few years, some within the last few months. Other girls and their families had lived their entire lives under the Taliban.

As we talked more, I realized how fortunate I was to have parents like my Baba Jan and Mother Jan. They had nurtured, taught, and encouraged us our entire lives. They raised us to be equals, living with the belief that society should be free and just.

Many of the girls I talked to did not have the same level of support and encouragement from their families. Their fathers and brothers may not have been on the streets with the Taliban gangs, but they believed in the puritanical elements of Taliban ideology. These girls were forced to be subservient to men. It had been drummed into them that their place was in the home, caring for children; if they went outside they risked bringing shame down upon the family. Many of the girls had been beaten by their fathers and brothers for not showing sufficient modesty or for speaking out. Other girls had to sneak out of their homes without their fathers and brothers knowing to take the test, and they prayed it would be over before the men got home. Seeing the fear in these girls' faces and hearing their stories broke my heart.

The time for the test came, and my sister and I were sent into two different rooms. We wished each other luck and hugged our father, who told us to relax. We were ready for this, and we'd do well.

I sat at my desk in the classroom and was given a test paper with one hundred questions on it. They covered everything: math, science, history, biology, Dari, Pashto, comprehension, and other subjects. Initially I felt a sense of unease, but as soon as I started, my confidence swelled. I knew these subjects and I knew the answers. After all the hours of study and practice, I was taking my very first school exam.

Two hours later, I set my pencil down and turned in my paper. We were told our scores would be posted outside the ministry in three days. Of course, I was impatient to know if I'd passed, but there was nothing I could do but wait.

Once my sister and I exited the ministry and were outside with our family, my father took us to eat at a restaurant near Cinema Pamir downtown. I had a beef kebab followed by a scoop of shir yakh, which is similar to American vanilla ice cream, except it's also flavored with saffron and cardamom and often topped with ground pistachios. It's simply delicious.

Our day wasn't over. On our way home, my father stopped in a corner store and bought two kites. Flying kites is usually just for boys—it's considered improper for girls to fly kites—but my father promised I could fly one.

The next day, we divided into two teams, and I was paired with my father. We were going to have kite fights from the roof of our house. The goal was to get your kite in the air and then dive and swoop with enough speed and force to cut the string of your opponent's kite. It's like a kite dogfight.

I don't remember who won that day, us or my brother's team, but I do remember feeling elated when my kite sailed into the air and I pulled the string so the kite soared high into the sky. It felt liberating to be up there, even if I was on the roof simply holding the spool.

At eleven, I realized what was most significant for me in life. Things were changing in Afghanistan. The Taliban was gone, foreign investment was pouring in, schools for girls were being built, and there was the promise of progress. After so many years in darkness, fighting to stay alive, we were happy, and I felt I had an opportunity to do great things.

12

SCHOOL

———

THE DAY FINALLY arrived when our test scores and associated placement would be announced. I barely slept the night before, staring at the ceiling in my room with the lights off and the covers pulled up to my chin, wondering how I did.

I knew I was smart, and I was confident I'd known the answers to most of the questions on the exam, but this was the first real test I'd taken. It had been created by actual teachers who knew the curriculum, and they would use the results to determine what grade level I should be in. Simply knowing these things made my mind race.

When it was time to get out of bed, I was almost as nervous as the day of the actual test. Afsoon felt the same way. For two little girls who had been educated by their mother, who were now awaiting their evaluations by the Ministry of Education, this was a lot of stress.

As the sun was coming up, my sister and I went with our father to the ministry building, where our exam results would be posted. It was twenty miles from our house. We walked the first four miles, took a bus for the next fifteen, and were back on foot for the last mile.

My father kept telling me to slow down, but it was like my feet were running on their own power, compelled to walk faster and faster and skip and jump.

When we reached the ministry, a crowd of parents and girls was already there. Everyone was trying to get close to see the test results that had been posted on the exterior of the building. I saw ten pieces of paper, but we were too far back to read any names or scores.

My father looked at Afsoon and me and told us to wait at the corner. He was going to make his way through the crowd and find our scores. He had a determined smile on his face as he turned and squeezed his way through the crowd. I kept sight of him for a little while, but soon the back of his head disappeared in the throng.

My sister and I didn't say much to each other while we waited. We were as close as sisters could be, but at that moment we were both in our own worlds, thinking about the exam. So much of our young lives had been focused around preparing for school and this moment. Now we were about to find out if all our hard work had paid off.

After a few minutes that felt like forever, our father came back through the crowd to our street corner. I remember seeing his beaming face; he was smiling from ear to ear, and his eyes were full of pride. He embraced both of us and said, "You did it! You both qualified for the sixth grade."

I screamed with joy, and so did Afsoon. We jumped up and down in our father's arms, shouting and laughing and thanking God. This was what we'd both hoped for, what we'd worked for, what we'd dreamed would come true. The sixth grade! We were going to school as sixth graders.

I had so many questions. When do we start? Where is our school? What does it look like? Will I wear a uniform? How many other girls will be in the class? Books, when do we get our books? And pencils and paper—I need supplies!

My father didn't know these answers; he'd only seen our names and our scores on the posting outside the ministry. He told us again to wait patiently. He would go inside the ministry to get all the information.

More time passed before he finally came out of the building with the details about when school would start, where to go, and what we needed. We left, but rather than going straight home, my father took us to Cinema Pamir again. In celebration, he bought my sister a lovely pair of new shoes and a stylish new jacket for me. These were wonderful and generous gifts, and I thought to myself how far we'd come.

I'd heard the stories about my parents fleeing Kabul during the aftermath of the Soviet-Afghan War, and I remembered how destitute we were in the refugee camps. We had nothing to our name, at times not even enough food to eat. But now we were shopping in a bustling Kabul market, celebrating our chance to go to school.

When we arrived home, I ran to my mother and embraced her, telling her the news. Like our father, she was overjoyed, and she began to cry. I knew none of this would have been possible without her tireless efforts. She'd taught us every day for years, never once complaining.

I owe everything to my parents, and even back then I knew it. I will never forget what they did for us.

———————

My first day of school was on a Monday. I got up extra early that morning since, again, I couldn't sleep the night before. It took me over an hour to get dressed. We had to wear a school uniform—black pants, black dress, and a white scarf—and I wanted to make sure everything was perfect.

Looking at myself in the mirror, part of me still thought this was all a dream and not truly real. I feared I would wake up, the Taliban would be back, and I would be less than human again.

But this *was* truly real.

Both my sister and I were ready to go at 8:00 AM, although school didn't start till ten. My father had already gone to work at the shop, so my mother was the one to walk Afsoon and me to school. It took twenty-five minutes, and I remember looking up into the sky as soon as we set off, taking in a beautiful and sunny morning. Everything around us looked fresh and alive; it was joyous, and my legs were as anxious as they had been that day we went to the ministry for the exam results.

As we got closer to the school grounds, we started seeing other girls in uniform accompanied by family members. Some were skipping, jumping, and bubbling with excitement like I was, while others walked more modestly beside their mothers or grandmothers. Other girls appeared quite timid, as if they were scared to go.

What I found most amazing was the number of women all in one place at the same time, with not a single man anywhere in sight. Honestly, I never thought I'd see anything like this.

Growing up under the Taliban had conditioned me to think that women should not be in public, they should never be in large groups, and they should always be covered and submissive. Seeing so many girls together was uplifting; it was inspiring and powerful.

We made our way across the school grounds, then hugged our dear mother and said goodbye; she left to return home, as she was not allowed inside the building. My sister took my hand to go inside. I recall holding her hand tight, not wanting to let her go.

Inside the main building it was rather chaotic since the school was still under construction and there were multiple unfinished classrooms. No one knew where to go, so we all gravitated to the courtyard. There was a sea of smiling faces, and I wanted to make friends.

Most of the girls were like me, amazed that there were so many of us, that we didn't have coverings over our faces, and that there were no men. Some of the girls talked about how their families were happy that they were going to school, but there were also quite a few girls who were not so lucky.

Some girls couldn't tell their fathers and brothers they were here or that they'd taken an entrance exam or that they had even the slightest desire to get an education. They had to hide their uniforms, lie, and leave their homes in different clothes so their male relatives wouldn't suspect anything.

The scars from life under the Taliban remained. Many people still believed if women were outside the home they would dishonor the family and that women should always be covered from head to foot. Even women who were married or girls who were engaged should not leave the house. They should be prisoners for their own safety and the honor of the family.

Hearing these stories, I couldn't help but feel for these young women. Their hardships under the Taliban made me want to cry. I wanted to believe that eventually their fathers and brothers would be happy for them, proud that they earned an education. But I also knew and feared that it would take a long time for these lingering beliefs to change. There are social and religious behaviors in Afghanistan that are deeply ingrained from the years of oppression; it will take generations to change the thinking.

One of our new teachers quieted us down and told us to get in a line. No one knew if we were to line up by age or by height or some other method, so it was more of a cluster than an actual line, but soon enough the teachers started calling out names and directing us into groups.

They called Afsoon first, and I watched her walk across the court-yard looking so mature in her school uniform. I remember praying that we wouldn't be separated. I wanted to be in the same class with her—she was my sister and I loved her.

They then called my name and sent me to the same group. I was so happy I rushed toward her and hugged her, telling her over and over again, "I'm here too, I'm here too." I think I was saying it to convince myself that all of this was really happening.

There were twenty of us in the sixth-grade class, but our classroom was in one of the buildings still under construction. A teacher collected us and led us under a tent on the other side of the courtyard. It was a huge tent, and it reminded me of the ones in the refugee camp. When we sat down on the ground I giggled and leaned over to whisper to my sister, "We're under the tent again." She smiled because she'd thought the same thing, but she also pointed to the classrooms that were being built and said we'd be inside soon enough.

One of our teachers introduced herself as Sohila; she taught history. She was about five feet, seven inches tall, with wide shoulders, and had a slight resemblance to my mother as she stood at the front of the class, ready to begin the lesson for the day.

I came to respect Sohila immensely, because she exuded professionalism, strength, and self-confidence. She wasn't afraid of being who she was, and on occasion she shared with us that her husband still wanted her to wear the burka. She refused. She was free, and no one would tell her what to do ever again. Like my parents, she inspired me.

That first day of school was the first time I'd been away from my mother for an entire day, and it felt a bit weird. For as long as I could remember, I'd been with my mother every day. She'd always been no farther away than a room or a neighbor's house, and I'd taken her presence for granted. Now I was on my own at school, interacting with other adults and having to make friends with strangers.

School was a new and sometimes unsettling experience. I wanted to be a good student, and I wasn't shy about raising my hand to answer the teacher's questions. Fortunately, I was bright for my age and familiar with a lot of the subjects because of what our parents had taught us. This wasn't work; I enjoyed it and loved learning.

I thought of our class as a group of friends who would be together for a long time, and I wanted us to have fun. Sometimes, as a joke, I'd squirt one of the other girls with my water bottle and we'd all giggle and laugh. I'd also help my classmates with their homework, because some of them struggled with math or reading. I'd let them see my notes to help them understand the material.

I helped a girl named Sonia who was having trouble with a few subjects. Sonia was the first real friend I'd made since the Taliban took my neighbor Samira, and we grew very close. But no one could replace my friendship with Samira. It was that young childhood type of friendship that lacked all the fears, uncertainties, and dramas that plague us as we get older. Our friendship had been innocent and pure, despite having been brought to an end by the murderous Taliban.

I eventually told Sonia the story of how the Taliban had shot and murdered Samira's father and taken her away. I never saw Samira again; even now, no one knows what happened to her or if she is still alive. Part of me hopes she isn't. I can't imagine the hell she went through as a Taliban slave or what they did to her. But perhaps she escaped from her captors in the middle of the night and fled to some place in Pakistan or Iran.

Maybe someday Samira and I will meet again, though as of the writing of this book it hasn't happened. After nearly twenty years, I still think of her.

———————

Despite how much I loved learning and how free I felt at school, I was confused and uncertain about what it was all for and what my future held. Most of my school friends, even if they enjoyed school, ultimately wanted to get married and have a family. Afghan society expected its women to be good wives and mothers.

There were a few girls, however, who aspired to be either doctors or teachers, which were acceptable professions for women in Afghanistan. As doctors they could treat other women, and as teachers they could educate young girls like me. Men were barred from doing either one of these things.

In light of the turmoil and tragedy that Afghanistan had endured over the past twenty years, our country desperately needed women to join these professions. The role and presence of women in society needed to be reconstituted, and it would take smart, brave young girls to do it.

Neither of these possible careers inspired me. I didn't want to be a doctor or a teacher, and the thought of staying at home as a submissive wife and obedient caregiver didn't enter my mind. I yearned for something else, though I didn't know what it was.

Without a TV, a phone, access to the Internet, or even a public library, it was hard to learn about what was out there in the world. School handled the mechanics of my learning—math, science, reading comprehension, languages, history—but my education about what life offered beyond the confines of my home and school was lacking.

Fortunately, every night during dinner our father would ask us what we learned at school and talk to us about other life issues. Often he would give us a topic and we'd have two minutes to write down everything we knew about the subject and what we thought about it. We'd have a lively discussion as a family, learning from each other and listening to what my father had to say.

We'd talk about life, our goals, our plans for the future, and how we could achieve what we wanted. One evening he told us the story of Abdul Ahad Mohmand, Afghanistan's first astronaut, who had been a pilot in the Afghan Air Force before any of us children were born. In 1988, during the Soviet era, he'd been part of a three-man crew that went to the *Mir* space station and spent eight days and twenty hours in space.

Stories like this inspired me. I wanted to do great and exciting things with my own life. I wanted to be *up there*, in the clouds. As I walked to school and saw the American warplanes flying overhead, I dreamed of someday being high in the skies over Afghanistan.

I didn't dare share my dream with anyone. I'd be laughed at and mocked; Afghan women don't become pilots or anything of the sort. Thinking I could be the exception was absurd.

13

NOT EVERYTHING CHANGES

―――――

IN THE YEARS FOLLOWING THE AMERICAN-LED INVASION, Afghanistan's society and culture went through profound changes. It began to feel like the country I'd dreamed about when I was a small child, the country my parents grew up in before the wars and devastation. I used to think if I squinted really hard and brought to mind the stories my Baba Jan and Mother Jan had told me, I could see the exotic bazaars with men and women chatting over tea, hear the music coming from car radios and shops, and smell the incense and spices wafting through the city streets.

I no longer needed a man to escort me if I wanted to go outside; no longer was I a prisoner in my house while the Taliban terrorized people on the street. Those days were over, and I felt like a human being. We had freedom, and we could raise our voices if we wanted to. I finally felt unrestrained.

As I went to and from school each day, the roads were full of young girls in their black-and-white uniforms hurrying to class or dashing home. Stores and businesses for women were opening—places to buy clothes, household items, and other essentials. In the bazaars, Western clothing for women was displayed everywhere, and the dreaded burka was gone.

Though Afghanistan was back on the path to its former glory as the Paris of Central Asia, the trauma of the Taliban regime still lingered. For reasons I still can't explain, at times I feared there were Taliban lurking in the alleys, lying in wait for me. Sometimes at night when I closed my eyes, I could see their black turbans and Kalashnikovs as they prowled the streets. I could hear the screams of my friend Samira the day they took her and the sobs of my mother the day they beat her. Those visions are still with me.

Although the American and NATO forces were present and international aid was pouring into the country, there were still many families who held strict puritanical beliefs.

Many of my classmates lived in oppressive conditions. They had to sneak to school and afterward scurry home so that their fathers and brothers wouldn't know they were going to class. There were others whose fathers knew they were at school but still expected them to marry and start a family as soon as they were old enough. Their futures had already been decided for them, so these girls didn't try very hard, because they feared they would never graduate. Moreover, for some girls, all of this was compounded by extreme poverty.

This was my friend Sonia's situation. She came from a conservative family that didn't have a lot of money, so there wasn't enough for her to buy pens and notebooks. When we first started school, this wasn't a problem, because I had enough school supplies to share. But by the ninth grade, our studies were getting more rigorous, requiring more notebooks, paper, and pens.

Sonia was starting to lose interest in school, but not because she wasn't smart or didn't enjoy learning. She simply had no idea when her parents might pull her out and force her to get married. She knew one day it would happen, so why bother trying. She didn't want to ask for any money for supplies because she didn't know how long she'd be around.

When she shared this with me, I went home and talked to my father. We were having dinner, and I told my Baba Jan that I felt so lucky to have our family and our livelihood. He'd started as a farm laborer, established a successful shop, and was now working with a construction firm as an engineer. After twenty years, he was doing what he loved, and we were living comfortably as a consequence.

I felt uneasy asking, but I told him about Sonia and that I was afraid she wouldn't be able to continue her studies because she couldn't afford the most basic needs. I asked if instead of giving me new clothes for Eid al-Fitr, a tradition in my family, he would please lend me money so I could buy Sonia a few school supplies.

My father got up from his place on the floor and walked over to hug me. I think that moment made him very proud; I could see it in his eyes. He'd raised us well, to care for others and to be kind. He gave me twenty rupees and said to buy whatever I needed. My father is the most generous man I know.

The next morning, my sister and I left the house early. Along the way, we stopped at a store and I bought four notebooks and six pens. When we got to school, I waited for Sonia to go into the bathroom to change, and then I put the supplies on her desk. I didn't leave a note or say anything to anyone else.

When Sonia returned, a look of surprise came over her face as she picked up the notebooks and pens and looked around the classroom to see who might have put them there. Class started, and I saw her take a piece of paper and write a short note on it. She passed the note to me, and I saw the tears in her eyes.

The note said, "Thank you, Niloo. I know it was you."

I was glad to help Sonia, but there were other girls in similar situations. When we started together in the sixth grade, there were twenty-five of us in the class. But by the ninth grade we only had seventeen.

Most of the girls who dropped out had been forced into arranged marriages—girls who were thirteen, fourteen, fifteen years old. Their parents had chosen whom they would marry, either for economic reasons or familial connections. Sometimes they were forced to marry older men, often ten or twenty years their senior. Love was never a factor in these marriages, and neither was affection or happiness. Some of the girls may have eventually found these things if they were lucky, but for others it was a life of abuse and subservience.

At this stage in my life, I couldn't imagine being married, neither to a boy my own age nor a man as old as my father—not to anyone.

Despite all the changes that were happening across the country and the newfound freedoms I experienced, there were times when I thought life for some Afghans was no better than it had been under the Taliban. It troubled me down into my soul.

14

DREAMS FORM

EARLY ONE FRIDAY MORNING, when I was a teenager, I went into my brother's bedroom and closed the door. Since he was the only boy in the family, he had his own room, while we girls shared two rooms. He normally didn't allow me in his room by myself. These were his things and his space, and although he was a kind and generous big brother, he didn't like me invading his privacy. I didn't particularly care to. This was *boy* stuff.

But this morning, my father told me to go into Omar's room and get a few items. With the door shut, I went to my brother's dresser by the window. This wasn't the first time I'd searched through his dresser, and within a few minutes I found what I was looking for.

I selected a tan pair of loose-fitting pants and a tunic. I stood in front of the mirror and put them on, admiring how the clothes hung off my shoulders and hips, which was good. I meant to disguise my body. From a hook on the wall I took a pakol, a traditional Afghan wool hat that was round with a flat top. I put it on my head and tucked my long brown hair underneath, doing my best to remove any evidence of my hair.

When I inspected myself in the mirror again, I didn't look like a young girl anymore. Dressed like this, I could pass for a young boy, which was the idea. My father and I were going for a walk outside the city on a nearby hill, and I didn't want to draw attention to myself.

Walking in the hills was not something girls did, even if they were with their fathers. I was also getting older, which made it even more disgraceful. If the neighbors saw us heading toward the hills, they would make assumptions, perhaps that my father wasn't honorable enough to shield me from an activity like hiking—which women didn't do—or that my father was disrespecting me in other ways. If we were caught, it would bring shame upon my father and our family.

I couldn't fly kites anymore either. Since Afghan girls didn't fly kites, if someone saw me on a roof flying one, especially if there were boys around, I would disgrace myself. I didn't like dressing up like a boy. It made me feel ashamed of who I was, but I had no choice. This was still Afghanistan.

I loved these walks into the hills surrounding Kabul because they reminded me of our hikes in the Kirthar Mountains back in Karachi. I remember those being wonderful days, the times we had together as a family and the innocent joys of being a young girl.

These walks were the precious moments I had alone with my Baba Jan. We'd start early on Friday mornings, leaving the house before most of our neighbors were out and about.

We'd walk swiftly through dusty streets and alleys, heading toward the outskirts of the city. The edge of Kabul was less congested than the center, and we'd cross numerous open dirt lots that sat like massive dust puddles between the monolithic apartment buildings. Eventually we'd hasten through the last neighborhood, and before us would be nothing but an open expanse of struggling shrubs, rocks, and scarred earth leading into the foothills of the mountains that ring Kabul.

Soon we'd be climbing the hills, and once my father was sure no one was in sight, I'd remove my hat and let the cool breeze blow through my hair. I'd close my eyes and let the sun warm my face, and then open them to take in the view of the city below us. A constant brown haze always hung over the city, a consequence of the dust, smoke, smog, and choked air. But still, the city looked alive and bustling—a stark change from the dark days of the Taliban.

From my perch in the hills, I'd look up to the sky. Often we saw American warplanes and helicopters overhead. They were magnificent and powerful machines, soaring elegantly through the clouds or hovering gently a few hundred feet off the ground. I remember one time two Black Hawk helicopters circled nearby and I waved to the pilots. I have no idea if they saw me, but it was exciting to see those aircraft in the sky. These were special moments for me, with the snowcapped mountains in the distance and my Baba Jan close by.

My father and I would have long discussions during these walks. I was sixteen and would be graduating high school soon, so we'd talk about my future. He knew I didn't want to get married yet; I wanted to finish school and go on to university. And he knew about my burgeoning interest in flying.

I asked him if it would ever be possible for someone like me to learn to fly. At the time, there were no civilian flight schools in Afghanistan and women weren't permitted in the air force. Trying to be optimistic, he said perhaps one day. With the help of the outside world, Afghanistan was changing and growing; maybe one day soon someone would start a civilian aviation school. However, he said this with sadness in his eyes.

My dream of becoming a pilot had been brewing for a long time. Ever since I was a little girl, I'd been fascinated with flying and by the stories my father used to tell us about his own dream of becoming a fighter pilot. He'd flown in transport planes when he served in the army, and he would tell us how amazing it was to see the world from above—everything looked so beautiful up in the clouds.

I used to think only geniuses could fly, because only a genius was smart and skilled enough to keep something so heavy in the air. Planes are massive machines, with jet engines or propellers and large interiors to transport people or cargo. Military planes were sleek aircraft that could scream across the sky carrying bombs and rockets. They struck fear into the hearts of the Taliban.

When I would wash the dishes in our yard, it always amazed me when a plane flew over, because I knew a brave pilot was up there. I also imagined it could be a woman. I knew American women were pilots and that they'd come here to fight al-Qaeda. They had helped bring change to my country, and they inspired me.

By the time I was a teenager, my interest in flying had evolved beyond the simple majesty of soaring above the ground. Our parents had raised us to be confident individuals and to think for ourselves, and I had faith in my abilities. In school I'd proven I was smart, and among my friends I'd shown myself to be a leader. I wanted to do something important with my life, and I wanted to help people.

I especially wanted to help other girls and women. In the brief time I'd been on this earth, I'd seen and experienced a lot of horrible events and oppressive circumstances. I'd witnessed the terror of the Taliban firsthand and seen how they took women as slaves and brutalized others for revealing the skin of their ankles.

Even with the Taliban gone, I'd seen how fathers and brothers and male relatives intimidated and controlled their wives and daughters. I'd witnessed them beating their wives and daughters—family members they claimed to cherish, honor, and protect—and abuse them as badly as a Taliban wretch.

I didn't like how mothers were shamed if they gave birth to a girl. My mother had suffered this treatment. My father's parents had always looked down on my mother and my father for having four girls and only one son.

Afghan boys can have dreams and grow up and do whatever they want and make others proud, but girls aren't allowed to dream. Their place is in the home and their duty is to raise children.

I felt embarrassed for being a girl and wanting to fly. Who was I to think such things? But then I'd remember how our parents had raised us, how they'd educated us, how much they'd sacrificed for us, and how much they believed in us. They wanted us to follow our dreams.

One day after school, I told my friend Sonia about my dream of becoming a pilot. We were walking home, and I was glad she didn't have to rush away to beat her father and brother home. It'd been four years and they still didn't know she was going to school.

No one besides my mother, father, older sister, and brother had any idea that I wanted to be a pilot. I'd never shared this dream with any of my friends, but I trusted Sonia and wanted to tell her.

I asked her if she still wanted to be a teacher, something she'd mentioned to me once before. She quickly laughed this off, telling me she'd be lucky if she finished high school. Her father was determined to marry her off when the time was right. I felt sorry for her, hearing this, but I didn't know how else to start the conversation.

I blurted out that I wanted to be a pilot, maybe even serve in the military like the American women and the women from the other NATO countries. I wanted to do something meaningful with my life and help people, and I wanted to oppose those who were unjust. Whether I wanted to actually stand against the unjust or be a symbol—showing the world that we, as Afghan women, were strong and capable—I hadn't fully thought out. But I knew I wanted to be a pilot.

I remember Sonia's exact words: "You want to become a pilot? How, exactly, do you plan to do that? In Kabul, the only things that fly are pigeons and the Americans."

We both laughed, because in reality she was right. Only birds and Americans flew in Afghanistan. But despite my smile, her words hurt me. The first person outside my family I'd shared my dream with thought I was joking and laughed. When she realized I was serious, she responded incredulously.

Still, it felt good to tell someone. My parents had taught me that I could do anything if I was brave enough to raise my voice and speak up. I'd just done that, albeit in a small way. This was the first step, and I wanted to keep raising my voice, especially for those who couldn't or were too afraid. I knew the only way women in Afghanistan were going to have basic rights and freedoms was to speak up.

I wanted to be a pilot, and I was going to speak up, no matter what.

15

UNIVERSITY

MY HIGH SCHOOL CLASS was set to graduate in May 2009. I still didn't know if I'd ever have a chance to become a pilot; nonetheless, I was happy and proud to be graduating.

Afsoon and I had worked exceptionally hard over the years, taking extra classes in math and physics because those were subjects that would prepare us for university. We studied diligently and listened earnestly to our father during his after-dinner lectures. Our teachers assessed us as being very smart, while our family and friends all thought we had bright futures ahead of us.

My relatives assumed I would become a teacher. They knew I hadn't been betrothed to anyone, nor had I shown any real interest in getting married or starting a family. They presumed I'd go to university, perhaps teach for a few years, and get married later.

I never told them I wanted to be a teacher; they simply believed this is what would happen because that's what unmarried Afghan girls did: they became teachers or medical providers. God forbid my relatives ever asked me what I wanted.

Graduation day arrived, and there was a small party at our school. Considering my first memories were of life in the refugee camp and learning my numbers under a tent, I was very proud to finish secondary education in a real school with a class of seventeen girls. I was also happy to share this moment with my classmates. Most of them would be married soon, including my best friend, Sonia, but there were a few who hoped to attend university.

My parents were very proud of us. Given everything they'd endured over the past twenty years and the moments when all seemed hopeless, I can only imagine how they felt watching Afsoon and me in our school uniforms smiling and laughing with the other girls. Perhaps it was a dream for them; everything they'd done hadn't been a waste.

Once high school ended, life changed for me. Earlier that year, a young man who was an extended relative of ours saw my sister at a wedding. His name was Farid, and he claimed he'd fallen deeply in love with Afsoon. Over the next few months, his parents negotiated with my family for a possible marriage. My father believed Farid was an honest man and came from a respectable family. He would provide a good life for Afsoon, my father thought, so he agreed to the courtship.

Two months after Afsoon and I graduated, she married Farid. It was a small wedding—we were still poor—but it was a happy occasion with delicious food, music, and lots of dancing. I was very happy for her and believed at the time she, too, was happy.

But I was also sad; I was losing my sister. She'd been my closest friend and confidant my entire life, and now she was leaving. We'd been together every day our whole lives. We laughed together, we cried, at times we were terrified, and other times we were filled with joy and happiness.

The day of the wedding, she left to be with her new family, and for the first time in my life, I felt immensely alone. Her absence from our house was acute; it was as if a physical part of me had been cut out. Her footsteps and the sound of her breathing had vanished, her voice no longer mingled with mine. My sister and closest friend was gone. I missed her.

––––––––––––

That summer I continued taking classes, preparing to take the entrance exam for Kabul University. I was eighteen years old; this was a good age to attend university.

Kabul University was where my mother had dreamed of going. She'd aspired to earn a degree in journalism from here, but the wars got in the way. With my prospects of attending the university, she seemed to live a bit vicariously through me.

I didn't know precisely what I wanted to do upon getting a degree, but I knew I had to go—I *wanted* to go. Like our parents had ingrained in us growing up, I believed education was a necessity for opportunities, freedom, and justice in this world. Education opened doors, and I deeply wanted to learn and have more education.

Although the idea of becoming a pilot was a distant dream, my desire to help other women and work toward an equitable society was real. I couldn't do that without an education. With an education, I could stand up and speak out for the rights of women. I could be an advocate, championing the rights of girls to have careers and do more than serve in the home as obedient wives who take care of children. Perhaps I could find a way to encourage the founding of the first civilian flight school in Afghanistan.

A week after my sister's wedding I took the entrance exam. It was a difficult test, not unlike the placement exam I'd taken back in 2002. It covered a variety of subjects, but I was confident in my abilities, and when the results came back, I was selected to major in economics. Classes would start in September.

16

A COMMERCIAL

I STARTED MY FRESHMAN YEAR at Kabul University in September 2009. At first, I found my class load intimidating—I was attending a university, not a small girls' school on the edge of Kabul—but I knew I'd be all right. I'd prepared well.

I made new friends at university fairly quickly. I'd always been outgoing, and my time at university was no different. However, unlike my time in high school, the university was coed and most of the professors were men. This took some getting used to, and as a woman I had to wear a scarf, but in general I was accepted as an equal in the academic community. The American and international presence in Kabul had brought these changes.

Going to university was a significant time in my life, but there was one day in October that eclipsed everything. It was windy, overcast, and getting cold with the approaching winter. Kabul can be bitterly cold—sometimes there's even snow—and the air is so dry the skin on your hands will crack if you simply bend your fingers.

It was five in the evening and I was at home. Omar and I were in the main room of the house playing chess. He was teaching me moves he'd learned from our father, and I was listening intently because I appreciated the game's complexity. I found it intriguing how one needed to think two, three, four moves ahead, perhaps more. I wanted to play against my father, like Omar did.

Suddenly a commercial on the television caught my eye. My father had bought us a TV a few years earlier, and my sisters were watching a show I can't recall. The commercial seized my attention, though, and I couldn't look away from the astonishing images on the screen or ignore the announcer's voice, which drowned out my brother's.

The Afghan military was calling upon men *and* women to join the armed forces. The announcer said the US-led coalition was working to develop Afghanistan's security forces, and they needed everyone who was able bodied. The army needed soldiers in the infantry, in logistics, in supply, and to work as mechanics, engineers, and other specialties. The Afghan Air Force was also recruiting people to be mechanics, truck drivers, administrative officers, and many other positions.

Toward the end of the commercial, the announcer said something that would change my life forever: the air force was recruiting women to be pilots!

I yelled for joy and jumped around the room. I couldn't believe it. Here was my chance. I could become a pilot. I could enroll in the military academy to become an officer and train as a pilot in Afghanistan's air force.

I couldn't contain myself, wanting my brother and sisters to share in my joy, but they either laughed at me or ignored me. They didn't think this was serious. They'd seen the commercial like I had, but the idea of women becoming pilots in the Afghan Air Force was too radical. It was in contrast to so many aspects of Afghan life and culture.

But I wouldn't be dissuaded. I couldn't be dissuaded. This was my chance, my one opportunity to learn to fly and soar through the air, and I could do it as an officer in the Afghan military.

After dinner, I told my parents about the commercial and that the air force was recruiting women to be pilots. They already knew it, but I told them anyway—this was a dream come true for me. There were no civilian aviation schools in Afghanistan, so this was my one opportunity to learn to fly. Plus, I would serve my country as a military officer.

The Taliban had retreated from the Americans and their allies, who were fighting and dying to bring peace and justice to our country. I knew they wouldn't be here forever, nor did I want them to be. We as Afghans had to fight for our freedoms and liberties, and the only way that would happen was if Afghans served in the security forces.

I wanted to serve my country to defend those who couldn't protect themselves. I wanted to ensure Afghanistan's women had justice and equality and could stand up to speak their minds. "You raised me to be like this," I told my parents. "You made us strong, and you told us we must follow our own path."

My father listened intently but didn't say anything. My mother was concerned, and I remember her words clearly. "It's too dangerous," she said. "This is Afghanistan. Society is not ready to accept working women and will never let women wear a uniform. And people will judge you if you try this, and you will be shamed."

I heard her words and I knew the risks. She was right; this was Afghanistan, and even though the Americans were here and society was changing, the nightmare of the Taliban still lurked behind closed doors and in the countryside. Furthermore, it wasn't just the Taliban. Most Afghan men still believed women were inferior and had no business outside the house without their husbands, fathers, brothers, uncles, or cousins, escorting them like children. The men's backwardness ran deep.

That's precisely why I felt compelled to join the air force to serve my country. It wasn't only for me. I wanted to fight for all the women of Afghanistan. Justice and equality for women wouldn't be handed to us; we needed to prove we had the strength to do these things. I knew I would make a good officer and that I could learn to fly. I never had any doubt, and I wanted my parents to believe in me.

My father was silent for most of the discussion, but I knew he was proud. He wanted this for me as much as I wanted it for myself. He turned to my mother and said Afghanistan was changing. The Americans were here, and if the military was asking women to join up, then it could be done. It made me so happy to hear him say these things.

My parents eventually agreed I could join the air force, but they had a condition. My decision to join the military must be kept secret from everyone. Only my older siblings, Afsoon and Omar, could know, not my younger sisters. None of my friends could know, nor anyone else outside the house. I needed a story to tell our relatives and another one to tell my classmates at university to explain why I was leaving. If someone found out, it would bring shame upon me and our family, putting us all at risk.

Of course I agreed to this condition. As reprehensible as it was, it was true that my decision to join the air force would put my family and myself at risk. There were many people in Afghanistan who would hate me for entering the military, considering me a disgrace and perhaps someone worth hurting. Nonetheless, with a huge grin on my face I hugged and kissed my parents. I will always be thankful to God for them and how they raised us.

This was my chance, and I seized it!

17

RECRUITMENT

———————

T HE NEXT MORNING, Omar accompanied me to the recruitment center. He and I had become close in recent years; I was glad he was with me. He took after our father in that he had a kind heart. He respected women and considered them equals. He also possessed courage and would stand firm on what he believed was right, and in the defense of others.

The military recruitment center was located in a dusty, run-down compound on the southern edge of Kabul. The buildings were constructed of gray concrete or mud bricks, all one level. Some had windows, but most were broken or missing panes of glass. It was less than inspiring, though I hadn't expected much more.

Throughout the compound, hundreds of young men milled about; I assumed they, too, were here to join the military. They were dressed in a wide assortment of clothing—traditional shalwar kameez, jeans, slacks, wool vests, T-shirts, button-down shirts, pakols, taqiyah skull-caps, scarves, and a few baseball hats—indicating that the recruits hailed from the city as well as the surrounding provinces. They came from all different backgrounds, from the more devout to the more liberal urbanites. They were either waiting in line to go into buildings, absently standing off to the side or leaning against a building, or sitting together in small groups.

When Omar and I entered the compound, everyone stopped to stare at us. I had on a modest black dress with a scarf over my head, clearly a woman. I can only imagine what these men were thinking, seeing me there, but I didn't dwell on it. I put on a brave face and we went into the main building to register.

We waited a long time in a drab corridor that lacked any overhead lighting, and soon enough I needed to use the facilities. I asked a soldier for directions to the ladies' room, but he looked at me with disbelief. "There isn't a women's bathroom," he uttered, as if the idea of having one here was absurd.

His response didn't surprise me. Women hadn't been allowed in the Afghan military since the Soviets. A lot had happened since that time, not least of all the banishment of women from public life. Thus, there was no need to accommodate females.

Sometime later, another woman entered the building. She was accompanied by her father, a sickly looking man, and she wore a full burka. It heartened me to see her; I wasn't the only one who had the audacity to think they could join the military. But when we started chatting, a reality became apparent to me that was common for a lot of Afghan women who joined the military in those first few years.

She didn't say it directly, but she told me about her sick father and that he wasn't able to work or support the family. She didn't have any brothers or other relatives who could help. But her family of three girls, an aging mother, and an ailing father needed to survive. She was here out of desperation, the oldest of three girls with no marriage prospects. Her only hope was to join the military so she could send money home.

A lot of the women who joined the military during this period did so out of financial need, not because they had a strong desire to serve their country or become soldiers. Some joined because they sincerely wanted to serve—I wasn't the only one who dreamed of doing something important and independent—but not many. They viewed the military as a means to find stability and earn money that they could send to their family. Most men made this assumption about female soldiers.

The recruiter for the military academy called my name, and I went into his office. He was a paunchy fellow in his midfifties, his uniform faded and ill fitting. I imagined he'd joined the army as a private back during the Soviet-Afghan War. During the subsequent civil war and reign of the Taliban, he'd probably disappeared into civilian society. When the Americans arrived, I imagined he'd pulled out his uniform and dusted it off. Now, here he was, recruiting new soldiers.

He had a TV in the corner of his office, which he could view from behind his desk. He had on a Tom and Jerry cartoon. He was probably more interested in the antics of the cat and mouse than the recruits coming before him. When he saw me, he stared quizzically. He'd seen my brother through the doorway, but Omar remained outside in the hall. It was just the recruiter and me in the office.

I remember the exchange we had almost verbatim.

He took a long slurp of his green tea and said, "You don't look desperate. Why are you here? Is there no one in your family who can support you? No father, no brother?"

"I'm joining the military because I want to, not because I have to," I said. The recruiter scrunched his face at my comment, but I continued. "It is my choice to be here, and I will be proud to put on the uniform. If you think that is shameful, why do you wear the uniform, sir?"

My words and confidence put the man off balance. He stopped staring, averted his eyes, and reached for my recruitment paperwork. He signed it quickly and said, "Good luck."

That was the end of it. I was scheduled to report for training in two months.

18

BASIC TRAINING

O N DECEMBER 2, 2010, I reported for basic training. I packed a small bag and wore black pants, a long, dark-green shirt, and a black scarf over my head.

I said goodbye to my family in the morning. Afsoon wasn't there—we'd said our goodbyes earlier in the week—but everyone else was present. They were all sad, my mother crying.

When Afsoon got married and moved out of the house, it was considered normal. Newly married couples typically remain close to family to rely upon the associated support network. Afsoon had simply moved into another neighborhood in Kabul, and my parents saw her regularly.

My enlistment in the military, however, was something my mother never expected, and she was very upset for a host of reasons. I was not only going away; I was entering a new, hard life that could be dangerous. Her view of the military was also colored by her experiences in the Soviet-Afghan War and ensuing civil war. Although NATO and the Americans were currently advising the Afghan military to modernize it, she feared what might happen to me.

I hugged my mother tightly, trying to assure her I would be fine. I did the same with my father. I kissed both their hands, reminding them they'd taught me to be brave. I promised to maintain my honor and the family's, and to make them proud. I'd try as hard as I could in everything I did to become a military officer and a pilot—these were my greatest goals. I wouldn't let challenges or failures along the way stop me. I was strong because of them.

My mother was still teary, but my father looked at me with pride. He didn't say much, nor did I expect him to. I remembered everything he'd told me over the years; he had faith in me.

I was sad when I left the house, but eager to get things started. Omar accompanied me to the bus station where I'd find transport to the training facility. I was glad he walked with me. He'd always supported me and been a close friend. I told him this wouldn't have been possible without him; I was lucky to have a brother like him. He smiled and hugged me warmly, and I got on the bus.

There were nineteen women on the bus, including myself, ranging in age between eighteen and twenty-five. Later I found out seventeen of the girls were Hazaras; only one was a Tajik like me. Everyone was nervous and no one talked. None of us knew what to expect.

The driver drove east out of Kabul toward Pul-e-Charkhi, to an area roughly eight miles outside the city, where the Kabul Military Training Center was located. At the gate to the base, the guards stopped the bus to search the outside of the vehicle for bombs. One of the guards came aboard for a cursory search of us, after which he welcomed us to the base.

The driver began threading his way through the base. We were going to the Malalai Company, which was the female officer candidate school. Our training company had been named after Malalai of Maiwand, who was a heroine of Afghanistan from the Battle of Maiwand. In 1880 during the Second Anglo-Afghan War, Malalai rallied the local warriors to fight the British at Maiwand, Qandahar, helping Ghazi Mohammad Ayub Khan, the emir of Afghanistan, achieve victory. She's been called the Afghan Joan of Arc, and I was proud to be associated with a national hero like her.

Malalai Company was colocated with the Afghan National Army (ANA) Command and Staff College. We had two buildings containing classrooms and training spaces, and there was a barracks secured by metal doors where no men were allowed. Our entire initial training, including all our meals, would take place inside these two buildings and the barracks. We would be around the male trainees only when we went to the rifle range. Some weekends we'd be allowed to go home, but most of us lived too far away to make the journey, myself included.

When the driver stopped the bus in front of the Malalai Company buildings, my world changed. My journey toward my dreams had begun.

A female US Marine came on the bus and immediately started yelling. Her voice was harsh and loud, and she banged on the windows as she barked, "Get off the bus! Get off the bus! Do you understand? Get off the bus!"

She kept banging her hand against the window, pointing at us to get off. We scrambled down the aisle, down the steps, off the bus, and onto the pavement, dragging our belongings behind us. Drill sergeants were there waiting, directing us to get in line. All of them were yelling, pointing, and ushering us into formation.

When we were finally in a haphazard line, the female marine came in front and told us we looked like a spoiled rabble. We were sloppy and undisciplined. She couldn't believe we'd made it this far.

She pointed to our barracks and said we'd be issued uniforms there. The instructors marched us over to the building, and we went inside.

My father had told me stories about military training, but you never really understand what it's all about until you're in the middle of it. When the marine was yelling, I felt my pulse quicken and my gut clench, while some of the girls looked disoriented. None of us had experienced anything this intense before. We were nervous and scared, but not like when the Taliban came around, shouting orders and waving their guns.

The Taliban could strike terror in you, often making you wonder if you were going to live or die, be beaten or raped, or dragged into slavery. You did what you had to do to survive and get through the moment. You prayed it never happened again, taking pains to avoid the Taliban in the future.

But this . . .

I wasn't afraid of being harmed by this marine or the other instructors—men and women from Afghanistan, Jordan, the United States, and the United Kingdom. Yet their intensity, coupled with the speed at which they spoke and moved, along with their fanatic attention to detail, was intimidating. This, compounded by my deepest desires not merely to complete the training but to excel in it, made me very nervous.

In time I recognized my initial reaction served me well. My desire to exceed expectations, to strive for the top—not simply pass—would help me qualify for flight school and ultimately succeed. Drive, determination, motivation, perseverance—I already possessed these qualities, but these instructors were about to hone them into their strongest forms.

Basic training is fundamentally similar throughout the world. The uniforms might be different, and the language, the location, the length, and the level of intensity undoubtedly vary—but all initial training is meant to indoctrinate someone into the core elements of the military. My experience was no different, and those first few days challenged all of us.

For starters, we had no understanding of military discipline. The idea of being on time, working as a team with strangers, or being able to stand in line and march with rigid posture is fundamentally alien to Afghan culture. Rules are frequently bent or ignored, while timeliness is very fluid.

It was difficult for the nineteen of us to be dressed and standing in formation by 0700, to then march to the chow hall for breakfast. A few of the girls would fall asleep in the early morning classes or refuse to do their homework. Others would cry if they got yelled at.

But soon enough, we appreciated the regimen and discipline we were learning. We took pride in wearing our uniforms correctly, working as a team to clean the barracks, performing our physical training properly and with motivation, speaking clearly, following orders precisely, and respecting ourselves and others. We were getting stronger physically and mentally, gaining confidence.

Our training involved military vocabulary, English, computers, processes for logistics, administration, finance, military customs and courtesies, drill, first aid, communications, and physical fitness— always physical fitness. Both female and male instructors taught us. Although in Afghan society we might have been uncomfortable working alongside men in this way, here in training it didn't bother us. It was accepted, necessary, and made sense.

On training days we were up at 0430 for prayers. We'd square away the barracks (make our beds, sweep up, empty the trash, etc.) and march to breakfast at 0700. Our first class began at 0800, taking us to lunch at 1200. We'd continue classes until 1600, followed by afternoon prayers. Physical training came next. After PT, we'd clean the barracks again, have dinner, and do homework, with lights out at 2100.

For most of us, PT was our favorite training event. Under the Taliban, females were not permitted to exercise. Even after the American-led invasion in 2001, the idea of women going to the gym didn't exist. Physical activities like long-distance runs, push-ups, obstacle courses, and all the strength- and endurance-building exercises our trainers made us do were utterly foreign. Some girls struggled in the beginning, but like everything else, in time we got better.

Wearing a uniform was also a new experience, and in the beginning some girls were uncomfortable with it. Afghan women don't wear trousers, boots, and heavy button-down shirts. However, we increasingly took pride in looking sharp. The pants and blouse were green, and we tucked our pant legs into black boots. Since Afghanistan is a Muslim country, we wore black scarves over our hair. The uniform was simple, but we wore it with pride.

19

FRIENDS, REFLECTION, AND GRADUATION

ALTHOUGH THE NINETEEN of us were learning to work together while undergoing a transformational, shared experience, there were some aspects of Afghan culture that were hard to overcome.

Earlier I mentioned seventeen of the girls in our training class were Hazara, while one other girl and I were Tajik. Hazaras are the third-largest ethnic group in Afghanistan and primarily reside in central Afghanistan. They speak a form of Dari-Persian. Tajiks are the second-largest ethnic group, concentrated in the north, and speak Farsi. (Pashtuns are the dominant ethnic group across Afghanistan, but are concentrated in the south and east.) Kabul is composed of people from all of Afghanistan's ethnicities, but unfortunately, even in the country's urban capital, racial prejudices exist. The Afghan military isn't immune to these issues.

In the early part of training, Fatima Abteen was my only friend. She was from Kandahar and I was from Kabul, but that didn't matter—we were both Tajik. We would talk, share stories, laugh, and cry, and we were often paired together during training. Fatima also wanted to be a pilot, which made me feel less alone because now I had someone to share my dream with.

The one other friend I had during basic training was Zahra. She was a Hazara and one of the older women in training. She was also the tallest. Whenever we lined up in formation, we did so by height; she was always first in line.

She was a kind woman, and I came to view her as an older sister. I think she took pity on me because at the start of training she thought I looked very young and small. She didn't think I would last a week; I'd either quit or fail the training.

We spoke for the first time one evening after I'd torn my scarf. I asked some of the girls if they could help me sew it—it was part of my uniform, and I needed to wear it the following day—but everyone I approached ignored me. That's when Zahra came over, took my scarf, and said she'd mend it for me. She had a seven-year-old son and knew how to do these things. She went on to say if I ever needed anything, I could ask her.

In time I proved her wrong—I wasn't too young or too small—and she saw how strong and determined I actually was. This didn't mean I didn't appreciate it when she looked out for me. The other girls wouldn't talk to me unless they had to, but she never let them say mean things about me or sabotage my duties.

Zahra was a good friend. She made basic training a little more bearable.

———————

For many reasons, initial training was a time of immense growth and reflection for me. Perhaps I was naive, but for most of my life I wasn't mindful of the deep ethnic divisions that plagued Afghanistan.

When we were living in Pakistan, if someone asked me where I was from or who I was (as in my ethnicity), I would say, I'm an Afghan from Afghanistan. I was made acutely aware of this fact that day on the playground when that boy pushed me.

After we returned to Afghanistan, I still didn't concern myself with ethnic identity. I knew there were Pashtuns, Kuchis, Hazaras, Uzbeks, and Tajiks, but my day-to-day interactions didn't put these issues in conflict. Our neighbors and my friends in school were either Tajik or were not concerned enough about ethnicity to cause divisions.

We were people, first and foremost, and we were Afghans. Ethnicity, religion, skin color—none of that mattered to me. My parents raised me to see beyond those things, and I'm proud to be this way.

Basic training, however, opened my eyes to the ethnic divisions that rack Afghanistan and the rest of Central Asia. Ethnic and familial lineage often determine whether you will like, trust, or tolerate someone. It doesn't matter if you're smart, dumb, tall, short, good looking, ugly, charming, quiet, nice, or mean—what's in your blood is what counts.

Afghanistan is an extreme case for this kind of racism and prejudice. Wars have been fought between ethnic groups, and since Afghanistan became a country, the central government has typically been dominated by one group or another. (Only in recent years has there been a more diverse mix.)

The Afghan military is much the same. Although certain Afghan commanders have tried, and our NATO advisors have done all they can to instill national values to transcend ethnic divisions, these prejudices are ingrained. Given I was a member of one of the first female training classes post-9/11, it wasn't a surprise I experienced ethnic exclusion.

However, an intellectual understanding of prejudice is far different than experiencing it firsthand. Given only two of us were

Tajiks, anything that didn't involve our instructors or forced group involvement meant we were excluded. We were the other, and not to be trusted, talked to, or even acknowledged. It was lonely and hurtful to experience this, particularly because of the countless other stresses one must face during military training. Military training is hard for a reason, but rejection based on ethnic background makes it much harder. Nevertheless, nothing was going to hold me back from my dream.

Basic training reinforced my desire to become a pilot in the air force. I enjoyed the discipline, physical training, expectations, and opportunities to succeed that I found in these early days of being in the military. As time went on, I gained confidence in my abilities, who I was as a woman, and my new identity as a soldier.

I thought about these things often. Who was I, and who could I be? I wanted to prove that I could do "man's work" and excel at it. Maybe I'd be the best. Failure was not an option; my upbringing had taught me hard work and determination would carry me forward.

Just as important, I saw this as my opportunity to make sure the horror of the Taliban never returned to Afghanistan. Being born a female is not a crime, and no one should be discriminated against because they aren't a male. Being barred from education, prevented from walking outside without a male chaperone, excluded from politics, prohibited from speaking in public, and living in fear if we showed an inch of skin—it's madness!

Even now, it's not right that husbands claim they have the authority to abuse their wives or that brothers assert they have an obligation to shame and beat their sisters if they speak out or look at another boy. Whether I would fight the Taliban as an air force pilot or serve as an example to inspire other women to follow their dreams, I knew this was my calling. I could not allow this to happen to my homeland again. I would fight for women's equality.

———————

On a Friday in May 2011, my class graduated officer candidate school. It was a very exciting day for us because we were finally commissioned officers and able to wear the uniform of the Afghan military. Although this was only basic training and we still had a long way to go to learn our official job skills, we felt we'd achieved something significant.

Even though we were due all the respect and courtesy that comes with such a position, our celebration was muted. We graduated alongside three hundred male candidates, most of whom didn't think we deserved to be there. They thought it was shameful that women were being commissioned as officers to serve in the military. The military was a place for men who were strong and tough. As far as they were concerned, we should be at home or in some other profession—not soldiers.

Their lack of acceptance hurt, but it also motivated me. I would prove them wrong. Not only did women deserve the opportunity to serve in the military, but we could also do better than men. I would show them. I knew I could.

As we stood in formation inside a massive graduation hall, the master of ceremonies announced our names one by one. Candidates came forward to have their rank insignia—second lieutenant bars—pinned on their shirt lapels and to receive their commissioning certificate.

When they called my name, I marched up and stood before the academy's chief of staff, General Sher Mohammad Karimi. He handed me my certificate and congratulated me. As custom dictated, I turned around to face my fellow classmates and the audience and yelled,

"Za Afghanistan lepara kedmat kavom!" *I will serve my country with honor!* I marched back to my place in the formation and watched as the rest of the candidates went through the same routine.

When I yelled my oath and saw the crowd before me, I felt the pride beating against my chest like a drum, with goosebumps on the back of my neck and arms. No matter what our male colleagues said, they couldn't take away the honor and dignity I felt. I'd dreamed of this moment for so long, and now it was mine.

Yet every single one of the women in my class had to keep their position in the military a secret. If the Taliban found out we were soldiers, they would target us and our families for assassination. In addition, there were many people in Afghanistan—those who were not officially affiliated with the Taliban—who weren't ready to accept women in the military. They might do us harm as well, or look down upon and discriminate against our relatives and us. Only our immediate families knew the truth about what we'd done.

Our families attended the graduation ceremony, and it made me proud to see my brother and mother in the audience. They didn't recognize me at first. They only realized it was me when my name was announced and I walked up on stage. When I joined my mother and brother after the ceremony, both of them were so happy for me.

My father, unfortunately, couldn't be there because he was very ill and resting at home; I admit his absence made me sad. This achievement and my success was in no small part due to how he'd raised and supported me.

20

JOINING THE AIR FORCE

AFTER GRADUATION, we were allowed one week of leave to go home to see our families and await our first set of orders, which would list our initial assignments in the Afghan Armed Forces; we'd be directed to serve in the army in one of the numerous job fields open to women (logistics, communications, administrations, etc.) or in the air force. The air force was my first choice, and given I'd graduated from officer training at the top of my class, I believed I had a good chance. I'd find out in a week.

Being home on leave should have been restful and gratifying—a chance for me to look back on my experiences in basic training, see how I'd changed, and take pride in the challenges I'd overcome and the rank I'd earned. I'd seen other relatives and neighbors come home from military training or a deployment, and how people were impressed by the new soldier coming home, admiring his accomplishments. The respect and satisfaction for me existed only in part, because no one knew I'd joined the military, and no one could know. A dark cloud hung over my family.

My parents knew what I'd accomplished and who I now was—a commissioned officer in the Afghan military—and so did my older brother and sister, but we didn't tell my younger siblings out of concern they might accidentally reveal this secret to someone outside the house. We couldn't tell any of my extended family, because my father knew that not only would they disapprove, but they also could very well shame my family and disavow us. The extremist views of the Taliban still existed, even in a place like Kabul and among my relatives.

If the Taliban found out, they would certainly threaten my family, perhaps by letter or through a stranger. They might go so far as to try to kill me. Targeted murders by the Taliban against women were (and still are) a real threat, and there are many ordinary Afghans who condone these acts. It's unnerving, because you never know if the person you encounter on the street, in a shop, or even in the uniform of a police officer or soldier is secretly a Taliban fighter, spy, or supporter.

The fact of the matter was, I had brought this upon myself and my family by joining the military. If I had married or continued my studies at university, this threat wouldn't have been hanging over our heads. The Taliban might not approve of women seeking an education, but in Kabul it was widely accepted. We could have told people I was at university without fear of reprisal.

Part of me regretted bringing this secret burden upon my family. But joining the military to become a pilot was my calling; I believed it was a righteous one, and something I *must* do. I will not deny I personally wanted to become a pilot for myself, but I also viewed my aspiration to fly as a greater service to my homeland.

Afghanistan and its people had suffered immense hardship for over thirty years. Except for the Soviet occupation, which occurred before I was born, I'd experienced the brunt of these things as a refugee, as a child under Taliban rule, and then when 9/11 happened and NATO came. Most significantly, I was a woman who'd seen the brutal oppression imposed by the Taliban and their sympathizers. I wanted to do my part to oppose these barbarians and their hateful ideology.

If I didn't stand up for my country and for the equal treatment of women, who would? I needed to show Afghanistan and the world I was strong and capable of doing "man's work," because by doing so I hoped to inspire other women to follow *their* dreams. From my perspective, this was the only way things would change in Afghanistan—if I and other women like me fought for what we believed in.

I knew my parents and my siblings, Omar and Afsoon, believed this as well. It would not be easy and it could be dangerous for us all, but it was necessary. I am truly grateful for my family's love and support, because I never would have succeeded without them.

For as long as possible, we would explain my absence to my younger siblings and our relatives as an extended stay at the university to focus on my studies. That was the lie we lived.

After my week of home leave, I reported to the Ministry of Defense along with the nineteen other women from my class. I wore my camouflage uniform, my black boots, and my black scarf, and sat with the others in a waiting room. We would be called one by one to receive our assignments.

I wasn't a little girl anymore. Whereas in the past I might have been bopping around talking with the other girls and playing jokes (my way of dealing with nervousness and the unknown), I sat quietly without fidgeting. Military officers are disciplined; I would carry myself appropriately. It was important I behaved precisely how I'd been trained—I never wanted anyone to criticize how I presented myself or have a reason to say I didn't deserve to wear the uniform.

But despite that, my palms were sweaty and my insides were stirring with nervous anticipation. When they called my name, my heart jumped and practically lodged in my throat. I stood, marched into the commander's office, and reported in.

The man behind the desk, a captain wearing army insignia, handed me my orders and said I'd been assigned to the Afghan Air Force. It was all I could do not to shout for joy, but I kept my composure and dismissed myself, only allowing a hint of a smile to appear on my face.

I'd done it! I was an officer in the Afghan Air Force, one step closer to becoming a pilot. I knew there were many challenges to come and nothing was certain, but I'd made it. It was official!

———————

In addition to myself, seven other women were assigned to the air force. We were told to go outside where a bus would to take us to the Kabul air base, which is colocated with the city's commercial airport. The drive was short, and we rode in silence. When we arrived at the base it was already lunchtime, so we went straight to the chow hall.

Up to this point, we'd been considered unique, being some of the first female officers in the Afghan military, but during our initial training we'd been made to feel like we belonged. This was in no small way attributable to the NATO advisors who ran our training and worked side by side with the Afghan command structure.

When we walked into the chow hall as members of the larger military establishment—no longer in the artificiality of a training environment—it was clear things would be different from here on out.

As we entered the chow hall, everyone—and I mean everyone—stopped to stare, and it wasn't out of simple curiosity. The looks we received from the men were harsh, unwelcoming, and borderline threatening. They also said things, some in hushed tones to the person next to them, but others spoke to no one in particular in loud voices.

"What are you doing here?"

"You don't belong here."

"Don't you have a family that can take care of you?"

"You must be shameful to have joined the military."

"You shouldn't be an officer."

"Who do you think you are?"

I heard these things as I walked to the chow line. So did the other women. None of us could escape. Hundreds of eyes fixed on us, ogling and sneering at every part of us—our uniforms, hair, bodies, faces. We were on our own and might as well have been circus animals. There was no training advisor nearby, no other senior officers who might quell the jeers and taunts.

I felt more uncomfortable than I'd ever felt in my entire life. Part of me wanted to shout at them to stop staring. We were commissioned officers in the Afghan Air Force. We not only had every right to be here but should have been accorded the same respect as the male officers.

Another part of me wanted to run, to get out of the chow hall, away from their prying eyes and hurtful words. I wanted to bury my face in my hands and leave.

My friend Fatima must have sensed what I was contemplating, because she touched my shoulder. I turned to see she was also uncomfortable, but our eyes met and a rush of unspoken strength and encouragement passed between us. Being together gave us courage.

I never thought about running away again. We deserved to be here, and I wouldn't let the sneers of ignorant and backward men intimidate me—ever.

Later that afternoon, we started in-processing; the first step was a medical examination. All eight of us had volunteered for pilot training, so our medical exams would be flight physicals. These exams would be much more comprehensive than the typical military physical because the air force needed to determine if our bodies could handle the stress of flying. We would undergo the same exam given to the men.

At the hospital, we reported to the chief of staff, Dr. Rasool, a stern man in his late fifties who had a beard a fist long (the minimum length for a beard under the Taliban). Dr. Rasool called us into his office and started asking questions about why we wanted to be pilots, making snide remarks about how women should be at home caring for the family. He made fun of us, saying we were too small and weak to fly, that even if we did pass the physical, we'd never make it through training.

We couldn't do anything but stand there and take it, answering Dr. Rasool's questions simply and directly. He begrudgingly divided us into pairs and sent us to different departments for our exams. It was humiliating.

In Afghan society, only women are supposed to examine other women, but there were no female doctors in this hospital, only two elderly female nurses. Men would have to perform the exams, and some of the tests would be quite invasive. It was going to be very uncomfortable, but I told myself it had to be done. I'd have to overcome a lot more than this if I was going to fly military airplanes.

They started with basic measurements like height and weight, then performed vision, hearing, blood, and urine tests; X-rays; joint and muscle exams; and so on. I'd never had men around me in this way, doing these types of things, touching my body, but I kept telling myself not to flinch.

When it finally came time for heart and chest examinations, we—the seven other women and I—asked the female nurses to be the ones to set up the sensors on our bodies. We couldn't let the men see us unclothed. The male doctors could administer the tests once we were covered back up, but we couldn't let them see us exposed and touch us in such a way.

Fortunately, the doctors agreed and we completed the flight exams. I was very glad to put my uniform back on, no longer being poked and prodded.

Afterward, the eight of us waited for the exam results outside Dr. Rasool's office. As the chief of staff, he would deliver them. He called me into his office first. I fortified my demeanor as I'd been trained, marched in, and stood at attention in front of his desk.

I could see my medical folder in front of him. He looked me directly in the face, but in his eyes I detected a sense of cruel satisfaction. He told me I had a heart condition that would prevent me from becoming a pilot. He went on to say there were plenty of desk jobs I could do, but I would not go to pilot training. Then he told me to get out.

21

MEDICAL TEST AND
MORE TESTS

———

WHEN DR. RASOOL told me I was medically disqualified for pilot training, it felt as though the world crumbled around me. I walked out of his office, and there was no more spring in my step or strength of purpose in my bearing. His words echoed in my ears: *heart condition—disqualified—never be a pilot—too weak—should be at home—raise children—shouldn't be here.* I was devastated. I wanted to scream and shake my fists in the air!

But despite the shock, I kept myself together.

I went into the bathroom. Thankfully, no one was in there. I grabbed each side of the sink and stared at myself in the mirror. I kept it together, I didn't cry, I didn't yell—but I saw the pain in my eyes. I told myself to breathe and calm down. I couldn't let anyone see how upset I was, especially Dr. Rasool or any of the other men in this place. I would not give them the satisfaction of seeing me weak or emotional. Never.

Once I collected myself, I emerged from the bathroom only to bump into one of the other girls, Amina. She was crying and told me she'd been disqualified for color blindness. Six other women were also medically disqualified—too short, diabetes, scoliosis, and so on. Only one of us passed the medical exam, Ferozi.

Interestingly, none of us who were disqualified had any idea about our conditions before this moment. We thought we'd been healthy all our lives. None of this had come out in our initial military physicals either. We then learned not a single one of the men had been disqualified, all of them deemed fit for flight duty with perfect bills of health.

This didn't seem right, not at all. I knew I was healthy, and never once in my life had anyone—neither my parents nor a doctor—ever said I had a heart condition. I started to wonder if Dr. Rasool lied, purposefully disqualifying us for pilot training because we were women.

When I went home that evening, despite the conclusions I'd made about Dr. Rasool possibly making false claims about my medical fitness, I burst into tears as soon as I opened the door and saw my Baba Jan. A wave burst forth of everything pent up inside me since the experience at the hospital. I hugged my father, held him tight, and kept repeating, "I hate these men. This is so unfair. Why would they do that? How could they destroy me like that? Why do they hate women? They say we're welcome and part of the armed forces, but we're not. Why, why, why, why . . ."

I must have worried my father terribly, because he took me in his arms and kept asking, "What's wrong? What's wrong?" He implored me to tell him what happened.

With tears running down my cheeks, I asked if he knew if I had a heart condition, and the look he gave me—even before he opened his mouth to respond—told me he'd never heard of such a thing. It was absurd. There was nothing wrong with my heart. I then explained that I'd been medically disqualified for flight training.

My tears of sadness turned to tears of anger and determination. I was furious, perhaps more so than I'd ever been in my life. I'd been angry before—at the Taliban, at the boy on the playground, at my friend Sonia's father—but never like this. I believed in my heart of hearts this was my one chance, perhaps the only chance I'd ever have to become a pilot. I would not let Dr. Rasool and his lies, or any other ignorant, chauvinistic man, keep me from what I believed were noble aspirations.

I wanted a second opinion about my health; my father agreed. My family knew a doctor in the neighborhood. We went to him that night. I told him what kind of tests the military doctors had done, and fortunately, he knew what they were and performed the same exam.

My heart was fine, perfectly healthy.

———————

The next day, I took the test results from our local doctor to an American advisor with the US Air Force 438th Air Expeditionary Wing (AEW), Lieutenant Colonel Daryl Sassaman. I'd been introduced to Lieutenant Colonel Sassaman on my first day, before the medical exams. He was the officer in charge (OIC) of the Thunder Lab, the English-language training center where I'd begin flight school.

When I handed him the results and explained what happened at the Afghan hospital, he maintained a cool demeanor. I couldn't tell what he thought one way or the other. He was impassive, remaining silent as I told him my story. When I finished explaining the situation, including my belief I'd been treated unfairly along with the rest of the women, he said three words: "Come with me."

Lieutenant Colonel Sassaman escorted me to the US-run military hospital and requested an American doctor administer the entire exam a third time. Again, the test results confirmed I was fine. Lieutenant Colonel Sassaman gathered these new results into a folder and accompanied me back to the Afghan hospital to see Dr. Rasool.

When we entered Dr. Rasool's office, I could see he was caught off guard, unnerved by my presence and that of an American advisor. He quickly regained his composure and asked how he could help, in a decidedly different tone than the one he'd taken with me the day before.

Lieutenant Colonel Sassaman showed Dr. Rasool the results and stated I was cleared for flight training; he expected me to start at the Thunder Lab immediately. Lieutenant Colonel Sassaman wasn't accusatory, nor did his statements sound like a request. He was matter of fact, as if there was no doubt about my health and there had never been a disqualifying diagnosis. This was the end of the matter.

Dr. Rasool didn't flinch. He shrugged it off, claiming he didn't know what happened. Perhaps I'd taken some kind of drug without telling them; that's why my test results were off. No big deal.

Liar.

With Lieutenant Colonel Sassaman standing over him, Dr. Rasool signed my orders. I was approved for flight training.

22

ENGLISH IS A REQUIREMENT

BEFORE I COULD start actual flight training, there were a few other training courses to complete. First was the air force orientation course. Although I'd graduated from officer training a month earlier, that course was considered basic military training intended to indoctrinate raw recruits into military life. Marching, physical fitness, discipline, customs and courtesies, how to wear the uniform, and following orders were all part of our basic training.

Air force orientation, however, would teach me the uniqueness of the air force, a distinctly different military service compared to the army and the other security forces. Air force ranks look slightly different than army ranks, commanders of units have different titles, and the air force has a unique administrative and personnel system. Whereas the army focuses on ground operations while the security services engage in law enforcement, the air force conducts air operations.

It was akin to my orientation at Kabul University. There are multiple universities in Afghanistan, and they all impart knowledge, but each institution is unique in its specialties, curriculum, graduation criteria, physical layout of campus, and so forth. Before you can do anything at the university, you must receive an orientation to know what is unique to your specific school.

Air force orientation was interesting, and I enjoyed learning about my military service, but it was relatively straightforward. I never once thought I wouldn't pass the orientation course. I completed it on July 14, 2011, and was ready to move on.

The next prerequisite for flight training was achieving proficiency in English. NATO was advising the Afghan Air Force, and NATO pilots were running the flight training; there would be no Afghan instructors in flight school. All Afghan Air Force lieutenants selected for flight school had to attend Thunder Lab, which was a special course inside the Kabul English Language Training Center (KELTC). Lieutenant Colonel Sassaman was the OIC for Thunder Lab, and my class consisted of seventeen male and eight female students.

Proficiency in English at a high technical level was an absolute requirement for all trainees, and we had to complete a rigorous exam to demonstrate mastery before we could get anywhere near an aircraft. If you couldn't understand or communicate aeronautical terms and orders in a high-speed and high-stress environment—like flying a plane in combat—then you wouldn't make it through flight school.

A typical day at Thunder Lab began at 0500 with physical training, then breakfast at the chow hall, followed by English classes for the rest of the morning. We'd eat lunch, and in the afternoon we'd have professional development and leadership classes, which were aimed at enhancing our military knowledge and skills. After dinner, we had unstructured time with our advisors, chatting over tea, watching English-language movies, or playing games. During this phase of training, we didn't do anything involving real aircraft, but airplanes and flying were frequent conversation topics. And everything was in English all the time.

Thunder Lab was total immersion, meant to teach us not only to speak and understand English but also to actually *think* in English. Anyone who has ever learned a second language knows thinking in the new language is key. That's when things start to click. Rather than mentally translating what is being said into one's native tongue, coming up with an appropriate response, and translating it back into the second language, it's automatic and faster to keep oneself in the same language. This is critical for a pilot, because split seconds matter.

To move on to flight training, I needed to pass Thunder Lab with a score of 75 percent. From the beginning, I knew I would make it, because I genuinely enjoyed working with the instructors, learning from them, laughing with them, and sharing my own personal experiences and culture. Luke, Joseph, Amber, Chris, AMANDA, and CAROL—they were great instructors and truly cared about our performance and who we were as people.

Language school in Kabul was a great experience, but in March 2012 we were surprised to learn Thunder Lab was moving to Shindand Air Base, located in western Afghanistan in Herat Province, seventy-five miles from the Iranian border. At the time, it was the largest Afghan Air Force base in Afghanistan, and it also housed a NATO contingent for combat and support operations. The reason for the move: Shindand was being made into the pilot training center of excellence for the Afghan Air Force.

———————

The move of Thunder Lab from Kabul to Shindand took about a month. A group of instructors went first to inspect the new facilities and arrange the training spaces and living accommodations. In military terminology, they were called the advance party. As students, we would travel to Shindand over a three-week period. We were known as the main body.

The new Thunder Lab would occupy a building that previously served as a morale and welfare facility for another air advisory group, so it needed to be modified to suit the needs of language training. In addition, the class size of twenty-five (my class) would eventually grow to support upward of seventy-five students once fully operational; NATO was making a major investment in the training of Afghanistan's air force.

The night before I was scheduled to leave, I went home to get some last-minute belongings and say goodbye to my family. That night was tough; I knew training would last a very long time, more than a year, and I wouldn't see my family until I finished. This would be the longest I'd ever been away from home.

It was a bittersweet evening. I was excited to continue my training. I'd been in the military for over a year now—between basic officer training, air force orientation, and the initial months of language training—but being transferred to Shindand was a big jump. I was a lieutenant in the Afghan Air Force, my country was at war, and I was being assigned to an operational base to learn to fly combat missions.

My parents were happy about what my future held, but they were sad about my leaving. My mother was very anxious, still coming to grips with her daughter being in the military, but she was supportive. I held her hand and told her I was happy, this was what I wanted to do, and she'd raised me to be a strong woman. I wanted her to be proud, and she was.

My Baba Jan also expressed his feelings about what I was about to do. He hugged me, and I still remember the words he spoke: "I have faith in you, and I know you will do great. You are making *my* dream come true. You are like a son to me and I am grateful to God for a daughter like you. I know you will make me proud, and I am not worried about you as my child, even though you are going to be away from me."

Reading my father's words, you might consider his comment about me being a son to him as odd, even disrespectful. But I didn't take it that way, nor do I perceive it as disrespectful now. I knew what he was trying to say—even in this male-dominated, patriarchal, and misogynistic society, I was a strong, independent woman who could do anything, just like a son could.

His words made me feel good, not because I wanted to be compared to men, but because my father believed gender didn't matter. The individual person is what is important.

The next morning, I said goodbye to everyone, including my younger sisters, who still didn't know the truth. They believed I was going back to the university campus, not to a military base hundreds of miles away in western Afghanistan.

My brother, Omar, drove me to the Kabul air base and dropped me off. When we said goodbye, I hugged him close, said I would miss him, and asked him to pray for me. I told him, "I wouldn't be here if it weren't for you." I meant it.

Like my father, he was different than most Afghan men. He'd believed in me, supported me, and stood up for me. Omar was my Lala Jan, my dear brother.

23

MOVE WEST

ON A COOL MORNING IN APRIL 2012, I linked up with Lieutenant Colonel Sassaman, our remaining instructors, and my classmates on the flight line at 0700. The instructors quickly divided us into three groups and directed us to board the waiting Cessna 208s.

The Cessna 208 Caravan (C-208) is a single turboprop aircraft that essentially performs utility functions, like carrying people and cargo. It can hold upward of fourteen passengers or a cargo load of a few thousand pounds, depending on elevation, distance, environment, weather, and a host of other variables. It's one of the few fixed-wing aircraft in the Afghan Air Force's inventory, and in addition to transporting people and cargo, it has conducted ground attack and intelligence, surveillance, and reconnaissance (ISR) missions. It's also a great aircraft for training new pilots.

This would be my first flight in an airplane, and I happened to sit next to Lieutenant Colonel Sassaman. As we strapped in to prepare for takeoff, at one point he leaned over and said, "This will be you soon. This is the airplane you'll learn to fly." His words made the butterflies in my stomach flutter like crazy.

From my seat, I watched everything the pilot and copilot did for the preflight checks. Their gloved hands moved swiftly over the controls and gauges, ensuring everything was set correctly and in order. I couldn't hear what they were saying, but I saw their lips moving as they spoke to each other and the control tower.

A ground crew performed their last-minute checks outside the aircraft, verifying all the compartments were secure, then removed the blocks from under the wheels. Everyone—both the pilots and the ground crew—knew exactly what they were doing, what they were looking for, and how to work together as a cohesive team.

We received clearance to taxi to the runway for departure. I recall the plane nudging forward, rolling across the tarmac with a slight bounce; it was bumpier than I had imagined. It was also loud, but the headsets we wore muffled most of the noise. With these headsets we couldn't listen in to the cockpit, but we could talk among ourselves.

We rolled to a position at the end of the runway. As soon as we were lined up, I saw the pilot push the throttle forward, making the engine whine. We gradually picked up speed, hurtling down the runway, with the plane rattling as we accelerated. I bounced around in my seat, almost knocking into Lieutenant Colonel Sassaman, grateful for the safety belt.

When we lifted off, everything went magically still and peaceful. Gone was the bumpy runway jostling us in our seats and the crosswind rocking the plane—we were in the air, flying smooth and fast, gaining altitude.

I looked out the window as we soared above Kabul, quickly trying to find my bearings and wondering if I would see my house. I found our general neighborhood, but the plane banked before I could find my street.

I'd never seen the city like this. I'd had a decent view when I went walking in the hills beside my father, but this was totally new. The cars, the houses, the buildings, the roads—they looked like tiny

Niloofar Rahmani in flight school at Shindand Air Base, 2012. *Courtesy of Kristina Wong*

Niloofar Rahmani with her parents in Pakistan in 1994. *Author's collection*

Niloofar Rahmani, six years old, in Pakistan in 1997. *Author's collection*

Niloofar Rahmani (center) with her older sister, brother, and father in Pakistan. *Author's collection*

Niloofar Rahmani in flight school at Shindand Air Base, standing beside a Cessna 208 Caravan (C-208), 2013. *Courtesy of Kristina Wong*

Niloofar Rahmani with her classmates at Shindand Air Base, 2012. *Courtesy of Kristina Wong*

Niloofar Rahmani with her classmates and Captain Lauren Stewart (third from left) at Shindand Air Base, 2012. *Author's collection*

Niloofar Rahmani with flight instructor Jarrod Hollander beside a C-208 at Shindand Air Base, 2012. *Author's collection*

Niloofar Rahmani with Captain Carly Reimer at Shindand Air Base, 2012.
Author's collection

Niloofar Rahmani with Captain Lindsey Bauer inside the cockpit of a C-208 at the Kabul air base, 2015. *Author's collection*

Niloofar Rahmani at the ceremony for the International Women of Courage Award with First Lady Michelle Obama and the other recipients, Washington, DC, 2015. *Courtesy of the Barack Obama Presidential Library*

Niloofar Rahmani with lawyer Kimberly Motley (right) and Fox News anchor Martha MacCallum in New York, 2018. *Author's collection*

Niloofar Rahmani flying with the US Navy Blue Angels in San Diego, California, 2015. *Author's collection, courtesy of the US Navy's Blue Angels*

toys that kept getting smaller and smaller the higher we climbed and the farther away we flew.

As new vistas appeared, I spotted snowcapped mountains to the north, which up here in a plane looked very close but were in fact miles and miles away. Afghanistan's sandy plains also caught my eye, desolate and dry, stretching to the horizon. The plains were dotted with pockets of lush green oases, with houses, farms, and towns located nearby. I imagined families tending to the fields, working in their gardens, cooking fresh bread in wood ovens, and grilling kebabs over an open flame.

Although I'd heard my parents and relatives talk about it before, up here I finally got to take in the magnificent natural splendor of my Afghanistan, with all its diversity. Up here, my homeland was beautiful and peaceful—I was speechless.

Then I heard my headphones crackle and Lieutenant Colonel Sassaman's voice come over the intercom. He announced this would be the aircraft we would learn to fly and to enjoy the view; once we were in the cockpit, there'd be no time for sightseeing and we'd be too busy to miss home. We all laughed.

When we landed at Shindand Air Base, I felt like we'd entered another world. Where the bustle of city life had been right outside the gates of the military bases in Kabul, here there was nothing but a military footprint.

Afghan, NATO, and US military aircraft were scattered across the airfield and inside the hangars. There were Mi-17 helicopters, Cessna C-182s and C-208s turboprop aircraft, C-130 Hercules transport aircraft, massive C-17 Globemasters, F-16 and F/A-18 fighters, and others. Some of the aircraft were in rows while others were clustered, but all of them were spaced far apart to mitigate the effects of an indirect fire attack. (If the aircraft were too close together and one of them got hit by a mortar and started burning, the others could go up in flames.)

Nearly everyone I saw was in uniform. There were airmen and soldiers from a variety of countries working in the mechanical yards, driving trucks or Humvees, walking with rifles slung across their backs, and going in and out of buildings carrying out their assignments. Paved roads and concrete slabs broke up the flat, sandy terrain. There was no foliage, and there were barely any colors besides gray, brown, tan, and green camouflage. Fences and guard posts lined the base perimeter and were also scattered throughout the interior of the base. Depending where you needed to go, you might have to pass through two or three internal checkpoints along the way.

Shindand was solely a military base and had been in operation since the time of the Soviets. After 9/11 it'd been built up to handle the NATO mission—supply, transport, ISR, close air support, and training. Aircraft were constantly taking off and landing, while soldiers and equipment were continuously going on and off the base, heading out to conduct combat operations against the Taliban and terrorist fighters, who still posed a serious threat to the Afghan government, population centers, and NATO personnel.

Shindand was a massive military machine that I'd heard about but never actually seen, until now. This would be my home for the foreseeable future.

The new Thunder Lab was contained inside the Shindand English Language Training Center (SELTC) in its own section of the base. There were multiple buildings that housed classrooms, as well as a separate building with a large hall. All the male students would stay in a nearby barracks with other Afghan soldiers and airmen, but as a woman it was not safe for me to live in the same building with them.

I was assigned to the barracks that housed the American and British female advisors. I had a concrete room with one window, two beds, and two wall lockers. Next door was the communal bathroom and shower, which was still a concept I was getting used to. I'd experienced this kind of arrangement in basic training with the Afghan trainees, but now I would share facilities with the Western advisors.

Although this would be a new experience for me—living in close proximity to foreigners—I wasn't bothered by it. All the advisors were very accepting and approachable. These Western women were tough, without a doubt, but they were polite and welcoming. I felt safe here.

The next morning I woke up at 0400 to start physical training at 0500. By 0600 I was formed up with the other students to march over to the US compound for breakfast. After I had my pancakes (one of my favorite foods, which my American advisors introduced me to), I sat with a group of the instructors, who were curious to know what I thought of Shindand so far.

I told them it was too soon to have much of an opinion, but Shindand seemed like a great place to continue our training and learn from the advisors. It was also fascinating to watch how the rest of the base functioned and to see how personnel from the United States and other NATO countries conducted themselves. What struck me was the universal confidence they all seemed to have, and it didn't matter if they were male or female. They walked purposefully, spoke strongly, and knew exactly what they were supposed to be doing. This in many ways was in stark contrast to a wide swath of the Afghan military, though I didn't say this out loud.

The instructors commented on the general activities of the base, which were separate from SELTC, and how this was a full-fledged operational base conducting real support and combat operations. They also talked about some of the attacks the Taliban had made against the base. The Taliban had primarily conducted rocket and mortar attacks, launching rounds from nearby villages or farm areas. They typically would fire from civilian areas, both to mask their activities amid the population and to limit our ability to respond without incurring civilian casualties.

Fortunately, these attacks weren't very accurate. Although people had been wounded and killed and buildings had been damaged, the rockets or mortars often missed the base entirely or hit an open area. I'd grown up during a civil war and endured the violence of the Taliban, but the idea of indirect fire attacks, complex ambushes, and ground engagements was sobering. The war was still going on, and I was training to fight in it.

After breakfast, we returned to the SELTC area, but rather than heading into class, we stayed in formation in the courtyard. Lieutenant Colonel Sassaman stood before us and announced he had been reassigned to another command and would no longer be the OIC of Thunder Lab. His replacement was US Navy lieutenant commander Matthew Pescador, who was a naval aviator. We watched the change-of-command ceremony, where Lieutenant Colonel Sassaman formally transferred authority to Lieutenant Commander Pescador.

After the ceremony, we went into class and continued language training in almost the exact same manner as we'd done in Kabul. We were immersed in English through classroom language instruction, professional development, leadership classes, meals, and social interaction with our instructors. This went on for two more months.

On May 31, 2012, I took my final exam for Thunder Lab. I needed to achieve a score of 75 percent to start the academic portion of flight training. I was well prepared and eager to take the test.

The exam was quite comprehensive, with well over a hundred questions and activities, including reading comprehension, writing, listening, and speaking. It took most of the morning, and although I was confident in my abilities, I found the process exhausting and stressful. I didn't want to merely pass; I wanted to do well and believed it was important to be near the top of my class.

Once we handed in our test sheets and materials, we had to wait two hours to receive our scores. When it came time to find out how we'd done, three names were called before mine. Lieutenant Commander Pescador then called my name, Lieutenant Rahmani, and said I'd achieved a score of eighty-nine and successfully graduated Thunder Lab.

One of the British female advisors and pilots, Lieutenant Lauren Steward, was present and came forward to give me a hug. I was so excited and so was she, and she told me now I could start *real* pilot training.

Later that afternoon, I ran out to the courtyard to see if I could get a signal for my phone. Coverage was spotty at Shindand and we didn't have regular access to the Internet, so I'd only talked with my parents a handful of times since arriving.

It took me fifteen minutes, but I got through and heard the phone ringing on the other end. My father picked up, and I told him I'd passed my language training; I'd start flight training soon. I said I would have never made it this far without him, and I was so grateful for his faith and trust in me.

Although I couldn't see him, when he spoke I could hear the smile on his face. He said he was so happy for me and that his prayers and love would also be with me.

24

FLIGHT TRAINING

———

I AGAIN WOKE UP EARLY to prepare myself. It was June 3, the first day of actual flight training. The new classroom was about two miles away from my barracks, and I would need to walk there. The sun was starting to come up and there was a slight breeze in the air, causing the dust to swirl a few feet above the ground. Although it was summer, at 0530 it was cool outside.

I didn't know what to expect. Even though I'd been in the military for well over a year, my knowledge of aviation was quite limited. I would have a lot to learn and would need to learn it fast if I was to make it through training. I also knew I couldn't fall behind; I needed to be on par with, or ahead of, the men.

I kept hearing my Baba Jan's voice in my head telling me I would succeed and not to get discouraged if I encountered challenges or failures. My dream would come true, and he would always be proud of me. I took this as an auspicious sign.

About a half mile away from the new training area, I spotted four large tents, one of which would serve as our classroom. As I drew closer, I recognized some of the instructors going in and out of the tent and saw some of my fellow students making their way there in small groups. There would be ten of us, but I was the only woman. Two other female students had made it to SELTC as well, but they still needed to pass their English test and would be there for another year.

Inside the tent, I saw the instructors preparing the classroom. They immediately welcomed us and started showing us around. The instructors were either retired military or contract civilian pilots—Rowe, Bostrom, Baker, Klemm, and Osmon, to name a few—and they all came from the United States. But no matter who they were or what their background was, they presented themselves as genuinely excited to be training us.

The classroom had tables and chairs for all the students and a blackboard at the front. There were also fans to circulate air. Although the tents were air conditioned (they were massive canvas structures), we would soon find out how stifling they could get during the hot, dusty days of Afghanistan's summer.

Next we went outside, and the instructors escorted us over to the flight line so we could see the aircraft used for training: C-208 and C-182 fixed-wing aircraft and Mi-17 helicopters. We would learn to fly the C-182, a four-seat single-engine light aircraft, which looks very much like a Cessna you would find on any small airfield in the United States.

However, even though the instructors were introducing us to the planes and giving us teasers about what lay ahead, we'd have to pass aerodynamics in ground school before getting anywhere near the cockpit.

Back in the classroom, I was thinking I'd have to work harder than all the other students to succeed. The men would have each other's backs and do whatever they could to help each other make it through the training. Some of their fathers had been pilots, so they had more advanced insight about what to expect. They conveniently shared this with each other, but not with me.

I was from a society that had one of the highest rates of domestic violence and gender inequality in the world. I could practically feel the disdain my male colleagues projected at me. They wanted me to fail and said as much, either in the conversations I overheard at the chow hall or in previous classes, or every time they looked at me with scorn in their eyes. I'd go so far as to say some of them hated me.

Even with the support my parents gave me, being brought up in a society that sees women as weak and undeserving of respect can destroy someone's confidence and self-esteem. Admittedly, I struggled with these things, especially around other Afghan men who were determined to oppress me any way they could.

I was very aware of how Afghanistan's culture, my confidence, and my self-esteem affected my performance during flight school. I told myself I couldn't control what other people said or thought, but I could control my mind, my heart, and my response. I didn't have to believe the words they threw at me; I needed to stay positive no matter what. I could do this.

We were designated Class 12-04, and we were the first class to include an Afghan woman. There were a lot of eyes not only on me but also on the instructors. How would Afghanistan's first female student pilot fare?

The first phase of training was called IFS, or initial flight screening, and lasted six weeks. The curriculum consisted of classroom instruction to teach us the basics. We trained six days a week, starting with early morning PT, followed by lectures in flight terminology, aerodynamics, airport markings, flight procedures, basic aerial maneuvers, flight patterns, and emergency procedures. Our instructors also taught us about S-turns, stalls, slow flight and military approaches, and forced landings.

There was so much to learn and they were delivering it at full throttle, so I told myself not to be afraid if I didn't understand something. If I didn't know the answer or didn't grasp a concept, I needed to ask questions until I understood. At the end of each day, I made sure I knew what had been taught and what would be expected of me the following day. I never made any excuses.

But as each day ended and another one began, training got more difficult and the pace got faster. The lessons and exercises built upon each other, and we had to recall what we learned on day one even if we were in the middle of week five.

I started using flight terminology in my normal conversations. Full throttle, the deck, crash and burn, milk run, bogey, visual . . . it was an entirely different language.

Unfortunately, despite my best efforts, I struggled in the beginning. I felt everyone was learning faster than I was and asking fewer questions because they already knew the answers, while I was always trying to put it together. They were smarter than I was, spoke more confidently and authoritatively than I did, and carried themselves more assuredly.

Part of the reason I struggled was my self-confidence. I was a woman trying to do a "man's job," and despite what I told myself about staying positive and that their words shouldn't bother me, for twenty years Afghan society had told me I was inferior to men. Moreover, when physically compared to other people, I'm relatively small and appear petite—perhaps weak. How could I possibly make it through flight school?

The lowest I felt during training was near the end of ground school. One particular day, I'd stayed after class a little later than usual because I was struggling with a concept. (I don't remember what it was.) I was very fortunate our instructors came from Western societies, because they never hesitated to answer my questions or keep working with me to make certain I understood the material. Once I was satisfied I understood what I needed to, I hurried to the chow hall to get lunch before they shut the doors.

The chow hall was three miles from the classroom, and it was scorching hot that day. The wind felt like a hair dryer blowing in my face, and the sun's rays felt like an open oven. By the time I reached the dining facility, I was out of breath, hot, and sweaty. I got in line, but most of the food had been picked over, so I settled for some vegetables, got some water, and found a table.

I was sitting by myself, as usual, until four Afghan lieutenants from my class—all men—entered the chow hall, grabbed some food for themselves, and sat down at the table next to me. They didn't say hello, didn't even acknowledge me, except by casting sidelong glances in my direction. They whispered among themselves, talking softly and laughing, occasionally looking over at me. Then they got louder, cracking jokes about how every time a woman does something outside the home, she fails. They went on to say respectable women stay at home, and any woman who has to do something other than raise children or care for her husband is shameful. As for women in the military, they deserve no respect and are a disgrace. They come from shameful families and are no better than beggars and whores.

I sat there listening, but I didn't say anything. I acted as if I couldn't hear them, couldn't even see them, and continued eating my lunch. My father told me it's better to ignore mean and ignorant people—they're looking for a reaction or a fight, so don't give them one. Still, what my classmates said hurt.

When I finished eating, I got up without so much as a glance in their direction, put my tray in the scullery, and walked back to my room. Since it was Thursday, study had finished for the week and would begin again on Saturday. (Friday is the weekend in Afghanistan.)

As soon as I closed and locked my door, I pulled my scarf off my head and let it drop to the floor. I fell on my bed, buried my face in my pillow, and began to cry.

I'd been keeping everything pent up for so long, trying to be strong and telling myself they couldn't hurt me, but I needed to let it out. It wasn't enough that training was hard and stressful. Being the only female student and being alone—with no one to truly confide in, not one real friend—was weighing on me.

I'd heard people talk about the camaraderie found in the military, where soldiers have each other's backs and stick together. I didn't have that. I was on my own. I gripped my pillow and cried.

I don't know how long it was, but soon someone knocked at my door. I had no idea who it could be, so I quickly dried my tears and put my scarf back on, trying to erase any evidence of the last few minutes.

When I opened the door, I saw Lieutenant Lauren Stewart standing there. She was a British pilot in the Royal Air Force and had been one of my mentors in Thunder Lab. She was an attractive woman, somewhere in her early thirties and about five feet, five inches tall, with fair skin, blonde hair, blue eyes, and an average build. She'd always been nice to me. During my time in Thunder Lab, she had always gone out of her way to check on me and see how I was doing.

Finding Lauren outside my door brought happiness to my heart, and I felt my cheeks stretch from smiling so big. I was so glad to see her, and her presence helped push away the sadness I'd been feeling just seconds before. I have no idea if she could tell I'd been crying, but I suspect she could. I imagine my eyes were still red, and I know my scarf was disheveled from my haste in putting it back on.

To my surprise, with a genuine smile on her face, she said she was planning a girl's night for that night, Thursday evening, and asked me to come. She'd invited a few women from the other NATO commands, and there would be eight of us. I enthusiastically accepted her invitation.

After dinner, I put on a traditional Afghan dress and went down to the common room in the barracks. I had an extra dress that I gave to Lauren, who hugged me and thanked me for the gift.

The six other women were Americans, and they did various jobs on the base, ranging from logistics and administration to flight operations. I'd never met them before this evening, but they were so friendly and talkative. We chatted about our cultures and families, drank tea, and snacked on little sweets and nuts.

I laughed so much that night, not necessarily because things were funny, but because I felt accepted by these women in a way I hadn't felt in months. They were warm and engaging and expressed their support for what I was doing as a pilot trainee. Without me having to say it, they knew it was hard and that I had to fight for everything. I could tell they'd experienced similar hurdles in their own careers.

Hearing their stories and their perspectives was so uplifting. I wasn't alone. I knew I wouldn't see or talk to these women often, and I knew come Saturday I'd be back in the thick of it with my male classmates. But knowing these women were nearby, especially my friend Lauren, strengthened me.

25

FIRST FLIGHT

———————

A FEW WEEKS INTO GROUND SCHOOL, I started going to the base gym on Friday mornings to do Insanity workouts. For those unfamiliar with the program, it's a form of high-intensity interval training for endurance and agility, but without any weights or equipment, only body weight. You can do it alone, but I liked the group classes because everyone was so excited and motivated and pushed each other to get better and stronger. It was fun too.

One particular Friday in June 2012, I was extra motivated during the workout because of what we'd be doing the next day during training. We would finally get up in the air to conduct our first training flight. I was thrilled!

As usual, I could barely sleep that night, and on Saturday morning I woke up early to prepare myself for the big day. I wore my tan flight suit and tan boots and put on my black scarf; this was a distinctly different-looking uniform from the green utilities I normally wore. This uniform—the flight suit—was for pilots.

I showed up in class with my flight bag like everyone else. (A typical flight bag holds everything from emergency items to batteries to gum to an extra scarf and pair of sunglasses.) But before we could get into the planes, we needed to review the day's agenda, talk through emergency procedures one more time, and perform other routine preflight activities, like reviewing the weather. Bad weather, not to mention factors like crosswinds and slick landing conditions, can make even a commercial airline flight quite harrowing. Fortunately, the day's forecast was for sun and clear skies with a slight breeze from the northwest.

The advisor in charge of our class overall, Flight Commander Jarrod Hollander, chose me to read the weather to the rest of the class, which had been the daily routine since the first day of training. As I'd done a few times before, I stood and read off the weather data: "OASD 160900Z VRB05KT—"

But instead of letting me get through the entire report, one of the instructors barked, "Speak up, Lieutenant Rahmani. We can't hear you. Can anyone hear Lieutenant Rahmani?"

The other students shook their heads in the negative, and I saw the smirks on their faces. They thought the instructors were picking on me. They'd heard the instructors ask me to talk louder in class before. But I knew the instructors weren't picking on me. They were trying to make me more confident. They were trying to take away my fear and timidity. They were helping me overcome years of being ignored and dismissed as a woman.

My male Afghan colleagues didn't understand this, but I did. In response to the instructor, I raised my voice and announced as firmly as I could the rest of the weather data. When I sat back down, we were each assigned an instructor to fly with. I would fly with Instructor Pilot (IP) Major McMannis; his call sign was IP Smack.

———————

IP Smack was one of the older IPs, probably in his early fifties, and I was glad to make my first training flight with him. He was a good instructor—experienced and mature—and he had a sense of humor, which I appreciated.

As we walked to the flight line, he reviewed everything we'd covered in the classroom, as well as what we needed to do before getting into the aircraft. We walked around the C-182 to perform a visual inspection not just of the aircraft itself but also of the area around the plane. We confirmed hatches and panels were secured, no debris was around the wheels, and no tools had been left behind by the mechanics who serviced the aircraft.

We got into the cockpit and buckled ourselves in, but before we continued our preflight checks, IP Smack reemphasized one of the most important, yet simple and obvious, interactions between a pilot and copilot. It's imperative before starting the engine or anything that involves flying the plane for pilot and copilot to confirm with each other who has the controls. You do this by stating, "I have the controls," or "You have the controls," and the other person verbally acknowledges control. It's simple, and it may seem excessive, but it would be really unfortunate if both the pilot and the copilot thought the other person was flying the plane when they weren't.

Next, IP Smack told me if I started to feel airsick to let him know immediately so we could land. He didn't want me to mess up the aircraft, because it would be a real pain to clean. We both laughed, which helped make me a little less nervous. He said, "Fear is your enemy." I needed to be brave.

It was a good lesson. As I would come to find out when I started flying combat missions a year later, wit and a sense of humor were good ways to calm passengers' nerves, stop them from panicking, and inspire confidence. Leaders need to be cool under pressure, and a pilot is the leader and commander of the plane. I would never forget IP Smack's wise words nor that moment of levity during my first training flight.

We completed our preflight checks and started the engine, and IP Smack told me to call the tower. I keyed my headset and said, "Shindand Ground, Baaz 11 clear to taxi for departure to MOA with information Charlie."

A male voice from the tower crackled over the radio, "Baaz 11, clear to taxi via Charlie. Hold short runway three-six. Advise run-up complete."

We taxied to the runway, joined the lineup, and made our final checks. We were ready for takeoff but still awaiting clearance from the tower. It would be our turn soon.

My heart was racing. I was about to fly a plane! Once the tower said go, I would be the one on the yoke and pushing the throttle, maintaining control of the aircraft as we sped down the runway and then taking off into the air. My palms were sweaty and I was breathing faster than normal, but I was also assured by the presence of IP Smack. He would back me up if I missed something or if we had a problem.

Finally, the tower gave us clearance. "Baaz 11, cleared for takeoff runway three-six. After takeoff fly runway heading."

This was it. IP Smack told me to maintain the center line on the runway and to keep my left hand on the throttle and right hand on the yoke. He would call out my speed to let me know when we could lift off.

I took a breath, released the brakes, and pushed the throttle forward. We picked up speed, and I felt myself getting pushed back into the seat. I kept the yoke steady, my eyes trained on the runway before us, as well as on the horizon.

About midway down the runway, IP Smack called out our air speed at 55 knots, which was the ground speed we needed for the plane to lift off. I'd already noticed the odd sensation of the plane feeling lighter, like the aircraft wanted to get into the air.

With my instructor's concurrence, I pulled back on the yoke smoothly, as I'd been trained, and felt the wheels leave the ground. We were flying!

_____

If I were to pinpoint one thing about flying I truly love, it's the thrill of takeoff. You're speeding down the runway, feeling a slight bounce as the aircraft's tires roll over the asphalt. With your hands on the controls, you manipulate the yoke for liftoff. Everything on the ground is whipping by very quickly, and then almost effortlessly you start climbing higher and higher into the air. As the ground disappears beneath you, the horizon becomes your focus while you continue to increase speed and gain altitude. The experience is totally exhilarating, and it feels the same when I fly now as it did way back then.

Even in the moment, I knew I'd done something extraordinary that day. I was an Afghan woman and a newly commissioned lieutenant in the Afghan armed forces, and I was executing my first training flight in a fixed-wing aircraft.

Women hadn't flown in the Afghan Air Force since the 1980s, and those few who had been pilots back then flew rotary-wing aircraft (helicopters). It'd been nearly twenty years, but now here I was, piloting a fixed-wing aircraft for the first time over western Afghanistan. I don't consider myself a proud or arrogant person, but the significance of the event was not lost on me.

_____

For this initial training flight, all students were to transit to an area called the MOA (military operations area), which was a section of air space reserved specifically for pilot trainees who were practicing maneuvers. Once in the training area, we'd practice steep turns, stalls, spins, simulated engine failures, and other aerial drills. These were maneuvers that we'd need to be able to handle reflexively and instantly.

In flight, things can happen extremely fast and with catastrophic consequences, so it was imperative we perfected these maneuvers. Since this was the first day, IP Smack had me practice each maneuver again and again.

I think I did well for my first flight. There were no major problems and I maintained control of the aircraft the entire time, but it went by so quickly. It seemed like time disappeared, until we had to return to the airfield.

But we weren't quite done. Now we were going to practice touch-and-go landings. IP Smack demonstrated the first landing. He took control of the aircraft and talked me through everything he was doing on final approach and touchdown. He made it look so simple, casually conversing with me while also working the controls gently with his hands and feet. He was an accomplished pilot and a great instructor.

It was my turn, but unlike my takeoff and performance during the aerial maneuvers, I let the pressure get to me. I so wanted to do well, but I ended up working the controls too hard. On my approach I soon realized I had too much airspeed and was too high. I knew if I tried to land it would be rough—I might even crash. I quickly made the decision to wave off and requested permission from the tower to come around again to rejoin the pattern.

As I did this, IP Smack took control of the aircraft. He wanted me to focus and listen. He told me to take a deep breath and think about what happened. He said I'd done exactly what I should have done. My approach was off, and rather than risk driving this little plane and us into the dirt, I made the correct choice to go around and try again. That's what a pilot is supposed to do. We're responsible for the aircraft and everyone on it, and we have to make life and death decisions every moment while we're flying. I'd made the right call.

This gave me some consolation, but I was still frustrated. I wanted to do well. I'd been working so hard in class and had been preparing my whole life for this. At last, here I was, flying a C-182 airplane over Afghanistan, but landing was proving difficult for me.

We went around a few more times, but I had problems with each attempted touch-and-go. If it wasn't one thing it was another, and if I didn't wave off to go around again, my touch was too hard or the aircraft was at a bad angle. I was approaching too fast or too slow, or unable to reduce my vertical speed. Nothing was working right, no matter how hard I tried. The time came to return to base (RTB) and get back on the ground. IP Smack took control of the aircraft and brought us in.

After every training flight, the IP would debrief us on how we did, and the lead instructor for the day would provide a grade for each maneuver and for the conduct of the flight overall. IP Smack gave me high marks for my takeoff and aerial maneuvers, but I needed to work on my landings. I wasn't surprised; I knew this, but I looked forward to my next opportunity to get into the air. I needed practice.

In the weeks following my first training flight, I flew with many different instructors. Like my first time, I was very good at taking off, the full spectrum of aerial maneuvers, and emergency actions. I was becoming a good pilot, and my instructors all graded me accordingly. They encouraged and supported me, and I truly believed they would do everything they could to help me succeed. But as I continued to struggle with landing, I was getting very concerned.

I thought I was doing everything exactly as I'd been trained, but I still couldn't get my landings right. In fact, I feared I wouldn't pass my upcoming check ride (a flight evaluation, or test) and continue to the next phase of training. My confidence was starting to falter.

One day during a break in class, I heard some of the other students talking about me. They were saying of course I couldn't land the plane. I'd never graduate. My hands were too small, I was too weak, and my brain couldn't handle everything I needed to do in the cockpit. I was a woman, and Afghan women couldn't handle being pilots.

I knew some of my classmates were having their own problems. None of them were perfect, and I wasn't the only one struggling with landing. But I was hurt by what they said, and this particular day I couldn't ignore it or keep it in.

I excused myself from the class to go to the bathroom. Once I was outside and out of sight from the other students, I sat down on the stairs and began to cry. I tried to hide my tears with my arms, but the tears kept coming. I felt alone and like I was failing. I was, to an extent. I hadn't received a passing mark on any of my landings.

After a few minutes, I heard footsteps approaching and looked up to see IP Bostrom coming toward me. He was a retired US Air Force fighter pilot. I'd flown with him a few times, and I liked him. He asked me if I wanted to talk. I stood up, and we went to walk around the tent.

IP Bostrom said he had a daughter about my age, and he knew this training was hard for me. It wasn't hard because the material or the activities were too difficult; he knew how hard I was working and that I was a good student. He also knew women not only could learn to fly but also could be great pilots and fly the world's most advanced aircraft. When he was on active duty in the US Air Force, he had flown alongside many women who were outstanding aviators.

He knew it was tough because I was the only woman in the class and because I was a young Afghan woman surrounded by Afghan men. He understood I was fighting against a lot of ingrained cultural behaviors and deep-seated customs and attitudes that had oppressed Afghan women for decades. IP Bostrom had been serving in Afghanistan for quite a few years, and he had seen firsthand how women were treated.

He told me I was very courageous for doing this, and not to let my classmates bother me. He said they were mean and ignorant to disrespect and criticize me, and they weren't as good as they thought. I shouldn't let what they said discourage me. IP Bostrom wanted me to succeed, and he told me I needed to focus on doing everything I possibly could to finish training. That's what was important: finishing training and becoming a pilot.

Were I not a lieutenant in the Afghan Air Force and an Afghan woman, and were he not a male unrelated to me, I would have hugged IP Bostrom. Anyone who has been really down at one point or another in life can likely imagine how much his words meant to me at that moment. I needed to hear them, and I thanked him deeply.

The day after my walk with IP Bostrom, I was scheduled to fly with our class flight commander, IP Hollander. But rather than going to the MOA to practice aerial maneuvers, he wanted me to stay in a flight pattern around the airfield so I could practice landing.

When it came time to execute my first touch-and-go of the training flight, he told me to make sure I kept the end of the runway in view the entire time until I touched down. I responded, "OK." This was the standard technique.

But as I was coming down during my final approach and about to execute the landing flare, IP Hollander asked me if my eyes were still on the end of the runway. I told him I was trying, but it was hard for me to see past the nose of the aircraft when I flared.

A landing flare is a maneuver that occurs right before touchdown. In short, after final approach and when the aircraft is very low to the ground but still in the air above the runway, the pilot raises the nose of the plane to slow the descent rate of the aircraft and make a softer landing. I understood the concept and theoretically knew how to execute the maneuver, but this was where I usually encountered trouble in my landings.

After I told IP Hollander I was having trouble keeping my eyes on the end of the runway during the flare, he told me to go around again and to give him control of the aircraft. He instructed me to put something on my seat to boost me up so I could sit a little higher. A C-182 is a small aircraft, and there wasn't much inside for me to sit on, except my flight bag. So I did as directed: put my flight bag on my seat and sat on it. IP Hollander passed control of the aircraft back to me.

We went around again to attempt another touch-and-go, and IP Hollander reminded me once again to keep my eyes on the end of the runway during final approach and the flare.

I must say, compared to all my previous landing attempts, this experience was unbelievable. Rather than struggling to watch the end of the runway, which helped with orientation and timing and direction (everything you need to monitor when landing), I could easily see the end of the runway with a clear view while simultaneously manipulating the aircraft's controls. I touched down nicely without ballooning (bouncing off the runway rather than sinking into it), executing an excellent landing.

Up until this point, my average landing had been graded at 40 percent. This particular landing, however, earned 70 percent! I couldn't believe it. All this time, my problem had simply been my inability to see past the nose of the aircraft—I was too short. But with a boost in my seat, I was golden.

In that moment, I not only knew I would pass my check ride and proceed to the next phase of training—I truly believed I was going to graduate and become a full-fledged pilot in the Afghan Air Force.

26

THINGS CHANGE

———

AFTER I GRADUATED FROM FLIGHT SCHOOL, I found out a few things I was unaware of during training. In short, my instructors were very concerned I wouldn't pass, but not because they didn't think I could learn the material or master the skills required to fly a plane. They all knew I could be trained to do those things.

Their principal concern was whether I could gain the self-confidence and assertiveness needed to be a pilot, not only in title but also in actual presence and ability. As I've mentioned before, the pilot is ultimately responsible for the safety of the aircraft and everyone on board. The pilot decides when to take off or land, determines whether to fly this course or that one, and, in an emergency, is the one ultimately responsible for performing immediate action and making decisions that could result in life or death. Any hesitation or timidity could be catastrophic, especially when split seconds matter.

All of my instructors, whether they were active duty, retired military, or civilian pilots, were highly skilled and experienced. They knew my biggest challenge would be whether I could overcome the oppressive, hostile, and dismissive elements of Afghan culture so I could carry myself and fly an airplane with true confidence and command authority. Apparently, I was a frequent topic of conversation for them at the chow hall when no other students were around.

Fortunately, once I learned my struggles with landing were due to my height, things changed. I wasn't mystified anymore as to why I struggled with particular maneuvers. In fact, I not only realized I needed to sit higher but also started looking at my relationship with the aircraft more intimately.

If I was in the cockpit, it was *my* aircraft for as long as I was in the seat. I made certain the instruments, my view outside, my positioning in the cockpit, the positioning of the copilot (my instructor, at this point), and everything about the aircraft made sense and was set up so I could exercise total control of the machine and ensure the safety of my passengers.

The IPs had trained me well, and I knew the material. I'd worked hard to make sure I didn't simply know the answers to questions but fully understood the concepts, the theories, and the connections between them. When class was over and my classmates left for the day, I was the one staying behind to ask more questions and put in the extra effort to learn all I could. I wasn't satisfied with the minimum; I needed to know it all.

With this new mindset, my outward demeanor also changed. When I spoke over the radio to the tower or other aircraft, I knew what I needed to say and what I expected to hear in response. I no longer sheepishly asked permission to get my plane into the sky; I told the tower I was ready and standing by clearance.

It didn't matter if I was speaking to my instructors, the NATO personnel working in the tower, the ground crews, or my classmates. I was an officer in the Afghan Air Force, and it didn't matter that I was a woman or whether I was speaking to a man. I had a job to do and I was going to do it.

The change in me became unmistakably apparent when I did my check ride at the end of the general handling phase of training. During this check ride, pilots would be required to perform the full range of maneuvers, both in the air and during various types of simulated emergencies and landing situations. On completion of the check ride, our performance evaluations would determine if we could proceed to the next phase.

What made this particular check ride unique was that it would not be with our instructor pilots, with whom we'd been training all along—our evaluators would be pulled from the larger air group at Shindand and the other flight classes. Their evaluations would be objective, unbiased, and rigorous. My classmates and I would either pass or fail.

On the morning of our check ride, we learned who our evaluators would be. When my name was called, I was surprised—if not shocked—by who I was paired with. The other students were also shocked at my pairing. My evaluator would be USAF colonel David Gossett, the commander of the 838th Air Expeditionary Advisory Group at Shindand and the senior ranking pilot for the entire base. He was an F-16 fighter pilot with a no-nonsense demeanor, making him a formidable examiner for any airman.

Although being selected to fly with the group commander was intimidating, I knew it meant my instructors had confidence in me. If they didn't, they wouldn't have assigned me to fly with him; I would have flown with someone else. I also knew assigning me to the group commander was a big risk.

My flight class, 12-04, was already under the spotlight because I was the first female trainee. Although I didn't think of myself this way, I was essentially a test case for NATO to determine how best to train Afghan female pilots. If I tanked my check ride, everyone would know, and it would be a significant embarrassment not only for me but also for my instructors. I knew I was representing not just myself but my entire class and all the future female pilots for Afghanistan.

Not surprisingly, my classmates didn't think I was up to the challenge. In fact, one of them was so bold he blurted out, "Sir, how could you risk letting her fly with the group commander? She's going to kill herself and him and crash the plane."

The other students laughed and snickered, but Flight Commander Hollander didn't flinch. He simply said, "Lieutenant, I know what I'm doing and think she's ready. You should probably think about your own flight."

The flight commander's words bolstered me, and these kinds of comments from my male classmates no longer troubled me. I had my confidence, and they weren't going to shake me anymore. I also knew actions speak louder than words.

We talked briefly in the classroom with our evaluators before heading to the flight line. Colonel Gossett was a tall man (at least six feet) with close-cropped brown hair, a weather-lined face, broad shoulders with a solid build, and fair skin. I think he was in his early forties, and he had a highly disciplined look about him in his tan flight suit and with his alert demeanor. He *looked* like a commander.

Speaking with Colonel Gossett, I wasn't nervous, which surprised me. I probably should have been anxious, given who he was and that he was about to evaluate me, but I knew what I was doing and believed I was good in the cockpit.

The two of us walked to the flight line with minimal small talk, strapped ourselves in, did the preflight checks, and were cleared to taxi to runway one-eight for takeoff. It was a beautiful sunny morning with the wind speed at only 5 knots—ideal conditions for flying.

Once our turn came in the lineup, Colonel Gossett gave me the nod. I pushed the throttle forward and we headed down the runway, doing everything exactly how I'd been trained and precisely how my

IPs had taught me. I made a course straight to the MOA, where I'd perform most of the maneuvers, and we got right to it.

We started off with some pattern work and basic instrument maneuvers, and then moved into more challenging actions: steep turns, stalls, slow flight, slips, and so forth. I also talked through everything as I was doing it to further demonstrate my mastery of the tasks I was being evaluated on.

Then, without warning, Colonel Gossett pulled the throttle back to simulate an emergency engine failure. I knew this drill would happen at some point during the check ride, but I hadn't known when.

For this task, I had to go through the full gamut of actions as if the engine were not going to restart. After performing the initial engine failure procedures, I identified a suitable spot to land (we were not near the runway) and set the aircraft on a glide path to take it down. Although this was a training environment and Colonel Gossett was a highly experienced pilot, it was still a risky maneuver; one miscalculation by the trainee (me) and I would lose control of the plane and crash.

I did everything by the book with calm efficiency and coolness as I told Colonel Gossett what I was doing and how I planned to land the aircraft safely on a patch of desert not far away. Satisfied, Colonel Gossett said the engine "magically" restarted, and he directed me to return to the airfield so I could perform five touch-and-go landings.

For the first one, I came in nice and easy as directed and touched down, but Colonel Gossett said there was a moose in the middle of the runway and I had to take back off right away. I've never seen a moose in real life, but I understand they are quite large animals and would cause a significant problem if the plane collided with one.

The next landing was standard with no surprises, then I demonstrated a short-field landing (landing on a short runway), followed by a soft-field landing (rather than a hard surface runway, landing on a soft surface like a grassy field or stretch of dirt), and finally a no-flaps landing (landing without the use of flaps to simulate a mechanical or electrical failure). On this last one, I made a full stop and taxied back to the tarmac. The test was over.

I felt I'd done everything right. I felt I'd nailed each maneuver and done everything exactly how I'd been trained. I'd also been relatively calm during the actual flight. Yet, at this moment, sitting in the cockpit with the engine powering down, I was nervous. I thought I'd done well, but did my evaluator think so too?

I didn't have long to wait. Colonel Gossett turned to me and said, "Good job, Lieutenant. I'm proud of you. You passed."

Over the radio I heard, "Oqab 62, good job." It was the flight commander for my class. I knew at that moment I'd not only passed—my check ride was outstanding.

Later that afternoon, the flight commander told me my grade was "excellent," the highest rating I could have achieved. For that day, three other students received grades of "excellent," and one received a "good." As for the student who'd said I would crash and burn, I just smiled at him.

27

UP WHERE I BELONG

ETWEEN MY CHECK RIDE with Colonel Gossett in August 2012
and the end of September, we moved into more advanced phases
of training. Classroom instruction, simulator flights, and supervised
flights (flying with an instructor beside you in the cockpit) still focused
on general handling and basic emergency procedures—stuff we'd been
learning all along—but now we were expected to do more on our
own without constant input or guidance from the IPs. The IPs were
still there throughout everything we did, but the training wheels were
starting to come off.

There was a reason for this; we needed to become more independent and able to think through problems on our own. We weren't
always going to have experienced instructors by our side—either as
copilots or talking to us on the radio from the ground—to affirm our
decisions or put us back on course if we were off azimuth.

In short, we needed to operate on our own and with confidence.
It was very important we learned to do so, because in a few short
weeks we'd make our first solo flights. An instructor would make a
practice run with us to ensure we were good to go, but then they'd

get out of the cockpit and we'd be on our own to take off, perform general handling maneuvers, and land.

This would be the ultimate test. The solo flight wasn't the end of flight school—after our first solo, we'd move on to more advanced academics and handling and eventually transition to flying the C-208, the advanced trainer—but to me the first solo flight would determine whether I had what it took to be a pilot. I'd been dreaming about this day for a very long time. When they finally announced the date for our solo flights, I felt the excitement growing inside me.

On the morning of September 30, 2012, I sat in the cockpit of the C-182 alongside Colonel Bands, the commander of the training squadron. I'd just completed a practice flight, which he supervised, and everything had gone well. I'd taken off, flown a bit, and landed. Simple and smooth.

The time had come for me to pilot an aircraft on my own. My dream was going to come true. In a way it was surreal, because I recognized I was living my dream. I took a deep breath to savor the moment and also to pass the time.

I was waiting for Colonel Bands to get out of the plane, but he hadn't moved to unbuckle himself, and I wondered if he had something else to tell me. Then, unexpectedly, he removed the aviation wings from his flight suit and pinned them on my chest.

"I know you'll keep these safe for me and make me proud," he said. With the edge of his mouth upturned in a small smile, he looked in my eyes. He saluted me and got out of the plane.

I was dumbfounded. The American squadron commander had entrusted his wings to me? Never in a million years would I have expected him to do that, but it filled me with confidence as I watched him walk back to the control tower where he would monitor everything, to ultimately assess whether I would pass or fail.

I thought, *So be it. The warm-up is over. I am on my own now.* I took another deep breath, expelling the air slowly through my pursed lips. I could feel my heart pounding like a sledgehammer. I needed to calm down. I'd trained for this. I'd prepared every part of my body and soul for it.

I was about to make my first solo flight, and I'd been selected to go first for the entire class. No pressure.

I wiped the sweat from my hands and took a deep breath. *Courage is not the absence of fear; it is the ability to overcome it.* The IPs had taught me that, and I believed it down to my core. I also remembered my classmates, who still said I shouldn't be here, that women couldn't be pilots, and that they'd never follow me. *Well, that's OK,* I thought. *You don't have to follow me. I will bring you along.*

I looked down at the airplane's control panel to go over the preflight checks once more. Since before 0500, I'd been mentally reviewing what I had to do to fly this plane, and this was my final check. The practice touch-and-goes I'd done with Colonel Bands had gone well. I'd done fine then, I'd do fine now.

With a fleeting thought of my father—his warm smile of encouragement, the man who had supported me in every way to reach this moment, my lifelong dream—I spoke into the mic. "Shindand Ground, Baaz 11 ready for taxi, pattern."

"Baaz 11," came the crackling response over the radio, "taxi to runway one-eight via Foxtrot, Bravo, hold short runway one-eight. Altimeter two-nine tac nine-two."

"Wilco," I replied, nudging the throttle forward and heading back out onto the taxiway.

I took another look at the wind sock and saw the wind had increased to 6 knots, coming perpendicular to the runway. Not ideal, but a light breeze never hurt anybody. That was my hope, at least.

When I reached the end of the runway, I called over the radio again. "Shindand Tower, Baaz 11, holding short runway one-eight at Bravo, ready for takeoff, pattern."

"Baaz 11, winds zero-three-zero at one-five, runway one-eight cleared for takeoff, left closed, report base."

I took another breath, felt the light perspiration on my face, and adjusted my black headscarf, the one I wore every time I flew. It had become my trademark, my good luck charm. It's the little things that comfort us, help us to stay calm.

I settled into my seat and pushed the throttle forward. The plane began to move. The aircraft picked up speed, accelerating down the runway, and everything my instructors had ever told me rushed through my mind.

More speed, faster, faster. The single-engine aircraft approached 55 knots, roughly 60 miles an hour. Outside, the ground whipped by. The plane started to feel light, the outside air passing faster over the top of the wings' airfoil to create lift. The wheels began to pull away from the runway. Moments later they lifted off, and I knew if I made one tiny mistake, I could drive this 1,600-pound aircraft into the deck, which would result in a spectacular mangle of aluminum, plastic, and glass. It would be the end of my life.

At that instant, the anxiety of my first solo flight, all the stress and pressure leading up to it, should have been whirling inside me, setting me on edge, perhaps making me panic. But it didn't. My fear dissipated, like it had in previous flights.

As soon as the plane lifted into the air—with my hands firmly on the controls and my eyes fixed on the horizon—a complete sense of calm washed over me, and I suddenly noticed how quiet it was. No instructor chattering next to me, no cars honking, no devastating explosions from across the city, no one yelling or gesticulating, no one criticizing me. There was nothing but me and the airplane, up where I belonged.

Life, people, problems . . . they stayed on the ground. Up here in the sky, where the birds flew, I felt incredible freedom and unbridled euphoria. Niloofar Rahmani, daughter of Abdolwakil and Tahera Rahmani, Afghan woman, sister, former refugee, dreamer—I was flying all by myself, a lifelong aspiration I'd dreamed about since I was a little girl!

The minutes passed as I took the plane to greater altitude and leveled off, and when the initial excitement waned, I gathered myself and focused on the task at hand. To pass my solo flight I had to perform basic navigation, execute two touch-and-goes, and land the airplane back on the ground without crashing.

Keeping major landmarks in sight to maintain my flight path, I called over the radio to request permission to attempt my first-ever solo touch-and-go. The tower responded, identifying the runway and clearing me for the maneuver. Just like I'd practiced hundreds of times before with my instructors, I put the Cessna into a bank and lined up on the runway. I double-checked the extra cushion I was sitting on, making sure it was positioned right and sitting high enough. (I'd opted for a cushion to act as a booster rather than my flight bag.)

I performed both touch-and-goes flawlessly, maintaining the proper airspeed and descent rate for soft landings each time before accelerating back up into the sky. My final landing was one of the best I ever executed. I put the aircraft on the runway like I was laying a baby in a crib for an afternoon nap.

And that was it. I completed my first solo flight. It took me thirty-five minutes.

I believed I'd done well. I had that feeling you get when you think you've aced a test or executed a perfect maneuver, and you see the smiles and nods from the IPs. An instructor came over the radio and commented on my nice landing, which absolutely cemented my confidence. I knew I'd passed.

I taxied off the runway toward the apron and saw over two hundred people waiting for me. It was overwhelming, to say the least. It was a sight I'll never forget.

When I powered down the aircraft and climbed out of the cockpit, with my feet back on solid ground, Colonel Bands walked up to me sporting a big grin. I handed him back his wings, pride welling inside me, and I could see it in his eyes too.

The Afghan commander of Shindand Air Base, General Shams, handed me a bouquet of flowers and congratulated me. My fellow classmates stood in the crowd, some smiling and clapping while others frowned, but I ignored their negativity. The people who mattered, the ones who'd trained and mentored me as a pilot and a military officer, they were ecstatic and cheering.

Then something very sacred happened. Because I am a woman, my male classmates were not allowed under Afghan custom to physically touch me. But the female instructors from the USAF's 838th Air Expeditionary Advisory Group could.

Carol and Amanda, both USAF pilots and friends of mine, picked me up and tossed me in a pool of water, drenching me and completing a time-honored tradition. *Everyone flies solo, and everyone gets dunked*, as the saying goes among pilots.

Although embarrassed at first, dripping wet, with my clothes sticking tightly to my skin, I immediately embraced the moment. It was my moment. I'd done it, and no disapproving glares from my male Afghan colleagues were going to ruin it.

Yet, with all the excitement and revelry, a tinge of emptiness tugged at me. None of my family had been here to witness my solo flight, and it'd been a long time since I last talked to them. I'd been intensely focused on the training, and I hadn't called as often as I should have. The connection was usually bad; sometimes I couldn't get through at all. I felt guilty.

Although family members were allowed to come observe the solo flights, there was no way my family could have come to see me. Just like back in Kabul when we told everybody I was at university, the risk of exposure was too great. If they'd traveled from Kabul to the base, someone would have known and asked questions. If that happened, I would have been outed, and my family and I would have been put in jeopardy. All our lives would be in danger.

But today I would call home, because I needed to share this moment with my father. Later that afternoon, I finally made the call and let out a sigh of relief when the phone started ringing. When my Baba Jan answered and I heard his voice, my heart warmed.

"Baba Jan," I said, "I completed my solo flight, and I get to move on to advanced flight training."

My father's voice was filled with joy, and I could picture the smile on his face, stretching from ear to ear. It touched me deeply as I fought back the tears. I could feel him bursting with pride, and I'd never felt so respected and loved. Just like me, he knew I could accomplish this. He had always encouraged me, never doubted me, and I knew he had been with me when I'd soared through the clouds.

28

OUTED

———

WHILE I WAS IN FLIGHT TRAINING AT SHINDAND, I was not allowed to take leave to go back to Kabul to see my family, and they couldn't visit me. For military training, this kind of situation is not unusual or unexpected; undergraduate pilot training (UPT) lasted a year, and there was a lot of material to cover. Not a day could be wasted. I missed my family, of course, but I also needed to stay focused on my training if I hoped to graduate.

I knew they understood this, because if I failed, everything I'd gone through and everything my family had done to support me would be for naught. That's what I honestly believed.

So, after my first solo flight, I told myself I needed to call home more often. It would be good to hear my father's voice, and I needed to hear it more often, along with my mother's, my brother's, and my sisters'.

Unbeknownst to me, in a few days this dream I'd been living was about to be shattered.

One night, I called my brother, Omar, to say hello, hear how the family was doing, and find out how university was going for him, but he told me something terrible had happened. There was a picture of me on social media—someone had taken it when Carol and Amanda dunked me in the water after my solo flight.

After I hung up, I quickly did my own search and found the picture on the Internet. It showed my two friends, Carol and Amanda, holding me up in the air on their shoulders. Their uniforms were unmistakably Western, and I was in my flight suit, soaking wet. But the comments below the image—hundreds of them—said something totally different.

The comments said foreign men were carrying me. Carol and Amanda had their hair pulled back and their uniforms were loose fitting, making it hard to tell they were female. Other posts said they were baptizing me, that I'd abandoned my religion and was no longer a Muslim, or that I was now a prostitute and shaming myself with foreigners. Some said the evidence of my betrayal warranted putting me to death and that my family was a disgrace for allowing this to happen.

I was both shocked at how such a proud moment had been savaged and grossly distorted, and scared for my family's safety. I feared that as the picture circulated and the news of my status in the air force spread, my extended family, my parents' neighbors, and our friends would find out. Once that occurred—questions about what would happen next roiled inside me. I feared my parents and siblings would be shamed and ostracized, perhaps even threatened with death themselves.

I didn't know what to do, but I needed to talk with someone outside my family to see what else might be happening. The only other person who knew about me joining the military and wanting to become a pilot was my best friend from high school, Sonia.

I called her, hoping she could give me some comfort, but when she answered the phone and realized it was me, her tone changed. She spoke as if we'd never been friends, never been close. I felt the tears coming, and a pain in my chest erupted almost immediately, even before she told me the news. Her parents had seen my picture on the Internet and found out I was in the air force. They forbade her to speak with me, and she was never to see me again. They called me and my family disgraceful and traitors to our culture and religion.

Sonia said she knew I would regret my decision to join the military and pursue my dream of becoming a pilot. She urged me to quit and come home immediately, otherwise my reputation and my family's would be irreparably damaged. Then she hung up.

That moment—this situation—felt like one of the deepest betrayals of my life. The childhood friend I'd trusted with my most precious secret had turned her back on me and told me it was all my fault. I was to blame for this trouble. The lies people were saying about me on social media were outrageous and brutal. I felt attacked by the entire world.

I cried myself to sleep that night, questioning everything I'd accomplished in the past two years, wondering what I'd done. I was truly terrified of what would happen to us—me and my family. I knew I hadn't done anything to dishonor myself or my family; rather, I was serving my country and doing something extraordinary. Yet I still doubted myself and couldn't shake those thoughts. It felt like my insides were being torn apart. I didn't know what I was going to do.

Over the next few weeks, I did my best to stay focused on my classroom work and training. I had to. I was distraught about the situation back home, but I had to keep going. I told myself if I failed now, all of this would be in vain, and I would truly bring shame upon myself and my family. For my own sake and for my family, I relied on the discipline the military had built into me. I showed up in class each day, just like always.

After our solo flights, we were deemed skilled enough to move beyond the C-182 aircraft and start training on the C-208. The C-208 is a single turboprop aircraft with a high wing, like the C-182, but it's considered a more advanced trainer and utility aircraft. It is larger than the C-182, able to carry up to thirteen passengers or be outfitted for cargo, and can be equipped with other types of payloads, including weaponry. I'd eventually fly this kind of plane all over Afghanistan supporting combat operations.

In addition to starting to work with the C-208, we also moved beyond basic handling skills, many of which can be done using visual techniques for navigation and maneuvers. Now we were being trained to use our instruments for navigation so we could perform longer and higher altitude flights, as well as night operations. The emergency procedure training got more difficult, because the increased size of the C-208 made it less forgiving if we made a mistake, and we had to be spot-on with our immediate actions and responses.

Even though the situation back in Kabul weighed heavily on me, I must admit that training and getting into the cockpit each day to fly an aircraft was my salvation. Unfortunately, I soon found out the situation at home was getting much worse.

―――――――――

In January 2013, I called home again and my younger sister Maryam answered the phone. She sounded worried and said our Mother Jan had fallen sick and was bedridden. Recently she'd been very depressed and scared; the situation was getting to be too much. Hearing this put me over the edge.

In the weeks that followed my solo flight, every time I'd called home my brother had said things were fine but that my picture was still out there and people were still making comments on social media, including threats. He hoped the situation would eventually quiet down and wouldn't extend to our relatives or neighbors. But things had deteriorated further.

As soon as I got off the phone, I reported to Flight Commander Hollander to request emergency leave to go to Kabul and visit my family. I explained the situation, and although he was concerned about me missing training, he authorized me to take a week of leave.

I flew back to Kabul on an air force transport flight, and Omar met me in the terminal. Seeing him after all this time truly brightened my spirits. He looked like a man now, similar to my father, and was finishing up at university. He would graduate with a degree in computer science. But more significantly, I noticed how he carried himself.

Omar walked with a certain amount of dignity and respect, and with a level of confidence I hadn't seen in him when I'd left home over a year and a half ago. Although we'd talked on the phone and everything seemed fine between us, now being with him, I wondered if things would still be the same. He'd always supported and believed in me; I hoped he still did.

Thankfully, as soon as I got in the car I knew everything was the same between us, as if we'd never been apart. I could see he was proud of me and happy I was home. I very much wanted to tell him about everything I'd done in flight school, but I knew there were more important issues to talk about.

I asked how things were at home and begged him not to hide anything from me. I needed to know what had happened since I'd been outed. He took a deep breath before he spoke, and to this day I can recall the sadness in his voice as he told me all that had gone on.

He said most of our extended family had found out about the photo of me and learned I was in the air force, training to be a pilot. He seemed very concerned about Afsoon, who was still living with her husband and his family. Once they learned what I was doing, they started harassing her and telling her she came from a shameful family. This upset our parents quite a bit and was one of the reasons my mother had fallen ill.

As for our father, his brothers and cousins had been calling him. They were furious, not only because I was a disgrace and an affront to Islam but also because he'd lied to them, telling everyone I'd been at university. They told him he'd dishonored his family and he would not get away with it.

At work, coworkers had confronted him, showing him the picture and all the accusations. They were disgusted and chastised him for allowing me to join the military. They questioned his manhood and told him he was a bad Muslim. Soon after, his boss told him he needed to look for another job because he wouldn't be allowed to work there anymore.

I couldn't believe what I was hearing. While at Shindand, I had no idea all this had happened, but now my worst fears were coming true, and I didn't know what to expect when we got home. Part of me wondered if I would even be allowed in the house.

It had been a few weeks since I'd spoken to either my father or my mother, and the darkest part of me wondered if they would expel me from the family. Rationally, I knew they wouldn't, but I was so scared and felt so ashamed for everything I'd brought down upon them. I loved my family, cherished them, and hearing this news broke my heart.

When we arrived home, my little sister Maryam opened the door. Her face immediately lit up, and she started yelling as she ran through the house shouting, "Niloo is here! Niloo is here!" My brother and I were still in the courtyard, but I could hear the commotion inside.

My mother appeared at the doorway, and after a moment's pause to get her bearings in the fading light, she rushed outside. With each step, I saw the tears welling in her eyes, and she took me in her arms and held me close. I buried my face in her shoulder and started crying. My Mother Jan held me tighter and told me it was OK, that they were so happy I was home, and they were so proud of me. "We will always support you," she said. "You're our daughter."

It's hard to explain how much my mother's words meant to me and how desperately I needed to hear them. I'd been gone for so long and been through so much, without anyone to talk to or turn to for support, so hearing my dear mother's voice warmed my heart and gave me a sense of comfort I'd greatly missed.

But in all the commotion of seeing and embracing my mother and sisters, I didn't see my father, my Baba Jan. I asked where he was. My mother said he was inside praying.

I pulled myself away from my mother and walked inside, finding my father in the back room, kneeling with his eyes closed, periodically leaning forward to touch his forehead to the ground as he whispered his prayers to God. I watched him silently, not saying a word or wanting to disturb him, but he knew I was there.

In the few moments while I waited for him to finish, I remember thinking I couldn't wait for him to hold me in his arms and tell me everything was going to be fine. I felt horrible about all that had happened and hoped he wouldn't be upset with me.

When he finished, I went toward him, immediately starting to mutter that I was so sorry, that it was my fault, and that I'd put everyone and everything at risk. His career, the family, it was my fault. I told him I would do whatever he wanted; I would quit the air force at that very moment and come home, if that's what he wanted me to do. I implored him to believe me, I'd done nothing wrong to shame myself, our family, our country, or God. Everything people were saying about me was a lie.

As my father took me in his arms and dried my tears, he shook his head as if dismissing my fears and apology. He said there was no need to apologize; of course he believed me. "I know you better than anyone else in this world," he said, "and I don't care that these people found out or what they're saying." He would always support me. He wanted me to go back to training, finish what I started, and make him a proud father.

My Baba Jan's words meant everything to me; I smiled and held him tighter. We stayed like this for a while, and having my father's arms wrapped around me made me feel more secure and protected than I'd felt in a very long time. I truly needed this moment.

———————

Over the next few days I stayed at home, telling my family stories about the military, my life in flight school, and what it felt like to fly an airplane. They also told me about how life had been in Kabul, with my younger sisters in school, my brother about to graduate from university, and Afsoon with her growing baby (she had a two-year-old son named Mustafa), whom I had yet to meet.

After that first night, we didn't talk much about me being outed or the problems that had resulted, probably because we were all so happy to be together again. But on the third night while we were eating dinner, the doorbell rang. My brother went to open the door and found Afsoon standing outside. She was crying and had a bag by her side.

My brother quickly brought her into the house, and my parents went to her, asking her what was going on. She said her husband and his family had seen everything about me and they were furious. They said we were a shameful family and no longer Muslim, and I was a prostitute for foreigners. They beat her, saying she had brought shame upon them as well. They kicked her out of the house, but kept her baby.

Afsoon was terribly upset as she told us these things, and I felt my heart breaking with each word. Then Afsoon turned to me and said it was all my fault. I'd been selfish to join the military. Her life was now ruined because of me.

I couldn't argue with her, nor did I want to. She was right; I'd been selfish to join the military and try to become a pilot, not thinking about the effect it would have on the rest of my family. I broke down and we both cried. At that moment I wanted to undo it all, wishing I could go back and erase everything.

Our Baba Jan came over to embrace us both, one in each arm. He looked at me first and said none of this was my fault, none of it. Joining the military and becoming a pilot was my destiny, and I should never doubt that, not even now. Next, he turned to Afsoon and told her everything would be fine. We would get her baby back and keep him safe from her husband and family. He said, "That man lost a valuable diamond, and he will never get it back."

My sister and I eventually calmed down, but a cloud of worry hung over my family for the rest of the night. When I woke the next morning, I still couldn't shake the disturbing feelings that were eating at me. Despite my parents' assurances, I felt this was all my fault and I had to do something to make it all stop. I'd ruined my sister's marriage, our extended family was threatening us, my father had been told to find another job . . . none of this would have happened had I not joined the military to become a pilot.

That morning I talked to my parents alone and told them I was to blame for everything. My choices and my actions—my selfishness—had brought this upon the family. I had to quit flight school and resign my commission from the military. I would tell my command I needed to be home to care for my family—where a woman belonged.

But my father stopped me right away, not letting me say another word. He told me I couldn't quit, I had to be strong, because if I didn't the bullies would have won. He didn't consider my dream of becoming a pilot and serving my country to be just mine. It was his dream, it was for the rest of the family, and it was for all of Afghanistan.

I thank God for my father and my mother and my entire family. It's not lost on me how much they risked, and in some ways lost, with me being Afghanistan's first female air force pilot for fixed-wing aircraft. If I hadn't chosen this path, our relatives would probably never have ostracized us, my sister would not have suffered such a horrific end to her marriage, and my father would never have lost his job and means for supporting the family.

They not only supported me but also encouraged me to go back and do this thing, become a pilot and serve my country. Every single member of my family is courageous and strong, and I believe that with every fiber of my body.

Although I carried guilt for everything that happened, I knew my father was right. I had to go back and finish the training. It wasn't only about me; it was about women across Afghanistan. If women were ever going to be treated fairly, it had to start somewhere.

29

GRADUATION

O N MAY 12, 2013, I passed my final check ride and completed undergraduate pilot training (UPT). In the final months of training, I'd mastered instrument navigation, night operations, low-level flight, crew and ground operations, and everything else required to be designated a full-fledged pilot.

I'd also completed UPT at the top of my class, outpacing the men in nearly everything. This was a point of embarrassment for them—a woman receiving higher scores and being rated above them—and their verbal criticisms, the way they shunned me, and how they disparaged me behind my back worsened.

At this point, I wasn't going to let their behavior bother me. I'd come this far, worked hard, and done well; I wasn't going to let their small minds and ignorance discourage me. I wasn't just a pilot, I was a good pilot, and they couldn't do anything about that.

The graduation ceremony for UPT class 12-04 occurred on May 14 in a massive hangar near the Shindand flight line. All of our instructors attended, as well as a good number of the air expeditionary group and base commanders. The chief of staff for the Afghan Ministry of Defense also attended, and there was a bevy of local reporters and national TV news crews present to report on the event.

I was Afghanistan's first female fixed-wing air force pilot, and the Ministry of Defense and NATO considered this important news. During the ceremony, along with the other students, I was promoted to first lieutenant. Chief of Staff Sher Mohammad Karimi gave me my wings and my diploma, and as he did this, he told me all of Afghanistan was proud of me and I needed to serve my country to the best of my abilities.

This was a very happy moment, being officially recognized as a pilot in the Afghan Air Force. There was lots of picture taking too. In the back of my mind, I feared this would cause my family greater problems—receiving this kind of publicity—but in that moment I did my best to ignore the fears. Graduation from flight school was a once-in-a-lifetime event, and I deserved an opportunity to be proud of my accomplishment.

What further brightened my day was seeing two Afghan women who were students in Thunder Lab. One was Ferozi (the only other woman who passed the flight physical back in Kabul), and Noori. Both were a few years older than I was, and they hoped to become pilots too. I was so proud to see them again and talk with them, because it gave me hope the situation in Afghanistan really could change.

Unfortunately, no one in my family was able to attend this event. The other students had invited their families, but I feared for the safety of mine. The situation in Kabul had not improved, and if they came to Shindand and were associated with me, I was genuinely concerned for their safety. In Kabul, they knew their surroundings and neighborhood and could spot trouble when it was brewing. But if they traveled to Shindand, there would be many opportunities for the Taliban to target them. I didn't want that.

Immediately after the graduation festivities ended, I called my parents. Both my father and mother were on the line, and I could hear the joy in their voices. They were so happy for me; they couldn't wait for me to come home to visit. When I told them I'd been assigned to the 538th Air Expeditionary Advisory Squadron at the Kabul air base and I'd be able to see them much more frequently, they were ecstatic.

I'd be home soon!

30

THE SQUADRON

I HAD ABOUT A MONTH OFF between graduation and when I had
to report to my operational command at the Kabul air base, the
538th Squadron. I spent most of my time at home with my family,
taking a break. I had been pushing hard for nearly two years and
really needed the down time.

However, both the US and Afghan militaries had their own agen-
das. They wanted to tout my accomplishments as a way to promote
the changes happening not just in the Afghan Air Force but also in
broader Afghan society, as well as the success of the NATO advisory
mission then in its twelfth year. The public affairs offices of the US
and Afghan militaries scheduled me for countless interviews with
local and international media outlets.

Although I was hesitant to do these interviews, not wanting to
attract more negative attention, I also saw them as an opportunity to
fight for the rights of women in Afghanistan. When asked about my
story, I tried to explain things in a way that would encourage other
young girls and women to pursue their dreams. I spoke about the
challenges I overcame and candidly shared how it was very difficult

to continue at times. I also said this was a new Afghanistan—a place where women deserved to be treated fairly, with respect, and as equals. Moreover, there shouldn't be any barriers put in front of us.

I never found out if these interviews had an impact. The military didn't share any data on female recruitment. Nevertheless, I hope I managed to inspire one or two people.

———————

I was scheduled to report to the 538th Squadron in June 2013, and on the morning of my first day I discovered my youngest sister, Manizha, wearing my flight suit. She was doing a very amusing impression of me, alternating between marching around and standing with her arms crossed, with a very serious look on her face, as serious as an eleven-year-old can be. Her antics made me laugh, but I told her I needed my flight suit back so I wouldn't be late. She could have her own flight suit one day, I said, but she turned her nose up at my suggestion.

As she unzipped my flight suit, my darling little sister said quite confidently she wanted to be a journalist and would rather interview me one day instead. We both had a good laugh at that!

My brother would drive me to and from the base most days because it wasn't safe for me to use public transportation. If I did, people would see me going in and out of the base and potentially target me.

As a precaution, when we neared the base I would duck down in the passenger seat so people outside couldn't see me. I also wore civilian clothes so that if someone did spot me, they wouldn't see me wearing a uniform. My brother would proceed to drive onto the base and drop me at my squadron building. I'd go inside to my office and change into my flight suit.

Although I had hoped things might be different now that I was no longer in a training command, my first day at the squadron was less than welcoming. Most of the pilots and support staff ignored me, only speaking to me if it was absolutely necessary. My commanding officer, Colonel Pacha Kahn, also gave me a cool reception. He was professional and respectful but expressed nothing beyond formalities.

There also were no bathroom facilities for women, not in the squadron building or anywhere nearby; the closest women's restroom was across the base at KELTC. I either had to hold it all day or use the men's room, which was extremely uncomfortable.

Nevertheless, I was on base, a full-fledged pilot, and couldn't wait to start flying real missions. The 538th was a combat support squadron, and I'd be flying missions throughout Afghanistan transporting troops to various outposts, flying the wounded back to hospitals (medevac flights), and delivering supplies to the combat units on the ground fighting the Taliban and other insurgent groups.

There was one type of mission, however, I was told I would not be allowed to perform: HR flights, which stands for "human remains." These flights transport the bodies of deceased soldiers back home to the next of kin. Apparently, this prohibition against women performing this sacred duty was enshrined in air force regulations and was directed not at me personally but at all female pilots.

There were two reasons for this prohibition: one, under Islamic law it is disrespectful for a woman who is not a family member to touch the body of a deceased male, and two, women are supposedly too weak emotionally to handle such a solemn mission.

While I respected the reasoning under Islam, I did not think this regulation was fair. As a pilot, I could easily fly the plane, perform all my duties, and never touch the remains of a soldier I was transporting. The notion that I was too weak because I was a woman was insulting. It was an affront to my status as a military officer, my professionalism, and my skills as a pilot. I promised myself one day

I would fight this regulation, but for the time being I just wanted to get in the cockpit and fly.

For my first year, I flew as a copilot. I needed to log 280 flight hours before I could be qualified as an aircraft commander (AC). Often, it takes pilots well over a year to log that many hours, but I purposefully volunteered for missions going to the farthest provinces or the ones with multiple intermediate stops, called hops. I wanted to be an AC as soon as possible.

Unfortunately, even my willingness to take on the more arduous missions wasn't looked upon favorably by the members of my squadron. The Afghan Air Force had only recently been reconstituted, which meant a lot of the personnel were relatively young. However, a number of pilots and officers had served in the air force during the Soviet era and before the Taliban came to power. My squadron included an interesting mix of experienced and newly commissioned pilots, some of whom were open-minded and others who were very much not.

To be on the safe side, I always arrived at base early so as not to be seen during high-traffic hours. Consequently, I would enter our squadron building before most of the other pilots. Before changing, I would immediately check the mission board to see where the flights were heading that day, which one I'd been assigned, and who I was paired with.

I would then change into my flight suit and take care of some of my preflight activities: eating breakfast, checking the weather report, gathering any supplies I might need, and so on. Often, when I'd pass by the mission board later in the morning, I'd notice someone had erased my name from one flight and put me on another. I never witnessed this happening directly, but I knew someone was making the switch; I was always there early enough to have seen the original assignments.

It didn't happen every day, but it occurred often enough that I knew it wasn't because friends were trying to fly with other friends. Rather, it was clear some of the pilots didn't want to fly with me. This bothered me. I hadn't encountered this kind of activity in training because the NATO advisors would never have allowed it. But here, in an Afghan squadron manned by Afghans and commanded by Afghans, my colleagues were deliberately excluding me and doing whatever they could to avoid flying with me.

Rationally, I knew whoever was doing this was bigoted and chauvinistic; however, it also made me question my abilities and made me wonder if I wasn't good enough. Had I done well in training only because the NATO advisors made sure there was an even playing field, but now in a real unit I wasn't made of the right stuff? I knew in my heart of hearts this wasn't true, but these doubts still crossed my mind.

Fortunately, not everyone in the squadron was averse to flying with me. One pilot in particular, Major Abdulrahman, didn't mind. He was in his early forties, of average height and build, and wore a trim mustache. But he had a baby face, making him look much younger than he actually was.

Major Abdulrahman always treated me with the utmost respect and didn't have any problem flying me, and soon enough I realized most men from his generation or older had no qualms having me as a copilot. From what I could gather, it was the younger pilots who didn't want to fly with me, and beyond the changes on the mission board, it showed in how they openly dismissed or ignored me.

During one of my missions as Major Abdulrahman's copilot, I asked him about this. I was very frank and inquired why he believed the older generations seemed much more accepting of me as an aviator and fellow officer.

He thought for a moment, then asked me if my father was different from most Afghan men and, if so, why I thought he might have a different perception of women. I told Major Abdulrahman a little about my father, how he'd always supported me and the rest of my family, and how he'd been raised to respect women. He wanted us to feel as he did.

Major Abdulrahman said that was precisely it. He said he grew up in a time before the Taliban and was raised to have a different view of women in society and the workforce. He didn't feel threatened because I was doing the same job as he was. He grew up believing everyone is equal and women should be free to do whatever they want.

The majority of the younger pilots, however, grew up under the reign of the Taliban. Whether they were intentionally raised this way or not, they grew up seeing women oppressed and abused; all they knew was war and violence. Afghanistan had essentially been in a state of war for over thirty years; the joy and beauty this land once possessed had been ravaged by decades of conflict, political strife, and religious extremism.

That was all these young men knew, he said. It was ignorant and wrong, but there was a reason the situation was the way it was. Abdulrahman was inspired by people like me. That meant there was hope and things would change.

I found Major Abdulrahman's perspective uplifting, because it helped me to further understand the challenges I'd been encountering since I first joined the military. Afghan society had been in turmoil for so long, and there were generations of people—men and women—who held these oppressive and harsh worldviews. From personal experience, they believed life was hard and the only way to survive was to live in a similar manner.

For the situation to improve—not just for women but for all Afghans—it would take a generational change; the only way that would happen was if people like me and Abdulrahman fought for it.

At that point, I resolved to log my 280 hours and become an AC as soon as possible. Once I was an AC, there would be a lot more opportunities to prove a woman could do as well as a man.

In July 2014 I reached my goal of 280 hours. I passed the qualification test and the check ride for AC, received my certification, and was promoted to captain. I couldn't wait to command my first mission.

31

FLYING OPERATIONS

MY PASSENGERS OFTEN didn't know a woman was piloting their aircraft. Once they found out, they usually assumed I was a Westerner and a NATO pilot. Consequently, I received more than a few shocked looks when I spoke to passengers or ground crews in Dari and they realized I was not only a woman but an Afghan.

Sometimes passengers' facial expressions showed disbelief, but they'd still board the aircraft and keep their opinions to themselves, often whispering to the person next to them. Other times I saw genuine admiration in people's reactions, happy to see an Afghan woman piloting an airplane and glad their country was changing for the better.

There were other instances when passengers were belligerent or disruptive and I, as the AC, had to manage the situation in a way that, traditionally, was highly unusual for an Afghan woman.

On one occasion during the summer of 2014, I was ordered to fly a mission to Kandahar. It was a routine mission and didn't involve any combat supplies or wounded soldiers. My copilot and I were merely going to fly some passengers from Kabul down to Kandahar, and then bring another group back. A milk run, so to speak.

At Kabul Airport, I sat in the cockpit performing my preflight checks while my copilot was on the tarmac supervising the loading of passengers and gear. About midway through the boarding process, I heard a commotion outside. I looked out the window and saw an army colonel arguing with my copilot, waving his arms and gesticulating, shouting he wouldn't board the aircraft unless a man was going to fly it. Somehow he'd heard the pilot was a woman.

It was one thing for my colleagues to criticize me or ignore me in the squadron building, but I found this situation totally unacceptable. This colonel was disrupting the flight line (which can be a very dangerous place with all the moving aircraft, noise, wind, and crazy things like spinning propellers) and threatening the conduct of an official mission. As the AC, I couldn't let this continue.

Not wasting another moment, I jumped out of the cockpit onto the tarmac and marched back to the rear of the plane where the colonel was making a scene. I went straight up to him, and even though he was a few inches taller than me and noticeably older and more senior, I spoke firmly, without any hesitation.

I said, "Sir, we're about to take off. If you want to fly to Kandahar today, you will need to board now. If not, go back to the hangar." I turned around, not waiting for an answer, and climbed back into the cockpit to continue my preflight checks.

Through the rear window, I could see the shock on the colonel's face. He was speechless, and he stood there for at least a minute gawking, but he reluctantly boarded the aircraft. I watched him take his seat and pull out a string of prayer beads, which he fidgeted with the entire time we were in the air.

The flight was smooth and clear, and we landed at the Kandahar airfield on schedule without incident. By this time, I'd moved on from the exchange, but as I powered down the aircraft and completed my postflight checks, I saw the army colonel waiting for me by the ramp.

When I got out of the cockpit, he approached me and said, "Captain, I shouldn't have doubted you. I am proud to see how an Afghan woman like you flew today, and I do apologize."

I never expected this man to say this. I'd become pretty callous to the negative comments made by others, and I rarely heard anything positive from my colleagues. For this Afghan colonel to compliment me as he did truly touched my heart. I replied softly but confidently, "I'm just happy to be serving my country and bringing change to Afghanistan."

Later that fall, I commanded a mission to Helmand Province. The fighting there had always been tough, but in recent months there'd been talk about the American military drawing down and leaving the bulk of the combat operations to the Afghan security forces. For weeks the Afghan army had been taking a lot of casualties in Helmand and the surrounding provinces.

I initially assumed this flight was another routine passenger run. I'd land at the airfield on Camp Bastion (today called Camp Shorabak), perform the pickup, and return to Kabul. Easy.

However, about midway through the flight the squadron commander called us over the radio and directed us to RTB in Kabul. When I asked why, he said the mission would require us to transport the bodies of soldiers killed in action back to Kabul for burial. According to regulation, I wasn't allowed to do this because I was a woman.

For a brief moment, I felt disheartened. Once again, because I was a woman, someone was telling me I was not strong enough or couldn't handle it. But I quickly stopped this line of thinking. A voice inside me said I must do this mission. I had to prove a woman was strong enough to accept and treat with honor and respect the remains of dead soldiers. Instead of acknowledging the order to RTB, I pretended the radio transmission was garbled and I didn't understand. I continued our flight plan to Helmand.

My copilot, Lieutenant Amiri, was stunned I was disobeying an order, and even though he had to follow my orders since I was the AC, he feared he would be reprimanded and dismissed from flight duty. I assured him this was my decision and he would not get in trouble, that I would take full responsibility for any fallout—but we were still going forward with the mission.

When we landed at Camp Bastion, we taxied to the hangar where the bodies were staged and prepared for transport. When I got out of the plane and the medical officer in charge, an army major, saw I was a woman, he directed the medevac team not to load the bodies onto the aircraft. He said military regulations didn't permit women to handle or be around the remains of deceased soldiers if they weren't family or next of kin.

I knew I couldn't let this happen, so I took a chance. As respectfully as I could, I informed the major my flight was the only one for the day and I was the only option. The families of the deceased were waiting for their loved ones, and it was our duty to transport them home. I would not leave with an empty aircraft.

Recognizing the social and religious issues of the situation, I assured the major I would stay out of the area during the loading of the bodies so as not to disrespect them. My copilot could supervise the loading and make sure everything was done with respect and honor. Once everything was secure, I would simply fly the aircraft back to Kabul.

To my satisfaction, the major and the medevac team agreed. Within a half hour, they'd loaded the six bodies and we were back in the air, heading back to Kabul. When we landed, I again distanced myself from the unloading process to accord respect to the remains of these men. Rather than performing the postflight checks, I left them to my copilot and headed to the squadron building.

Along the way, I spotted the line of families waiting to receive the bodies of their loved ones. I could tell some were parents, others were wives, and there were also some young adults, and likely someone's child. Many were crying, while others stood stoically.

I was glad I'd brought their loved ones back to them, rather than returning with an empty aircraft and putting them through another agonizing night of waiting. But I was also sad, as I could empathize with the sorrow they felt losing a father, son, or husband to this war. The war was now in its thirteenth year, with no end in sight. Many more soldiers—people's loved ones—would die in the months and years to come, and it pained me to think about it.

Nonetheless, I was a pilot in the Afghan Air Force and this was my job—my duty—and I was proud to serve my country. I held my head high and strode confidently into the squadron building to report to my commanding officer.

Colonel Pacha Kahn was waiting for me in his office. I suspected I was about to be severely reprimanded—I'd disobeyed a direct order; I deserved to be in deep trouble, no doubt about it—so again I decided to take a chance.

When I entered his office, I saluted, but before he could say anything, I said, "Sir, before you start, I'm going to be honest." I then proceeded to tell my commanding officer I had, in fact, heard him over the radio but decided on my own to continue the mission. It was an important mission, and I knew I could complete it with honor and respect. Although I understood the religious and social issues of me being a woman around the remains of deceased men, I didn't agree with the regulation and believed it should be changed. I continued on with the mission to prove I could do it, without disrespecting the fallen. I finished by saying it was now in his hands, and I would submit to any decision he made concerning my future.

I'd spoken for several minutes, pushing the words out as clearly and assuredly as I could. Once I stopped to catch my breath, a heavy silence fell between us. I remained at attention in front of my commander's desk, as he sat behind it with a stern and impassive face. He hadn't moved or said a word since I reported in. He sat there, his eyes boring into me.

All kinds of thoughts raced through my mind, many of them resulting in my losing my flight status and being transferred to another command, maybe even being demoted. I even started to question whether I'd done the right thing and if it really had been worth it.

But my commander smiled and stood up. He looked me in the eye and said our country was at war; these missions were critical and had to be done to honor our countrymen killed in action. Although I'd gone against regulations, Afghanistan was changing, and I'd done the right thing despite the risks. He thanked me and said he would talk to his superiors about getting the regulation changed to allow me to carry out more such missions going forward.

I was speechless.

Besides flying missions across Afghanistan, and despite the animosity some of my colleagues felt against me, I also had to perform numerous public relations activities. I was Afghanistan's first female pilot, and the Ministry of Defense wanted to use me as an example to show they were indeed recruiting women and that we were serving in some of the most demanding jobs.

Ironically, some of the senior officers pushing me to interview with national and international media outlets were also the ones who quietly, and sometimes loudly, complained about having a woman in their ranks. Nonetheless, I did as ordered.

Unfortunately, these PR events put me and my family at greater risk. I'd already been outed when my picture appeared on social media after my first solo flight. Now not only was my picture appearing on the news, but I was also being formally identified as a military pilot and closely associated with the Americans.

My extended relatives had already ostracized my family, but I feared this ongoing notoriety would put my parents, my siblings, and myself in much greater danger.

32

THE THREATS COME

SINCE OUR RELATIVES KNEW WHERE WE LIVED, and since some of them had already threatened us, my father decided we should move to a new apartment closer to the air base and keep it a secret from our extended family. We'd already changed our phone numbers, so he hoped we could hide in a new apartment while still getting on with our lives. I would continue flying, my younger sisters would change schools, my brother would continue to attend university, and my father would find another job.

Our plan worked for a time. My brother and father continued driving me to and from the base, and everyone else seemed to be settling in to their new routines and surroundings. I thought things were actually getting better.

Then, one night while I was helping my sister Manizha with her homework, my phone rang. The caller ID said the number was anonymous, but that wasn't unusual. Caller ID wasn't the most reliable service in Afghanistan, and people often blocked their numbers. I answered it.

The caller was a man, and I didn't recognize the voice. As soon as I said hello, the caller started shouting. He demanded I quit my job with the air force. If I didn't, I would be killed. I was a disgrace to Islam and Afghanistan, a traitor—I deserved to die.

I immediately hung up and did my best to control the alarm I felt. The call startled me, but I needed to stay in control. When my sister asked who called, I told her it was nothing. I knew if I shared the content of the call it would terrify her. I couldn't do that to my sweet, innocent little sister.

Later that night, as I thought more about the call, I wasn't surprised someone had my number. The men in my squadron had it, as well as the personnel office and countless others in the command, so someone was bound to either call me or give my number to someone else who would call and shout threats and insults. That kind of behavior is common in Afghanistan.

I knew that whoever it was hoped to intimidate me, scare me, compel me to quit and relegate myself to housework or some other job suitable for a woman. Fear and harassment were how Afghan men controlled women; I'd been dealing with this kind of treatment my entire life.

But I wasn't going to be intimidated by these faceless cowards. After that night, more calls came from different numbers and different people, but they were always done in this cowardly way. I ignored them and didn't tell anyone in my family. I didn't want to worry them. It was my burden to bear.

However, about the same time and unbeknownst to me, my father started receiving similar phone calls. The callers would threaten him, accusing him of being a bad Muslim and a disgrace. They said if he didn't stop me from flying they would assassinate me and my siblings. They would kill us all.

Then, on one occasion when my father picked me up from the base, he told me about one of these phone calls and asked if I'd ever received anything similar. When he asked me, I could sense the call had worried him. My father is not a man who scares easily, but these calls made him anxious.

I told my Baba Jan I had, in fact, been receiving occasional threats. I apologized for not telling him about them, but I deliberately chose not to because I didn't want to worry anyone unnecessarily. We'd all been through so much, and I knew everyone was under a lot of stress given our recent move, job and school changes, and the disagreeable situation with our relatives. I didn't want to add one more thing to the pile.

My father saw things differently. He was very upset I hadn't told him about the phone calls. These calls weren't jokes or empty threats. Physical violence and assassinations were real; someone could be plotting against us right now. It could be someone on the air base, someone who knew my whereabouts during the day, perhaps someone working with other extremists who could follow us and find out where we lived.

As I would later learn, it wasn't just the two of us. My brother received threats, and so did my mother and older sister. All of these threats were anonymous, and they started after we moved into our new apartment. This disturbed me because it meant that, in a very short amount of time, someone or a group of people had found out information about us that we'd tried to keep secret. Who knew what else they might know or, worse yet, what they might do?

I could not go on ignoring these threats, and my father believed I had to report the situation to my commanding officer immediately.

The next day I met with one of the senior commanders for the air force in Kabul, Lieutenant General Zafar. I reported to his office, a grand room with several Persian rugs, a table with chairs, a separate sitting area with a coffee table, a few bookshelves, tall windows (one with an air conditioner unit in it), and an expansive desk, at which he sat. A young officer whom I suspected was his military aide sat against the wall, along with a young boy in service clothes who likely spent his day fetching tea and tidying up the place when the general was out.

In standard military fashion when formally reporting to a superior officer, I came to attention three paces from his desk, saluted, extended a good morning, and waited for the general to put me at ease so I could explain the situation. He stopped reading the papers in front of him and raised his eyes, but the look of annoyance remained etched on his face. Although this man along with others had sung my praises in front of the TV cameras, I suspected he considered me a trinket to be put on display—not a *real* pilot.

When he finally asked what I wanted, I described the threatening phone calls that I and my family members were receiving. To preempt him from offering any sage advice, I told him about our recent move and that we'd changed our numbers. I then asked him for help, to provide us with some kind of personal protection.

The general thought I was making the story up, that I was just another woman being overdramatic, that I didn't know what I was saying. He might just as well have said, *All Afghan women tend to exaggerate or not understand such things. They're stupid that way.*

But I continued to press, assuring him these threats were real and that my father, who'd also been in the military and was a man of sound mind, also believed these threats must be taken seriously. We needed his help. I was an officer in the Afghan Air Force, and I deserved to have security.

General Zafar allowed me to finish, then leaned back in his chair and regarded me for a moment. After an uncomfortable silence, he finally said there was nothing he could do. These kinds of threats were normal. Most men in the military received them at some point. They came with the job, and if I wanted to continue serving in the air force, I'd have to get used to it.

He dismissed me with a wave of his hand, and that was it. My heart sank.

———————

General Zafar's response to my request surprised me. I knew it was common for soldiers and airmen to receive death threats because they were in the military, but this was different.

The Taliban and their insurgent network of supporters and sympathizers were deeply embedded throughout Afghanistan, even in Kabul. Fighters and terrorists routinely infiltrated the city to conduct attacks, and permanent residents—men, women, families, neighbors, relatives—as well as mosques, schools, and boardinghouses scattered throughout the city were giving matériel support. They provided places to hide or sleep, supplies, and food, as well as intelligence about targets, activities by the security services, and so forth.

It wasn't unusual for a neighbor or relative to find out someone they knew had joined the military, and pass this information to the Taliban to either intimidate the individual or to kill him. If the soldier was alerted to this threat—either directly, via a threatening phone call, or indirectly, through a neighborhood rumor—often the soldier was allowed to bring a firearm home for protection, and sometimes the command would conduct a small investigation or even assign a few personnel for security for a short time.

I was aware of this, but I believed my situation to be different. I was the first female pilot in the Afghan Air Force. That fact didn't make me any more important or deserving of special treatment than a private in the infantry, but it did make my family a bigger target. As a consequence of the publicity, I had a higher profile than most military personnel, further dangling me in front of the Taliban and anyone else who didn't like what I was doing or the direction Afghanistan was heading.

Without a doubt, the general's dismissal of my situation reiter-
ated that, despite everything I'd accomplished, I wasn't welcome in
the air force. This realization hurt, but what bothered me more was
that my career was also hurting my family and putting them at risk.
By joining the military, I'd chosen to put them at risk.

I can't put into words how much this weighed on me, every single
hour of every day. I felt it at home, when I helped my younger sisters
with their schoolwork, and when I saw my older sister crying out
of despair from being separated from her child. I felt it when I put
on my uniform, when I walked through the halls of the squadron
building hearing the whispers, and when I ate in the chow hall and
could practically feel the disapproving looks from other soldiers and
airmen boring into me.

The only time I didn't feel this crushing weight was when I was
up in the air flying. Up there—in the open skies—I was free and I
genuinely felt at peace. Flying meant everything to me; it had become
an integral part of my identity.

I also believed it was important for me to advocate for the plight
of women in Afghanistan. If I couldn't be strong and make sacrifices,
who would? My service as a pilot was necessary, not just because I
was flying missions but because I was a woman in a male-dominated
society proving it could be done. My efforts and my struggles were
for all of Afghanistan, and hopefully when my younger sisters were
grown they'd have a better chance to achieve their dreams, regardless
of their gender.

But early one morning, everything fell apart.

33

INDIA AND AWOL

IT WAS AUGUST 2013, and the sun was starting to come up. I was inside our apartment with my father, getting ready to drive to the air base. My mother was cleaning up after breakfast, taking the trash outside, when she noticed a yellow envelope had been slipped under our front gate. It was addressed to me.

My mother rushed inside with the letter. She was breathing fast, and I could see the fear in her eyes. She handed the letter to my father, and even though I saw my name written on the outside, he opened it.

The actual letter was very short. It read: "If you continue doing your job and if you don't stop working with the Americans and working in the military, you will be responsible for your death and that of your family."

As he read the letter, I watched my father's face fall. It was the first time in my life I'd ever seen him appear truly scared. He handed the letter to me, and I felt my throat constrict. No longer were they making cowardly phone calls, hiding behind the anonymity of a faceless voice—they'd found us and had been so bold as to deliver a letter to our front door.

My Baba Jan didn't hesitate. He knew this threat was much worse than anything we'd received before. We had no time. He told everyone to pack a bag, nothing more. We were leaving immediately. In less than an hour, we were in the car, except my brother, who'd already left for class. As we drove away, my father called Omar and said not to tell anyone; we were going to my grandmother's house to hide. Our home was no longer safe. Once he finished class for the day, he was not to go home but to come straight to my grandmother's place.

When we arrived, my grandmother took us in, but my father refrained from telling her the details of what happened. I believe she knew I was a pilot, given how the news had spread among our relatives, but we'd never spoken about it, and now was not the time. My father needed to focus on figuring out what we were going to do next.

Later that afternoon, my father and I went to the air base, but instead of dropping me off, he stayed with me. We went straight to General Zafar's office and requested to see him immediately. He was in a meeting, so we waited, but that was fine. My father would wait as long as necessary.

When we were finally admitted, General Zafar looked at us quizzically. My father was dressed as he usually was, wearing a pair of pants, button-down shirt, and a vest, but I hadn't put on my uniform for the sake of time and to avoid going to the squadron building.

My father explained the situation, hoping as a man he might have a better chance at persuading the general to help us. I didn't like the idea that General Zafar might take my father more seriously on this matter than me, but I knew how Afghanistan worked and knew my father was right to think this was the best course of action.

My father showed the general the letter with the death threat and repeated everything I'd already told the general about the anonymous phone calls we'd all been receiving. He implored the general to authorize an investigation and asked if there was anything he could to do to help protect us.

The general assumed that same look of annoyance he'd had with me and told my father there was nothing he could do. His tone changed to one of admonishment when he said no one had forced me to join the military—I'd known what I was getting into. "Did you think it would be easy? Did you think this wouldn't happen? We're fighting an insurgency; this comes with the job." He turned his attention back to my father and said I was free to quit whenever I wanted, but there was nothing more he could do. At this point, the general was clearly done wasting his time.

My father gave the general a defiant look, then turned to me and said we should go. On the drive back to my grandmother's house, my father discussed what we were going to do next, talking it out as he drove. We couldn't stay at my grandmother's for long. Whoever was after us would most likely track us there soon. It wasn't safe for my younger sisters to go to school, nor could my brother go back to university. It wasn't even a consideration for me to report to work. The likelihood someone would attack me on base was low, but both my father and I suspected someone was watching our comings and goings and could set up an ambush.

As for my dear mother, the stress was becoming unbearable for her. She was very nervous and no longer slept well. It was affecting her physically, making her sick.

To make matters worse, my father wasn't working. He'd been unable to find another job after his last employer told him to leave, and it was unlikely he'd find work in the near future. The word had spread—by our relatives and his former coworkers—that he was the father of Captain Niloofar Rahmani, a disgrace to Islam and a treacherous, shameful woman who worked with the American occupiers.

In light of our predicament, my father decided the only option we had was to escape to India for a few months. (Pakistan and Iran were not safe for us either.) He hoped after the passage of time and our disap-pearance, those threatening us would think I'd quit and drop the matter. Our disapproving relatives and neighbors might shift their attention to something else. Maybe we could return later and live quietly.

———————

Within a week, my father obtained visas for the seven of us, and we flew on a commercial flight to New Delhi the next day. This was the first time any of us had been to India, and when we took a taxi to a nearby hotel, we couldn't help but marvel at the city.

Although Kabul is a large city, New Delhi is much bigger, more modern, and packed with people. There are shopping malls, five-star hotels and restaurants, tall buildings, expansive gardens, and a host of other sights and sounds unique to this impressive South Asian city. But we weren't booked at the Ritz, nor were we here on a sightseeing tour. We were safe, but we needed to figure out how we were going to survive the next couple of months.

We stayed the first few nights in a hotel, though we knew this would not be tenable for the long term. Since we were here on tour-ist visas, we couldn't work to generate income. Also, we expected my salary from the air force would eventually stop. Out of precaution, I hadn't told my command I was leaving; I just didn't show up for work. Technically I was AWOL (absent without leave), and they would probably put a hold on my salary in a few weeks. We needed to find an inexpensive apartment where our money would last for a while.

A day after our arrival in New Delhi, a journalist from an Indian news-paper showed up in the hotel lobby. Through his immigration contacts, he'd learned I'd come to India, and he wanted to do a story on me.

It's important to note, as Afghanistan's first female pilot, I'd achieved a level of regional recognition in Central and South Asia. This was also the same time the Pakistani education and women's rights activist

Malala Yousafzai had been recognized internationally for her work. This journalist, whom I will not name, believed I was a good story too.

We spoke for about an hour, but ultimately I convinced him not to write a story about me. My family and I had fled Afghanistan for our personal safety, and we didn't know what the future held. If a news story appeared in the Indian press, our situation could become even more complicated. It was quite possible the people threatening us in Afghanistan, whom we assumed were from a Taliban cell, would follow us or use their international connections to target us here. I'm forever grateful this reporter did not run the story.

But the day after I spoke with the reporter, three men from the Indian government came to the hotel front desk asking for me. They also wanted to meet with me, but not for a news story.

The Indian government was willing to offer me citizenship if I wanted to stay in India. They said the government would protect me, and they believed in my advocacy for women and what I symbolized as a female pilot. While they seemed genuine, I suspected there was a geopolitical angle to the offer, given the regional rivalries that exist between India, Pakistan, and Afghanistan.

Although the prospect was tempting, I knew my family would not want to stay in India. Like me, my family loved Afghanistan. At the height of the Taliban's rule, we'd moved back to Afghanistan because it was our home. We all believed our time in India was temporary; things would eventually get better and we would return home.

Speaking for myself, I needed to go back to continue serving my country. Although I'd fled with my family, I wasn't giving up on my career as an air force pilot. I felt it was my duty, and I would not run away. I turned down the offer of citizenship, but I will be forever grateful to the Indian government for reaching out to me. Their concern meant we would be safe while we were there.

We continued our search for housing and found a place to rent. For the next two months, seven of us crammed into a small two-room apartment. Since we couldn't work, we had time on our hands, and with our limited financial resources we were very conscious about preserving what we had.

We thought we might receive the proceeds from the sale of our house (my father had put it on the market right before we left), but the security situation in Kabul was deteriorating rapidly. No one was buying residential property.

We couldn't ask any of our relatives to send us money. Most of our extended family had forsaken us because of what I'd done. My father and I also believed it was imperative none of us told anyone back home where we were or what we were doing. The risk was too great. If by chance the Taliban found out, they could come after us.

The prohibition on communication included any contact with my squadron too. I should have kept them informed and notified them where I was, but I didn't trust my leadership. Part of me even wondered if some of them were connected to the threats. I would never know, but for the time being I would not communicate with them.

Nevertheless, I realized I needed to let someone know where I was and why I was gone so that when I eventually returned, I would have sufficient proof I hadn't gone AWOL without cause. I reached out to two people I did trust, MAJOR OLIVIA JOHNSON and CAPTAIN SOPHIA RICHARDSON. Both were officers in the US Air Force and assigned to the advisory wing working with my squadron. They were my trusted friends; they would keep my whereabouts secret until I returned.

My family and I returned to Kabul in October 2013. Our visas were set to expire, and we were nearly out of money. Although we were unsure of the situation we were returning to, we hoped the threats against us had calmed down and the perpetrators had either forgotten about us or moved on to other matters.

We spent that first week of our return at my grandmother's house, but we did not return to our normal lives. My sisters did not go back to school, my brother did not go back to university, and my father didn't look for work. I didn't report back to my squadron either. But we knew this couldn't go on forever, so eventually my father and I arranged another meeting with General Zafar at the air base. As in our previous meeting, his reception was very cool.

My father did his best to explain our predicament. Because the air force would not help us, we had to take matters into our own hands. We had no choice but to go away for a while, hoping the attention on us would subside and the threats would stop. Now that we had returned, we would be living in a different part of the city, which we intended to keep secret.

General Zafar didn't care about any of this. Rather than discussing the matter with my father, he simply stated I'd gone AWOL and I would be reprimanded accordingly. The general dismissed us.

But both my father and I held our ground, and my father proceeded to lay the matter directly at the general's feet. He said we came to the general first because he was a senior commander for the air force in Kabul, and it was ultimately his responsibility to provide for the security and welfare of the people under his command. This is also a custom in Afghanistan—senior tribal elders and patriarchs have an obligation to protect the younger, less influential members of the group as a form of patronage.

By this time, my father's anger was beginning to show. He told the general he had believed him when he said women could join the air force, trusting the military would protect the people who served in it. After all, my father pointed out, he and my mother had taken a risk allowing their daughter to join the air force because our family believed in the future of Afghanistan—"But now you abandon us as if we are worthless."

General Zafar stood up from behind his desk and said, "War is no job for a woman. You are dismissed."

My father was irate when we left the command post, but when we got in the car to go home, I said I had not given up hope. I told him to go home and take care of my Mother Jan, who was sick again, but I would remain at the base. There was another option I could pursue. It took some convincing, but he believed me when I said that as long as I was on the base nothing would happen to me.

As I watched my father drive away, I felt immensely grateful for what he'd done. As the head of our household, he was expected to represent me in a situation like this, and it would have been the same if I were a man. These traditional elements of Afghan culture persist throughout the military, and I did not mind him stepping in for me.

Yet the traditional Afghan system failed us, so I intended to go outside it. I would go see the American advisors with whom I stayed in contact and would seek their assistance to get my flight status restored. Despite the prejudices of my own people against me, I would get back up in the air. I would not be beaten.

Before going over to the American side of the compound, I stopped at my squadron building to change into my uniform. As I expected, my colleagues greeted me with sneers and contemptuous looks, but a few of them asked where I had been. Most had assumed I'd resigned my commission or simply run away, never to return.

I responded by telling them about the threats to me and my family, and that we'd not received any support from the senior command. Consequently, we'd traveled to India.

I then told my colleagues I was back and intended to continue flying. Some of the younger pilots scoffed at this, echoing General Zafar by saying I didn't belong here. One of them said the only reason I'd been allowed to become a pilot was because of the Americans, and if I needed help I should run to them. Another chimed in and asked what I would do once the Americans left—I'd have no one to protect or support me anymore.

This interaction was probably one of the harshest I'd ever had with the other pilots in my squadron. I have no doubt some pilots were pleased about the threats being made against me, even if they weren't directly connected to them. However, there were other pilots, like Major Abdulrahman and Colonel Pacha Kahn—some of the older and more mature members of the squadron—who I know didn't feel this way. But they stayed silent.

After this exchange, I donned my flight suit and headscarf and went to the American advisors' compound, where I found Major Johnson and Captain Richardson. In contrast to my reception from my colleagues, they were thrilled I was back. I quickly told them my story, and shortly thereafter we headed back over to the command post, where they verified my story with the senior leadership. I was reinstated with my squadron and cleared for flight duty.

I know the Afghan leadership hated my relationship with the American advisors, and hated being advised to reinstate me. But it wasn't their call. NATO had been rebuilding the Afghan Air Force from the ground up, and they owed everything to the advisory group. The planes, the training, the funding—everything. The air force would not survive without the advisory group. The Afghan leadership had no choice but to acquiesce with a forced smile when the Americans "recommended" something.

This was one of those moments.

34

BACK IN THE AIR

BACK IN KABUL WITH MY FLIGHT STATUS REINSTATED, I attempted to straddle two very different worlds as two different people. One the one hand, I was a captain in the air force commanding an aircraft and responsible for the lives of everyone on board, flying missions throughout the country. On the other, I had to disguise myself coming and going from the base and out in public wearing a burka—something I thought I would never have to do again—while doing my best to remain invisible.

Being back up in the air was a joy. I truly felt free and alive when I was flying. I could be myself, confident in my abilities to fly the airplane and make decisions, and I didn't have to worry about someone criticizing or threatening me. In the air, I was where I belonged.

Yet even though I felt liberated soaring across the skies of Afghanistan, the situation on the ground was getting worse day-by-day, and my missions were increasingly more challenging and important to the wider war effort.

In the fall of 2014, as the Americans and NATO troops incrementally handed over the main combat operations to the still fledgling

Afghan Army, casualties mounted. We were also suffering a shortage of new pilots (I don't know why), so most of us in the squadron routinely conducted medevac flights to the more troublesome provinces, like Helmand, Kandahar, Paktika, and others.

One of my missions to Camp Bastion in Helmand was yet another medevac assignment. When I landed, my copilot and I got out and walked toward a waiting ambulance. Two Afghan doctors approached us and said we would be transporting them and four wounded soldiers back to Kabul, for a total of six passengers. The soldiers had been wounded in a roadside bomb attack and needed immediate trauma care.

Roadside bombs, also known as IEDs (improvised explosive devices), were killers in this conflict. Throughout Afghanistan there was an abundance of ordnance either left over from the Soviet-Afghan War, when thousands of artillery rounds had been abandoned as the Russian army fled north in 1989 or funneled across the Afghanistan-Pakistan border during the subsequent civil war. After 9/11 and the American-led invasion, more arms and ammunition came in from Iran and Pakistan to be used against the foreign invaders.

With a little training, the Taliban and their allies (the Haqqani network, al-Qaeda, and others) could fashion and deploy IEDs with lethal efficiency, some large enough to knock out armored vehicles as strong as the American MRAP (mine-resistant ambush-protected vehicle). The loss of limbs and massive head trauma were common injuries after such attacks.

I watched as the medical personnel carefully took the wounded men out of the ambulance and began loading them onto the aircraft. As I feared, these four soldiers had suffered extremely severe wounds, including the loss of arms and legs. They were on stretchers, which would take up most of the passenger space on the plane. The two doctors coming along would keep the wounded men stable during the flight to Kabul.

As I was about to step away from the ambulance to return to the cockpit, I heard someone yelling from inside the ambulance. Whoever it was started banging on the rear door. One of the doctors opened the door to reveal another wounded soldier, who I would later learn was Sergeant Mohammad. He'd also been hit in the IED attack—he'd suffered shrapnel and burn wounds to his face and eyes, and he was at risk of losing his eyesight. He was begging the doctors to put him on the medevac flight, afraid if he didn't get medical help he would be blinded for life.

I could tell Sergeant Mohammad was in his early twenties, just a young man. He was scared, and I didn't blame him. To be wounded on the battlefield is one thing—the pain, the violence, the uncertainty can be overwhelming, and even the strongest of men can wonder if they're going to make it out in one piece. But being blinded adds an entirely new level of fear to the experience. I felt for this sergeant and couldn't sit idly by.

I stopped the head doctor and told him to load Sergeant Mohammad onto the aircraft. We would leave one of the attending doctors behind—one on board during the flight would be sufficient—so there would be enough room for the sergeant.

At first, the doctor protested and said they both needed to get to Kabul, but I held firm. I had enough experience to know medevac flights required only one doctor to accompany the casualties and monitor their condition while in flight, even ones worse than this. I suspected the second doctor had another, nonemergency reason for going to Kabul. He could wait. There'd be another flight later today or tomorrow. He could be remanifested on one of those.

When the major kept insisting, I told him this aircraft wasn't leaving without Sergeant Mohammad. This was a medevac flight, not a passenger run; Sergeant Mohammad was wounded and needed medical attention at the hospital in Kabul.

Reluctantly, the doctor gave in and directed the nurses to put Sergeant Mohammad on the plane. My copilot went to help, to try to calm the sergeant down. We told him he was getting on the plane to go to Kabul, but he was so frightened he didn't believe it. He kept mumbling he was going to die here, that he was alone and blind and would die.

I spoke to him, assuring him he was getting on the plane and he would be OK, but he seemed to be in a state of shock, unable to hear or process what was going on around him. My heart went out to him; I couldn't imagine how scared he was.

Once we were fully loaded and had taken off, Sergeant Mohammad seemed to understand he was actually on a plane heading to safety. He calmed down, sitting quietly for the remainder of the flight. When we landed at Kabul Airport, I watched the waiting doctors and nurses help Sergeant Mohammad walk to the ambulance that would take him to the hospital. They loaded the other casualities in the ambulance as well. All of them had remained stable during the flight.

I felt I'd served my country well on this particular day. I would likely never see any of those men again (I hadn't encountered any of the other casualties I'd transported on previous medevac flights), but I felt I'd helped these particular soldiers in a vital way.

As for Sergeant Mohammad's situation, I was proud I'd demanded he come along. I believed I'd made the right decision. I had a responsibility to make those kinds of calls on the ground when the situation demanded it. Being a woman had nothing to do with it—I was a pilot in the Afghan Air Force, and I would carry out my duties accordingly.

———————

That evening, my father picked me up from the base, which was unusual. My brother usually did. There had been a time when such a change wouldn't have bothered me. I would probably have been glad to see my Baba Jan. But given the precautions we'd been taking since India, the change in pattern unsettled me. A tightness formed in my chest, and I felt the blood rush to my face; I was afraid something had happened. I'd been living on the edge of this fear for months.

After our return from India, we'd stayed at my grandmother's house for about a week before moving into an apartment across town. As before, we told no one. My sisters went to new schools and made new friends, and my older sister, Afsoon, still hadn't contacted her husband, because she feared what he and his family might do. She missed her son terribly.

My brother, however, needed to go back to class at the university; he was bound to run into people from before who would ask him where he'd been. Fortunately, he only had a few months left until graduation and believed he could avoid any trouble.

But one night after class, when my brother was walking home, two men on a motorbike drove by and shot at him. This was a typical tactic for assassinations in the city, and they sped away before my brother could identify who they were.

Omar was scared but on alert, and he ran from the area as fast as possible in case there was a second team or if the two on the motorcycle came back around. He spent the night hiding in an alley a few blocks from campus, afraid the perpetrators might still be out there. He figured if he waited until daylight, he'd have a better chance of spotting any new threats and could make it home safely.

My family wasn't aware of any of this. We feared the worst when we couldn't reach him. My mother had another breakdown and had to be taken to the hospital. We all went with her, and while there my father tried calling some trusted friends to see if they'd heard or seen anything about Omar, but he found out nothing.

It wasn't until the morning when my bother returned home to an empty house that we learned he was safe. He'd lost his mobile phone, so he used a neighbor's phone to call my father to find out where everyone was. Hearing the news, we were relieved, and my mother recovered enough to be discharged. We came home, all of us thanking God while also afraid of what might happen next.

Thus, when I saw my father in the car and not my brother, all sorts of fearful visions flashed through my mind. But when I got in the car, my Baba Jan said Omar was not feeling well, so he'd offered to come get me. Relief swept over me.

I dove right in, telling my Baba Jan about my day and the medevac flight with Sergeant Mohammad. I could see he was proud of what I'd done, and he said as much. He said no matter what happened, he would always support me. However, as he told me these things, I noticed a hint of hesitation in his voice, like there was something else he had yet to tell me.

We were about to drive off the base when the guard at the front gate stopped us. He knew my father and brother because of how I had to come on and off base, covered in a burka and ducked down in the seat. The guard approached the driver's side and said earlier in the evening someone had come up to him saying he was a relative of mine and wanted to come on the base to find me. The guard asked if I knew who this person was.

My father and I exchanged looks. No one we knew—no relative, that is—would have come to the base asking for me. Whoever it was, I had no doubt they were a threat.

I told the guard my father and brother were the only ones who would come to the base looking for me. If anyone else did, even if they were posing as a relative, they were lying and shouldn't be allowed onto base. If it happened again, I asked them to please call my squadron and let me know immediately.

As we drove away, my father turned to me and said there was more. After my brother had dropped me at the base that morning, two men had come to the apartment building asking about me. When the attendant at the front desk called our apartment, my father told him to say no one was home and they couldn't come in. As they left, the two men said they would avenge the dishonor I had brought upon Islam.

———————————

When we got home that night, we packed up to move to another apartment. There was no time to waste—we just had to go.

But we weren't at the new apartment for long. One morning, I was running late for work and went outside without wearing my burka. A neighbor who happened to be walking by stopped and stared. He said he recognized me from the television. A few days later, my father was buying vegetables from the vendor down the street, and the seller said someone was looking for my father and pointing at our apartment.

We packed up again. It had been only a month, but we had to go.

Out of options, my father called a trusted friend of his named Ahmad and asked him if we could stay in his spare room for a time. My father had faith Ahmad would keep it a secret, so we moved there.

Things went on like this for most of 2014. I felt like we were refugees again, without a place to call home. My father was having trouble working, and coupled with all the moves, we were living very destitute and uncertain lives. I watched my father's hair turn gray over a few short months, my mother suffer depression, and my brother and sisters struggle to grow up and live their own lives.

It was all my fault. This was happening because I became a pilot. I was selfish, and now my family was paying the price.

35

CONTACTS

———

MY FAMILY AND I FOUND OURSELVES abandoned by nearly all our relatives, friends, coworkers, classmates, and neighbors, and our lives were being threatened by our countrymen—the people I'd volunteered to serve and defend. Much of the happiness in our lives had disappeared.

Yet, while all this was going on in our Afghan lives, I began to find rays of hope in my contacts from the West. Some of these people, in fact, would come to save my life.

In the summer of 2014 I met a *Wall Street Journal* reporter named Margherita Stancati. She'd heard about me through one of the media events I'd participated in, and she wanted to do a story on me. She obtained my phone number through the public affairs office, called me, and asked if I would come to her house in the diplomatic quarter of Kabul in the middle of the city.

A couple of days after I'd conducted a mortuary mission, I went to meet her. My brother drove me to the diplomatic zone, and I again wore a burka to disguise myself. When not at the base or at home, this—the burka—had become my daily attire. I'd come to accept I was no longer free, and if anyone recognized me I'd be hunted down. So would my family.

When we arrived at the diplomatic quarter perimeter, we stopped at a fortified security checkpoint manned by both Afghan police and foreign security guards. It was an intimidating sight, replete with machine gun nests, hardened guard houses, vehicle lanes, drop arms, and most likely an impressive array of additional security features I couldn't see.

When one of the guards approached our car, my brother provided our names and identity papers. We were on the list to visit that day, so we were allowed through. Through the security checkpoint—the strictest security procedures I'd ever experienced—we traveled along the narrow roads that made up this international enclave filled with reporters, diplomats, military commanders, and international organizations.

After slowly weaving around blast walls, HESCO barriers, and numerous armored cars and SUVs, we arrived at a small gate with Margherita Stancati's address. She was there to meet us, standing outside with a scarf around her head. She had brunette hair, an oval face, a petite physique, and a pleasant smile complemented by her brown eyes. I learned she was Italian by birth and had earned a degree at Oxford before becoming a reporter and working across the Middle East and India.

She welcomed my brother and me warmly, and invited us inside for tea. It was a sparsely but beautifully appointed home, with a cosmopolitan feel both inside and out. She had decorated with Persian rugs and traditional Afghan serving ware, and flower baskets hung on her balcony. In her courtyard she kept a rose garden. I imagined this is what Kabul must have looked like before the Soviets came.

During this first meeting, we chatted about my life, my family, and how I'd come to join the Afghan Air Force, but it was more conversational than the focused interviews I'd done before. She shared as much about herself as I did with her, and she seemed genuinely interested in me as a person, not only as a story.

As our visit came to an end, she expressed she wanted to remain in touch and eventually write an article about me. She believed my story needed to be told and that it could inspire others. I liked the idea, and I felt she was becoming a real friend.

We would meet many more times over the years, and Stancati wrote a few articles about me. She also came to my aid in one of my darkest hours.

———

Another fortunate encounter occurred in October 2014. A contingent of senior military officers from NATO—Americans, British, Norwegian, and others—were coming to visit the Kabul air base to meet with some of Afghanistan's female military officers, including me. This was a typical command visit under the NATO advisory mission; they were coming to observe firsthand how we were doing as Afghanistan's initial crop of female officers.

Honestly, it was very hard for these outside observers to see the true reality of our situation. The NATO officers weren't going to meet with us in private. Rather, multiple members of our senior leadership would be present, including General Zafar. None of the female officers would dare say anything negative or controversial while he or any of his aides were around. If an observer asked a question, we would respond positively and with deep respect, saying it was an honor to be allowed to serve our country. We would maintain the party line.

When the day finally arrived, we met at the base command post inside the conference room. General Zafar introduced the six other women and me, and the NATO officers greeted us and started asking very simple questions about our backgrounds, military specialties, and such. I did my best to put on a strong demeanor as directed, but the struggles my family and I faced weighed on me constantly. We'd just moved again, and every hour I feared for the safety of my family.

To my surprise, an American, Colonel Holly Silkman, and a Norwegian, Colonel Tormod Heier, noticed the sadness in my eyes. As the meeting came to a close, both officers approached me on their own at different times and surreptitiously passed me their phone numbers and email addresses. They said to contact them if I wanted to talk.

I was surprised they'd slipped me their contact information in such a manner, but I also realized I had an opportunity here. That night, I emailed Colonel Silkman and told her a little about my situation, including the threats against my family. The next day, she invited me for tea at the NATO compound.

As he had with my visit with Margherita Stancati, my brother drove me to the NATO compound, and we went through a similar round of security checks before being allowed onto the facility. We were met by one of Colonel Silkman's security officers, a man named Michael Coleman, who was a retired US Army colonel. Coleman preferred to wear traditional Afghan clothing, like a pakol hat and patu blanket, and with his beard he looked very much like a local. My brother quickly took a liking to him, and they chatted while I met with Colonel Silkman.

Coleman escorted us to Colonel Silkman's office, and she and I spoke for quite a while. She told me to call her Holly and that this wasn't an official meeting. She was a public affairs officer, but she wasn't meeting with me because she needed a story or had to write a report. She wanted to hear what my family and I were going through.

I told her my father's story, and everything that had happened flowed out. I wasn't emotional, and I didn't break down and cry, but I conveyed the immense weight and sadness that had come into our lives. I also spoke about my love of flying and the dedication I felt to my country, and that I had a responsibility to serve as an example for other Afghan women who wanted to pursue their dreams. I told her how much it hurt me that my fellow pilots and my own countrymen hated me. I felt alone, targeted by everyone, and it was nerve-racking.

Holly simply listened, and it felt good to explain everything to her. She had a kind heart, and I will be forever grateful for what she did next. She wanted to introduce me to someone at the US embassy. She asked if she could share my story with one of the senior State Department officials and if I would be willing to meet with this official.

I said of course.

A week later, I met with Molly Montgomery, a senior Foreign Service officer at the US embassy. Molly was responsible for consular affairs, and she wanted to do anything she could to help me, thanks to Colonel Silkman's intervention on my behalf.

During our first meeting, I shared many of the same things with Molly that I'd told Colonel Silkman. But unlike before, it was much harder for me to hold back my tears. Afsoon's situation had been bothering me more and more in recent days. She'd finally contacted her husband, but he wouldn't allow her to see her baby boy—not even once. Each night, I would hear her cry herself to sleep, and I couldn't help but blame myself for her pain.

Molly listened intently to my story and everything my family was going through. She told me anytime I needed to talk, I could call her. From that day on, we met once a week for tea. Sometimes during our meetings, I would share other challenges I was contending with, while other times we would simply chat. She never hesitated to encourage me. She is a beautiful person both inside and out, with a kind heart. She told me courage comes through suffering and that I and my family were immensely courageous as a result of everything we had endured in our lives.

One time, she asked me if things were to get worse, what I would do. I told her flying was my life's dream and the one thing that felt good right now; the idea of giving it up was as painful as being ostracized by my relatives and friends. But I recognized I wasn't the only person who faced dangers or who had made substantial sacrifices. Given everything that had befallen my family, I was contemplating whether I should quit.

When I shared this with her, tears were streaming down my face. I was losing hope in the future. A long time ago, I'd felt free and cherished the idea of living in my homeland and serving my country. But now, after everything that had happened, I felt like I was a prisoner in my own life.

She hugged me and encouraged me to stay strong. She said things would get better in time. Afghanistan was changing; I was a part of the change, and I was an inspiration to others. She thanked me for what I was doing and said she believed in me.

I received a letter from the American advisory group in February 2015. It came through my squadron, and it said I'd been nominated by the US embassy for the Secretary of State's International Women of Courage Award. I was invited to travel to the United States in March to receive the award and be recognized with the other nominees. Receiving this letter made me very happy, and I felt joy I hadn't experienced in months.

As soon as I could, I called my Baba Jan and told him the news. He was also thrilled, and I could hear him announcing it to the rest of my family. That same day, I emailed Molly Montgomery to tell her, and she said she was one of the people who nominated me; she also said she wanted to see me again before I went.

General Zafar, however, did not want me to travel to the United States to receive the award, and gave me a direct order not to go. He said I was needed here to continue flying missions.

I knew he was lying; he didn't want me to go because I was a woman, and he didn't want me to receive any more recognition than I already had. He resented me, and I could hear it in every word he spoke.

When the US embassy found out I'd been ordered not to attend, the US ambassador "highly recommended" I be allowed to go. I'm not sure what was said, but General Zafar approved my orders.

36

THE UNITED STATES

———

I FLEW TO WASHINGTON, DC, in March 2015 to be honored with nine other women for the International Women of Courage Award. The other honorees hailed from Kosovo, Syria, Bolivia, Japan, the Central African Republic, and other countries. I found it fascinating to hear their stories. They had a range of backgrounds—investigative journalists, activists, lawyers, government officials—but they all had one thing in common: each of them had faced and overcome immense challenges and opposition, including threats to their freedom and life, but they had persevered.

Speaking with these women, I realized I was not alone. There were other women out there fighting for justice and equality who were willing to risk everything to do what's right. I knew my interaction with these women would last only a few days before we went back to our respective countries, but for a brief time my head was free from worry about my family.

The second night I was in DC, I had another surprise. Three women I'd become friends with during training or with the advisory wing, USAF Captains Sophia Richardson and Jessica Bishop and

Major Agneta Murnan, arranged to have dinner with me. They came from South Korea and the West Coast, and it warmed my heart to spend time with such dear friends. I was amazed at their willingness to come so far for me, because aside from my parents and siblings, no one had ever done so much to support me. Although my family couldn't be at the ceremony, these women were like my family.

Deputy Secretary of State Heather Higginbottom presented me and my fellow nominees with the International Women of Courage Award at a ceremony in the auditorium of the State Department building. We received the full VIP treatment, and the State Department protocol officer read a short bio about each of us during the ceremony. Put simply, I felt honored and immensely grateful to be counted among these women.

The following day, we were recognized by the American Women for International Understanding, followed by a visit to the White House to meet First Lady Michelle Obama. The First Lady took time to speak with each of us and thanked us for what we were doing and for our courage. She said to stay strong, that we were the ones making a difference in the world, making it a better place.

When I've heard other people say these things, sometimes it sounds like a script or a string of practiced phrases, all for show but without any real meaning. But with the First Lady, I had no doubt she meant every word and that she was a truly genuine and good human being. I'm lucky to have met her.

After the White House visit, the nominees and I went our separate ways. Some went back home to their home countries, but some of us stayed a few more days in the States. I went to San Diego, California, for a special surprise. I was going to fly with the US Navy's Blue Angels!

Never in my wildest dreams did I ever think I'd get to fly in an F/A-18! Rather than providing me with a G-suit to help me withstand the high levels of acceleration force, they gave me a basic flight suit and said it was a Blue Angel rule. I was totally OK with it. I got to fly with US Marine Corps captain Jeff Kuss, and we flew for about an hour over Southern California, reaching speeds and doing maneuvers that were over-the-top exhilarating. It was an incredible experience.

A year later, I learned Captain Kuss died tragically in a training accident in Smyrna, Tennessee, on June 2, 2016. When I heard the news, I was heartbroken. He was a true gentleman and a fantastic pilot. My prayers go out to his wife and two children; I will always remember him.

While in California, I also met with some of the people in the San Diego community, and Mayor Kevin Faulconer proclaimed March 10 as Captain Niloofar Rahmani Day for the city. I visited Marine Corps Air Station Miramar and met a C-130 air crew and got to see an F-14 Tomcat, the plane used in my favorite movie of all time, *Top Gun*.

In the final two days of my trip to the United States, I went to New York and visited the United Nations. I met up with my new friend and corecipient Arbana Xharra and her sister, and we spent our final hours in Times Square. We didn't sleep at all that night, preferring to remain awake and soak in the last few moments of our time in America.

My trip to the United States was thrilling on so many levels. I felt honored to meet important people, like the deputy secretary of state, the First Lady, and the countless other officials and aides who welcomed me and made sure I was taken care of. I was also flattered to be counted among such extraordinary women as my conominees. They are people of exceptional strength, courage, and determination. My time in California and New York was amazing too, and I got see and do things I'd only seen on TV or dreamed about—like flying with the Blue Angels, wandering around Times Square, and getting to experience firsthand how wonderful the United States is and how welcoming Americans are. But most important, I came away from this experience inspired. I'd always known my status as Afghanistan's first female fixed-wing pilot was significant, but I'd viewed it in the context of Afghanistan and the ongoing war. Simply put, *I* wanted to fly and *I* wanted serve my country.

The international nature of this experience, however, made me see more clearly that I wasn't just fighting for myself and my career, or for my family, or for other women in Afghanistan. I was a part of something that spanned the globe, and I was among the many women fighting for equality and freedom who came from oppressive countries. If we didn't stand up for our rights and the rights of others, and if we didn't fight for the opportunity to live free from fear and pursue our dreams, no one else would.

I truly believed that, and I still do. Someone has to do it. Someone has to be the first. I'm not the only person to think this way, nor will I be the last, but I am proud to be among those who have.

Unfortunately, when I returned home to Kabul, no one cared.

I wasn't surprised. I expected it. On my return, I saw the same animosity I'd experienced since I'd first put on the uniform. My squadron leadership never once acknowledged the award I received, and I suspect it caused them to resent me even more. What I hadn't expected was what happened to my family while I was away for those seventeen days.

37

MY RETURN

THE NIGHT I RETURNED HOME, I learned my brother was in the hospital after a second assassination attempt. He'd been at the bazaar buying food for the family. While walking home, his arms full with groceries, a car with two men inside came up from behind. As one drove, the other fired an AK-47 rifle at my brother. He dove to the ground and by the grace of God the bullets missed, but as the car sped past it clipped my brother.

Omar sustained a severe injury to his left arm and leg and could not move. Fortunately, some of the witnesses on the street came to his aid and carried him to the nearby Khair Khana Hospital.

My father had started a new job at an engineering firm. It was his first day. But when the news about Omar reached him, he left immediately to make sure his son was all right. My mother was at home when she found out; she suffered another panic attack and had to be hospitalized again.

The day I returned was my father's second day at work, but as soon as he arrived at the office his boss told him he could no longer work there. They didn't want him or any of his problems being associated with the company.

I'd had visions of telling my family all about what I'd seen and done in the United States, but upon hearing what had happened to my family, the happiness and inspiration I'd felt on the trip vanished. It was like a horrible nightmare, one I couldn't wake up from. But it wasn't a dream at all; this was my life.

I asked my Baba Jan to take me to the hospital to see Omar and my mother. When I entered their room, my eyes immediately welled up. I went to my brother's bedside and pulled out my award from my purse, clutching it in my hands before him.

I professed to my brother, my Lala Jan, that I never would have received this award or been able to accomplish anything in my life without him. "You never failed to support me, even at your own risk or by your own sacrifice. Yet I can't bear to see you like this." I begged for his forgiveness, and told him I was so sorry about what happened to him. I'd rather be dead than see him suffering in pain.

It's relatively easy to be brave when you're the only one at risk. It's easy to be bold and to fight when you only have to worry about yourself. But when your actions threaten the health and safety of the people you hold most dear—your family, the people you would do anything for—being brave and continuing on is not easy, and you might have to reckon whether the risk is worth it. Being brave or courageous or strong may no longer be part of the equation.

These were the questions I had to contend with as I saw my brother lying in the hospital bed with a bloody arm and leg and my mother nearby so overcome with fear and concern she was emotionally exhausted.

I couldn't do anything but turn to my Baba Jan and tell him I couldn't keep my promise. I couldn't keep flying and serving in the air force if this was going to keep happening to our family. And it would, I knew it would, and eventually someone could die—because of me. I could not be responsible for destroying our family.

But my father said, "No, you must stay strong, and you cannot quit. No one knew any of this was going to happen." We all believed what the military and our leaders told us, that Afghanistan was changing, that women could go to school, become professionals, join the military, and become pilots. "If you quit now, our enemies will win," he said. I couldn't give them an excuse to call me, or any woman, weak. As for our family, none of this would break us apart. We were strong and we would stay strong.

My father's words bolstered me, and I believed him to the depths of my soul, but I still wrestled with how my career was affecting the people I cared about most.

Resuming my normal duties at the squadron, I settled into flying missions throughout the country, bringing supplies to the combat forces, transporting personnel to the front and back to Kabul, and doing medevac flights.

On my second day back, I was to fly to Mazar-e-Sharif out west. When I exited the squadron building to go to the flight line, however, I saw a man dressed in a white shalwar kameez and a woman wearing a burka running toward me and calling my name. I stopped. When they reached me, they took a moment to catch their breath.

Finally, the man said, "Captain, my son has recovered. My son is Sergeant Mohammad, and he has his life back. He lost one eye, but you saved him. He wanted us to find you and thank you for what you did for him. He is our only son."

They went on to explain that although Sergeant Mohammad never saw me, he'd heard my voice and knew a female pilot had flown the airplane, and that she had refused to take off without him. From there, he'd figured out who I was and sent his parents to thank me. His parents then offered me a beautiful red scarf as a gift.

I told his parents I'd simply done my job. It was the doctors who saved him and returned his eyesight. I also told them their son was very brave and that it must not have been easy to go through what he did. I thanked them for finding me, and I was grateful their son had recovered.

As they left, the father said Sergeant Mohammad and they would be forever grateful to me. Given everything that had happened in the past few days, I needed to hear this.

38

EVERYTHING CRUMBLES

WHAT I'M ABOUT TO TELL YOU ILLUSTRATES the horror women face every moment of their lives in Afghanistan.

On March 19, 2015, I completed a long mission to Kandahar and back, and my father picked me up late from the base. He normally took side roads to avoid traffic, and it usually worked, but the drive between our apartment and base was now over an hour, and that was on a good day. We'd vacated my father's friend's house a short while ago—Ahmad said we must leave because our troubles were putting his family at risk—and we'd moved to another rental across the city.

But on this particular commute home, we found ourselves snarled in traffic with no cars moving at all. I was in the back seat wearing my burka so no one would recognize me, but it was still unnerving sitting in gridlock. My father didn't want to get out to see what was going on, because he feared what might happen if he left me alone in the car.

As time wore on, however, we started hearing angry chanting and saw hundreds of people—mostly men—flocking to whatever was happening up ahead. I was getting nervous, and I could tell my Baba

Jan was as well, but there was nothing we could do. We sat there and waited until traffic started to move again, which happened soon after sundown.

When we got home that night, we found out what had occurred and why that part of the city had come to a standstill. The story was all over the local news, and rumors were already shooting around the city like bolts of lightning. The story would hit the international stage soon: an angry mob of Afghan men had beaten, mutilated, and burned to death an Afghan woman. Her name was Farkhunda Malikzada, and she was twenty-seven years old.

Farkhunda was a religious studies student and an observant Muslim, but on this day she was arguing with a mullah near the Shah-Do Shamshira Mosque in downtown Kabul. The mullah accused Farkhunda of burning the Koran, which was later proved false, but at the time it didn't matter. She'd been accused by a religious figure, and everyone nearby had heard the mullah make the accusation.

Within minutes, hundreds of men—young, old, poor, middle-class, urban, traditional—rushed to the scene. They surrounded her, began calling to her, and hitting her. They started with their hands and fists, but some picked up boards, sticks, and pipes to hit her. Farkhunda couldn't get away, because the mob had packed in and there was nowhere to go. She was caged by a mass of enraged men shouting she was a blasphemer and she'd disgraced Islam.

The crowd grew, and other rumors began to circulate, including that she worked for the Americans, was an infidel, and was a prostitute. She was an agent sent to undermine Afghanistan and Islam.

In the first minutes, a few police officers tried to keep the mob off her, but they were overwhelmed and pushed aside. There's a video that shows a police officer trying to drag Farkhunda up onto a roof to help her escape. She was still walking at this point, but before she could break free she lost her balance and fell back into the mass of men. Other police officers seemed all too willing to let the mob batter the young woman.

By this time, Farkhunda was bloody, broken, and dazed. She fell to the ground, and men took turns hitting her with sticks and rocks. They were kicking her and stomping on her face and limbs. The mob dragged her into the street and ran over her with a car. Next, they tied her to the back of the same car and dragged her a short distance down the road, but the car didn't get very far given how large the mob was.

By now, traffic was backed up for miles, and we were trapped in it. I had no idea what was going on, but I could hear the mob. The yelling, which was angry and vicious, sent chills down my spine.

The car dragging Farkhunda stopped, but the mob kept beating her. More kicking and bludgeoning. Someone yelled they should throw her in the river. The Kabul River is rarely full, but at that time of year it's essentially a dry, stony riverbed that runs through the city, roughly thirty yards across, and with a wall dropping down and lining the edges. The mob tossed Farkhunda's body from the road over the side and down onto the rocks.

Farkhunda was probably dead at this point, but the mob began stoning her. They started with small, hand-sized rocks but moved up to large chunks of rock and concrete requiring two hands to lift. They raised the blocks of jagged rock over their heads and dropped them on her.

Then it was time to burn her, to completely destroy and disgrace this woman who had offended Islam, who had dared to argue with a mullah, who had burned a Koran, and who, in absolute truth and fact, was an agent for the Americans, scheming to subvert and undermine all Muslims and to corrupt Afghanistan's faithful.

They tried to light her clothes on fire, but the fabric was soaked with her blood and the flames kept going out. Enraged, men started removing some of their own clothing—scarves and vests—which they ignited and threw on Farkhunda's body. Someone eventually poured gasoline on her seared and bloody remains, and her body finally burned.

The crowd dispersed.

For the next few days, numerous mullahs and imams endorsed her murder, stating she had deserved death for her crimes. Others celebrated the perpetrators of the lynching as defenders of Islam and the Koran. Some of the police and local politicians applauded her murder as well. But it was determined Farkhunda had committed no crime; she hadn't burned a Koran, and she wasn't an agent of the Americans. In fact, she was a good Muslim and an Islamic scholar and teacher.

Other religious leaders now spoke out to condemn her murder, and in the coming days, thousands of women marched in Kabul in protest, demanding the perpetrators be brought to justice. Arrests were made and men put on trial. Four men received death sentences, and others received up to sixteen years in prison, but many of these verdicts were reduced during secret hearings after the trials.

Although there was local and international outcry over Farkhunda's murder, and the event exposed the plight of women in Afghanistan and the broader region, this was not the first lynching of an innocent woman, nor will it be the last. Nor is it the only way women are violated, brutalized, and murdered in my homeland. Domestic violence is rampant and considered normal. It's deemed acceptable and just.

This is Afghanistan. This is my homeland . . . the one I swore to defend and protect.

The graphic images of Farkhunda's murder on the television shocked me. Killings like this were commonplace and done in public under the Taliban, but I believed we had changed. It had been almost fifteen years since the American-led invasion forced the Taliban from power, and things should have been different.

Seeing the angry faces of those men in the mob—like wild animals in a feeding frenzy—I feared nothing had changed. Kabul is the most developed, modern, and liberal city in Afghanistan, yet this happened in broad daylight.

Part of me was furious that so many people allowed it to happen. And I was angry the ones who should have stopped it—the police—didn't. Part of me also regretted not helping Farkhunda. I know it's foolish to think that. I had no idea what was happening, even though I was little more than a mile away, and had I ventured into the mob I most likely would have met a similar fate. But I still felt I should have done something.

Mixed with all my feelings of anger and revulsion was a deep fear. Farkhunda and I were about the same age, which resonated with me. They'd accused her of offending Islam and being an agent for the Americans, which was false, but people still believed it. Even after she'd been publicly declared innocent and falsely accused, many people still thought she'd offended Islam. Someone could easily accuse me of something similar (some people already had in the threats I'd received), and there was ample evidence to support such a claim. If that happened, I could be next.

Farkhunda was an innocent woman falsely accused by a mullah, then brutally murdered by a wild mob. I, on the other hand, was already a target for the Taliban and countless others who thought I was betraying Islam and Afghanistan. There'd already been two assassination attempts against my brother, and strangers often showed up looking for me at the base or lurked around our house. It would have been easy for someone to incite a similar situation if they found out who I was and where I lived. And what would they do to my family?

Looking back on my life in Pakistan and Afghanistan, I realize there are many times I could have died—where I probably should have died: when my family first fled to Pakistan while I was a new-born, when we returned to Afghanistan under the Taliban, in flight school, and most recently with all the personal threats against my life. I could have easily been caught up in the mob that day if they had recognized my father or our car—we both would have been killed. I believe I am a strong person and have persevered through immense adversity and overcome countless obstacles, but Farkhunda's murder terrified me, both for my own personal safety and that of my family.

But even with the public outcry against Farkhunda's murder and the condemnation by the politicians and a few religious leaders, I no longer believed Afghanistan was on the path of change. The hatred of outsiders, the trauma from decades of war and oppression, the humiliation by foreign powers, and the ingrained paternalism that seemed to be in Afghanistan's DNA—it all ran too deep.

Change wouldn't happen in a few years. It wouldn't happen in a decade. Change in Afghanistan was going to take a generation, perhaps multiple generations, and there would be many more tragedies along the way.

What could I do besides fly?

39

OPPORTUNITY

ALTHOUGH FARKHUNDA'S MURDER had shaken the city and me, I reported to work and continued flying missions. I had a responsibility to continue serving my country, even if my view of it had been shattered.

Something inside me had changed, and in those first few days after the mob murdered Farkhunda, I couldn't look at my colleagues the same way. Some of them I couldn't look at at all, wondering if they had been in the mob.

A few days later, my friend Molly Montgomery invited me to the US embassy to talk. She asked me how things were since Farkhunda's murder, and I shared with her everything I'd been feeling, the anger as well as the fear. This touched her more than our previous talks, I assume, because she said she would be meeting with Afghanistan's First Lady, Rula Ghani, in the coming days. She planned to mention me to her. Given the target I'd become, she believed I deserved protection and felt there was no time to waste.

I hoped I might hear from Rula Ghani or someone else from the president's office, but I kept my expectations muted. I was right to.

No one ever contacted me, and Molly believed they disregarded the request.

I continued flying missions.

One of our squadron advisors, Colonel Craig, came to my office the following month and said the US ambassador had talked to the NATO commander, and US Army general John F. Campbell wanted to meet with me. Colonel Craig escorted me to the American advisor compound on the far side of the base, and from there I flew in a Black Hawk helicopter to the NATO compound opposite the American embassy. (The Kabul airfield and the NATO compound were a few miles apart, but the threat from ambushes and IEDs was real, and if there was traffic, the short drive might take more than an hour.)

Captain Jeffrey Rosenberry, a senior advisor with NATO, was waiting for me at the helipad, and he escorted me to the general's office. Naturally, I was nervous to be meeting one of the senior NATO commanders for all of Afghanistan, but General Campbell had a warm and friendly manner, and he quickly put me at ease. He wanted to hear my story, so I told him.

He applauded me for everything I'd accomplished, but he also realized I was at severe risk. Given some of the things he said, I think he was surprised I hadn't been killed already. He quickly identified the greatest threat I currently faced—my commute to and from the base—and directed his staff to provide me with an armored sedan. Although this was a grand gesture and I was immensely grateful, it was fraught with problems.

It was a new vehicle and looked like the other armored cars driven around the city by US personnel and senior Afghan officials. Parked near our house, it stuck out and drew unwanted attention to my family.

Also, since it was a NATO-provided vehicle, it needed license plates from the Ministry of Interior. But the ministry never provided the plates, which I suspect was intentional. We couldn't use the car in the city.

As much as I appreciated the generosity, I ended up giving the vehicle back to the Americans. I couldn't use it, and letting it sit parked near our apartment would only bring unwanted scrutiny.

By this point, I'd given up on getting outside help. Those who wanted to help me and my family—Margherita Stancati, Molly Montgomery, the American advisors, Major Abdulrahman, and a few of the other pilots—were either unable to help, were not in a position to help, or were prevented from helping due to some complication. Those who could help—my command, the police, the air force—chose not to. Consequently, all I could do was rely on myself.

I continued performing my duties in the squadron, but some days I didn't make it to work. Our family car—not the armored one—periodically broke down, and it was my only means of transportation. Other times, something suspicious would happen, and in consultation with my father or brother, we would decide it was too risky for me to go outside even if I wore a burka. Still other times, an attack or ambush in the city would block our route.

Then, in August 2015, I was faced with perhaps one of the most difficult choices I'd ever had to make, and it ended up changing my life forever.

One morning in the squadron building, the American advisors came in and announced five Afghan pilots would be selected to attend C-130 flight training in the United States. I was one of the five chosen, although General Zafar did everything he could to oppose it, including refusing to sign my orders. He wanted five men to go, not me. But since the American advisors had the final say, I was on the list if I chose to be.

The first thing I did was call Molly Montgomery and Margherita Stancati. Both of these women had become close friends and trusted confidants, and I wanted to hear their views on the matter. Although I knew it was a great opportunity—once in a lifetime—I was wrestling with what to do about my family. The training would take place in the States, and I would be gone for more than a year and a half. After everything I'd put them through and all the support they'd given me, I would feel guilty and selfish if I left.

Both Molly and Margherita didn't view it that way. They made the case that if I left the country, the threat to my family might diminish. They both thought I should go to the training, and strongly encouraged me to do so.

Later that night, I called home and spoke to my Baba Jan. I told him the US Air Force had offered me a chance to go to the United States and train to fly the C-130 Hercules. He knew this was a great opportunity, but I told him I was unsure about accepting the offer. It would be difficult to be away from him and the rest of the family for so long. Family is everything to me, and we'd been through so much together; I felt if I went to the United States for training, I would be abandoning them during hard times. I still blamed myself for everything that had befallen my family.

My father wouldn't hear any of it. Although I couldn't see him, his tone indicated he was smiling. He asked jokingly, "Don't you believe in your Baba Jan? Don't you think I can take care of us while you're gone?" He went on to say I should never blame myself for anything that had happened. I lived my life and did everything exactly as I should have and in the manner he raised us. "We are a strong family, and you are not selfish," he said. He believed I had to go—it wasn't even a question—and he would support me no matter what happened.

I had tears in my eyes, both of happiness and sadness. I thanked my Baba Jan, telling him I wouldn't let him down.

I left Afghanistan on September 8, 2015, for the United States to undergo C-130 training.

40

BACK IN TRAINING

I **ARRIVED IN SAN ANTONIO,** Texas, along with two other Afghan pilots, Captain Emal and Lieutenant Mohammadi. The two additional pilots would join us shortly. One was already in the States for another bit of training (he was General Zafar's son), and the other was expected to graduate UPT soon. We were a total of five.

Similar to my initial flight training in Afghanistan, we had to complete language training at the Defense Language Institute English Language Center (DLIELC) at Lackland Air Force Base. We needed a score of 89 percent to be cleared for the next training phase, which was notably more difficult than what we'd done at Thunder Lab. Fortunately, I didn't have any problem with the curriculum.

Being at DLIELC and living in the United States was quite an experience. Training ended at four every day, and then we were on our own. We had the weekends off too. Not surprisingly, my Afghan colleagues didn't approve of anything I did, but I essentially told them to shut up. I was an officer and outranked some of them. They needed to accord me the respect I was entitled to. They were not my father, my brother, my uncle, or any other relative, and they had no power over me. They needed to mind their own business.

After class, I spent my time getting to know the other international students, who came from all over the world, including Jordan, Kosovo, Iraq, Albania, and Turkey. I enjoyed spending time with them, learning about their cultures, hearing their stories, and socializing. A woman named Jasmina, who was from Kosovo, became like a sister to me, and we relied on one another a lot at DLIELC. We practiced speaking English together, we supported each other if we were struggling, we comforted each other when we missed home, and we laughed a lot. I still keep in touch with Jasmina.

The four other Afghan pilots and I graduated on February 12, 2016, and were cleared to move to the next phase of training.

From Texas we flew to Tampa, Florida, to begin the first part of flight training at CAE's C-130 Tampa Training Center. I would learn that CAE, an international defense company, is one of the principal vendors that provides training to both military and civilian personnel on the Lockheed Martin C-130 Hercules aircraft.

We spent six months in Tampa focusing on academics and simulator training. Although I was eager to learn, I also found the training much more intimidating than what I'd done at Shindand. The C-130 is a four-engine turboprop military transport aircraft, and compared to the Cessnas I'd been flying, it's a beast. But I knew if I worked hard and stayed focused, I would succeed.

Inevitably, I began to miss my family. Although I had access to a phone and reliable service, my family back in Kabul weren't as fortunate. I rarely reached them, and when I did, the connection would last for only a few minutes. It bothered me that I didn't know what was going on back home. Afghans traditionally have very strong family connections, but I think ours was stronger than most, given our circumstances. Being on the other side of the world was very difficult for me.

But by some stroke of luck, wherever I go in life I always find at least one person I can look to for support. In Tampa I became friends with a woman named Mary, a CAE employee. She would invite me out after work, have me over to her house for dinner, and introduce me to her friends and family. She was a genuinely nice person, and I will be forever grateful for her kindness.

By the time August rolled around, the other pilots and I had completed 432 hours of academics, 40 hours of flight training device (FTD) training, and 60 hours of simulator training. We hadn't flown a C-130 yet, but we knew as much as we could know without having strapped ourselves in and hit the throttle.

We graduated on August 25 and were at Little Rock Air Force Base in Arkansas by September. Here we'd actually fly the C-130 and, if all went well, graduate in four months.

In Tampa, I'd lived almost like a civilian, wearing civilian clothes, working at a civilian location, and living in civilian quarters with access to the surrounding area. It was very pleasant, and I enjoyed my time in Florida, but I was glad to get back into uniform.

In Arkansas, we were on a military base, wearing our uniforms, and training in a military environment with other military personnel. I always liked wearing my uniform, because it conveyed a degree of strength and respect, and here in the United States I wasn't dismissed because of my gender. I was treated like everyone else, including the American students. It's a good feeling when equality is not even questioned or an issue. I'd found this to be true the first day I'd landed on US soil for training.

As for the training itself, I felt confident about my abilities to fly the C-130, but I still had quite a few things to learn that I'd never been exposed to in Afghanistan. I had to learn the Federal Aviation Administration rules, because in Afghanistan we followed the International Civil Aviation Organization (ICAO) regulations. Not a huge difference, but it was important.

There were also technical systems we didn't cover at CAE but which I was expected to know. The biggest challenge I faced involved the nondirectional radio beacon, or NDB, which is used for long-range navigation on modern aircraft and maritime vessels. I'd never been trained on the NDB—they weren't used in Afghanistan—but during one of my check rides I'd be expected to use it. Unfortunately, I didn't have any way of getting up to speed on the NDB in Arkansas.

With no other option available, I contacted some of the instructors from my initial flight training at Shindand. I was fortunate to reach a few of them, and I explained the situation. They in turn sent me some instructions via email, and one of them created a short video he sent to me.

With their help, I learned what I needed to and passed my check ride without any issues.

By this point, we were nearing the end of training. It was November, and we had less than a month to go; we were all excited and could see the light at the end of the tunnel.

But for me, the situation back home lingered persistently in the back of my mind. Despite repeated attempts, I hadn't been able to reach anyone for weeks, and not knowing my family's situation was making me worry. One night after a training flight, I kept calling until my younger sister picked up on the fifth call.

I was so excited I'd gotten through, and hearing her voice touched my heart. I wanted to share everything I was doing and hear how everyone was getting on back home. But something was wrong. My sister sounded sad and had little to say, as if she didn't want to talk. I asked her if anyone else was home, and she put my mother on.

My mother tried not to say anything about what was wrong, but I kept asking until finally she gave in. She said she was very ill, and she didn't think she could do it anymore. I asked her what she meant, what was going on, but the line went dead. I tried to call back over and over, but I never got through.

I went to bed distraught, wondering what had happened to my family. Here I was, in the middle of an amazing opportunity and experience, something I'd never dreamed of, but my family was suffering. I knew they were. With everything that had happened over the years— the ostracism by our relatives, the threats, the moves, the attempts on my brother's life—I knew whatever was going on in Kabul wasn't good. Yet I had no idea what it was and I could do nothing about it. I felt helpless, like I'd deserted them when they needed me most.

The next day, a few of the American students noticed something was off with me, and Major Korry asked if I wanted to talk. I told him some of what was going on, mainly about the call with my mother, and shared with him how much I missed my family and that I feared for their safety. He acknowledged everything I was going through and said he could only imagine how difficult it was for me, but he also encouraged me to keep on with the training. We were only two weeks away from graduation. I'd come this far, and he knew my family would want me to finish what I started. Otherwise, all of this would have been for nothing.

Major Korry was right, and I did my best to remain focused, but I also explored other ways to find out what was happening with my family. I contacted my friend Margherita Stancati to see if she knew anything. She had since left Afghanistan, but she reached out to her friend Kimberley Motley, a renowned international human rights attorney who had been working in Kabul for over ten years, focused on domestic violence. I'd met Kimberley once at Margherita's house in Kabul. She was a very kind person, and she said she would try to check on my family for me before she flew back to the United States.

My last training flight was on a beautiful sunny day in December. Everything went well, and I felt truly at ease up in the air. These days, flying was the only thing that brought me joy and peace of mind. There was no time to dwell on anything else. I just flew, and it was wonderful.

But after I landed, finished the debriefing, and went back to my room, I saw a missed call from my father. I immediately called him back. I was so glad to hear his voice, but I could tell something was terribly wrong. He tried to sound cheerful, but I pressed him until he finally told me. Since I'd been gone, the family had moved three times. In their previous apartment, four men had tracked them down and attacked the house, breaking windows and doors and fighting with my brother and father. Luckily, the police showed up before anyone got killed.

He said there was nowhere else for them to go, and he didn't know what else to do. He had decided to move the family to Pakistan, which was where he was calling from. They'd left Kabul a week ago and were already across the border.

The news shocked me. I'd had my suspicions, but I had no idea how bad the situation had gotten since I'd left. My family was on the run again, maybe a step above refugee status.

Then another realization struck me. Once I finished training on the C-130, I would go back to Kabul. But unlike in the States, where anyone can rent an apartment and make a fresh start, a woman is unable to do that in Afghanistan. I couldn't simply use a realtor to find an apartment with vaulted ceilings and a nice view of the park. I wasn't married either, so I would need to stay with a male relative. But with my family gone and my extended family wanting nothing to do with me, I had nowhere to go. I couldn't stay on the base, because it was also risky.

I'd never be able to find a place to live and keep my identity hidden.

Tears streamed down my cheeks, and I asked my Baba Jan what I should do. "Where could I go? Where could I live?" I had no answers and feared there were none. Then my father said something I never thought I'd hear him say. With a very sobering tone, my father said I should not return to Afghanistan. If I came back, I'd be killed within days, if not hours. I had to stay in the United States and request political asylum.

I was speechless.

41

ASYLUM

BY GRADUATION TIME in mid-December 2016, I still hadn't decided what I was going to do. My father's words had rattled me. Never once had he suggested I stay away, which made me realize just how bad things were back home.

Whereas in the past he may have found a way to care for us and keep us together, it was clear that now he must have feared for our safety as he had twenty-five years ago when he packed up the family in the dead of night to flee to Pakistan. The difference now was by circumstance; I was already safe. If I returned to Afghanistan or tried to find them in Pakistan, I would only put them at more risk.

My choice was clear, but it pained me. I reached out to Kimberley Motley, who by then had arrived in North Carolina. I asked her about political asylum and what it meant. I knew generally what it consisted of, but I needed to know the extent of the potential consequences.

Among many things, I would essentially be giving up my ability to leave the United States throughout the duration of the asylum process, which could take years. And if I chose to seek American citizenship, it would be even longer before I could leave. This meant

I would have no chance to see my family in the foreseeable future, unless by some miracle they traveled to see me.

This was so hard for me to fathom. I'd been away from my family for long periods before, but it'd always been a given I would return to them. Now, I could potentially make a decision that would keep me away from them for years, perhaps forever.

I also had to consider my status as a captain and pilot in the Afghan Air Force. By seeking asylum in the United States, I would have to effectively resign my commission and put myself in a position where I would no longer be flying—stepping away from my career in aviation. After so many years of fighting to earn and maintain my status as a pilot, that very struggle was now the reason I might have to walk away.

This aspect of my decision, which some might construe as selfish, was, in fact, quite demoralizing. My childhood dream of flying, which I'd overcome so much to achieve and for which others had also sacrificed beyond their due, would be over. Everything I'd worked for, everything I'd done in the hopes of blazing a path for other young women, would vanish. Rather than continuing to fight and be an example for others, proving women were as capable as men and we could stand up to their bigotry—I'd be giving up.

This crushed my soul.

I graduated training as a certified C-130 pilot in December 2016, one of the few Afghans to have achieved this certification, and the only Afghan woman to have done so. The following day, rather than getting on a plane to return to Afghanistan and resume my duties in the air force, I waited for Kimberley Motley. She was driving from North Carolina to Arkansas to pick me up and take me to Washington, DC.

I filed for political asylum in late December, citing persecution for race, religion, nationality, and political opinion, and fear of torture. My interview was scheduled for January 4, 2017. Kimberley offered to be my lawyer, and she accompanied me to the interview.

I'd been to Washington, DC, before on my trip for the International Women of Courage Award, but that had been a time of celebration and recognition. This time felt different, and the nation's capital that had been so beautiful and inspiring during my previous trip now intimidated me. Without my uniform, I struggled with my identity, and I had no idea what the future held.

I thanked God for Kimberley; she stayed by my side. We rode in the taxi together to the US Citizenship and Immigration Services office on Massachusetts Avenue, and she sat beside me in the waiting room as I waited for them to call my name. At one point, she leaned over and whispered everything would be fine; she'd been through this process before, and she'd be beside me every step of the way.

Finally, a man in a dark suit, white shirt, and blue tie emerged from the back and called my name. I followed him into a small, windowless room, with a framed print of the Jefferson Memorial hanging on the wall. My interview officer asked me to raise my right hand and swear to tell the truth, the whole truth, and nothing but the truth. Sworn in, I told him my story and requested political asylum in the United States.

―――――――――――

Within a few days, the news broke that I had not returned to Afghanistan and had requested asylum in the United States. CNN, Fox News, the *Wall Street Journal*, the *New York Times*, the *Guardian*, the *Independent*, Al Jazeera, and numerous other international media outlets covered my story. The headlines seized on the drama: *Afghanistan's first female pilot seeks asylum, flees her homeland for her safety,*

threatened by her own government, Afghan government responds, she
quit and she lied, she gave up . . .

I was taken aback at how widespread the coverage of my story was. Some articles portrayed me as a victim, forced to leave my country and abandoned by the government and military I'd chosen to serve. Others took a human-interest angle, discussing how I'd been separated from my family, who had since gone into hiding. And other articles drew connections to the broader US effort in Afghanistan, questioning the success of the advisor mission and whether the US and NATO were having a real impact.

And there were also reactions out of Kabul, including from the government and air force. They smeared me, told lies about me, and said I was a traitor, and some were quoted as saying if I ever returned to Afghanistan I would be tortured and killed.

The following months proved overwhelming for me. Initially, I stayed with Kimberley and her family in North Carolina. I had nowhere to go and no family to help me, so I was extremely grateful for her hospitality. But I couldn't live with them forever. A decision about my asylum case could take over a year, maybe longer, and I couldn't stay idle in Kimberley's guest bedroom for too long.

Although I had many friends across the US military, nearly all of them were deployed overseas or at locations where I couldn't travel. I identified Tampa, Florida, as the place where I knew the most people and where I thought I might have the best chance of getting on my feet.

I reconnected with some of my contacts at CAE, and one of my friends from there offered me a room in her home with her family, to stay in for as long as I needed. This couple, Karen and Dennis, treated me like a daughter, going out of their way to make me comfortable and see to it I had everything I needed. And, just as important, they cared for me and listened to me as I wrestled with the immense upheaval, sadness, and fear racking my life.

I became active in the local and international community. I knew I wouldn't be flying a C-130 again anytime soon, but being a pilot was part of my core. I joined the Ninety-Nines, an international organization for woman pilots cofounded by Amelia Earhart in 1929. The organization promotes the advancement of women in aviation through education, scholarships, and mutual support. I also began speaking about my experiences at air shows and other aviation events, encouraging both men and women to become pilots.

I settled into the normal pattern of life in America as best I could, going to restaurants, making friends, exercising, watching TV, going to the beach, and attending barbecues.

I must say, it really is wonderful to live in the United States. I miss my homeland terribly, but to wake up every morning free from fear and violence, and to be able to travel around and do as I please, is truly amazing. I am genuinely thankful to be here.

———————

On April 19, 2019, CNN anchor Jake Tapper broke the news that I'd been granted asylum in the United States. Oddly, I hadn't been notified yet and had no idea my case was nearing the end. I immediately called Kimberley to see if the news was true, and she confirmed it.

The nagging fear that had been festering at the back of my mind about whether I'd be allowed to remain in the United States suddenly vanished. I could stay, and I was safe. I was only twenty-eight years old and had already lived a full life, but I was still young and believed there was much more to do. Now I could get on with it.

42

WHAT'S NEXT

S INCE BEING GRANTED ASYLUM, I have applied for US citizenship. America has graciously given me a new life, and I now consider it my home and my country. I will always love Afghanistan—it is and will remain my homeland—but I want to be an American and give back to the country that's done so much for me, my family, and my people.

Some said I quit when I resigned my commission and sought asylum in the United States, but they are wrong—dead wrong. I chose the only path I could. I have a long life ahead of me. My time as a pilot in Afghanistan was merely the first chapter.

In July 2020 I received an email from a friend, Leon Butler, who had been one of the administrators during my C-130 training. After I was granted asylum, he had reached out on my behalf to various flight schools so I could earn my commercial pilot license. His email said a school in Fort Myers, Florida, had offered me a full scholarship and an opportunity to teach at the school upon graduation. I will be forever grateful to Leon for getting me back in the air.

When I eventually become a US citizen, I intend to join the US Air Force to serve in any capacity I can. I would of course love to fly as a military officer again, but I will do what is necessary and wear the uniform with pride and honor, as I believe service to one's country is one of the highest callings in life.

Alas, where I don't feel relief is with my family. While my asylum case was pending, I spoke on the phone with them as often as I could, but the connection wasn't always reliable. Also, they didn't have the money or the time to keep making international calls.

For reasons I will not go into here, my older sister, Afsoon, came to the United States in July 2017. She also applied for asylum, and came to live with me in Tampa. Fortunately, she has been able to move a bit beyond the tragedy of her marriage and the loss of custody of her child. She's getting on with her life, and having her with me has been very uplifting. No words can express how wonderful it is to be together with her again. We're as close now as we were twenty years ago when we were children playing on playgrounds, cooking with our mother, and hiking with our father.

I have yet to see my father and mother, my brother, or my other sisters. It's been five years. For their own safety, I will not identify where they are in the world, except to say they remained in the region and are trying to live day to day in peace. The threats have calmed down, and my brother has a family of his own and works for an IT company. My father is once again working as an engineer and doing what he loves. My mother is healthy, and my younger sisters are about to finish school themselves. But I fear they will always live with the reality that someone could come after them.

Unless my family leaves the region entirely, I suspect this fear will always be with me. I pray for them every day and constantly worry about them. They made me who I am, and I will always be thankful for their support and encouragement.

I am very lucky. I also worked hard and followed my dreams. I didn't let anyone tell me I couldn't do it. I became Afghanistan's first female fixed-wing pilot—and this is who I am.

AFTERWORD

———

AFGHANISTAN'S FUTURE IS STILL UNCERTAIN, and eventually the United States and NATO will pull out. When that happens, it's almost certain the oppressions of the past will creep back into Afghan society. Other countries in the region are contending with similar situations, with governments and societies preventing girls from attending school, pursuing careers, being free from fear and sexual violence, and leading independent lives. And it's not just women—there are countless minority and disenfranchised groups facing discrimination and persecution.

This can't continue. If you come from one of these places—or anywhere, for that matter—you must fight for your freedoms and you must follow your dreams. Dreams are important. In many ways, they are what we live for. My dreams took me up into the sky, which is where I know I belong. Your dreams may be similar, or they may be totally different. It doesn't matter how big or small they are; you must follow them.

You will face adversity. It could be similar to what I experienced, with unequal laws that block you from doing what you want to do, cultural stigmas attached to behavior that others consider unacceptable, or violence perpetrated by barbaric and evil groups. Adversity could also be benign and passive, and may come from those claiming to be on your side, trying to urge or shame you into doing or not doing things. But I encourage you not to be afraid and not to back down. Work to change the laws, change the perceptions, and change your society. Stand up for what you feel is right and just.

When you pursue your dreams, you will also doubt yourself at times. You may think you're not smart enough, strong enough, brave enough, or worthy. This is normal. I felt these things as a young girl, during training, and even after I was a full-fledged pilot. But you need to stick with it. You can't quit. And when you make mistakes or fail, you must get back up and try again and keep working at it. Nothing of real value comes easily, and we all must believe in ourselves. And when your confidence falters, don't be afraid to lean on those who support and love you. They will stand with you.

Last, you will likely question whether it's worth it. I did on many occasions. I knew that my choices brought immense hardship and suffering to my family, and the weight on me was suffocating at times. I still feel guilty, knowing that my family remains at risk. This choice—deciding whether it's worth it—is probably one of the hardest you will encounter. I know it was for me. I personally could suffer and struggle, but when my actions affected the ones I held most dear, those I loved with all my heart, I seriously questioned what I was doing. You will need to contend with this in your own way; nevertheless, I implore you to see the bigger picture. Although my family endured much strife, they knew it was for a greater cause and they supported me. I was fortunate, and I hope you are too.

For all of you out there, change will come only if you choose to bring it about. You need to follow your calling in life, so others around you and who come after you can follow theirs.

We have so much to do—follow your dreams.

ACKNOWLEDGMENTS

M Y DREAM TO FLY AND THE REALIZATION of this book would not have been possible without the immense sacrifices my family made. My father, Abdolwakil; mother, Tahera; brother, Mohammad Omar; and three sisters, Afsoon, Maryam, and Manizha, never wavered in their support, and I will be forever grateful. I am thankful for my grandmother, Zakhira Ahmadi, and uncle Mirwais Ahmadi, as well.

I would also like to thank my flight instructors who taught me to soar, especially Jarrod "JROD" Christopher Hollander, Larry "Morris" Bostrom, Gerard "Skid" Rowe, and James Davey. I am indebted to Molly Montgomery with the US State Department; my lawyer, Kimberley Motley; Margherita Stancati with the *Wall Street Journal*; and Majors Lindsey Bauer and Jessica Colby of the USAF, who supported and stood by me in the toughest of times. I am appreciative of Leon Butler, and of Chris and Sara Schoensee and Jeffery Wolf of the Paragon Flight Training school for getting me back up in the air. And last, I would like to thank my editor Jerome Pohlen and the team at Chicago Review Press, as well as my agents, Judy Coppage and Sam Dorrance, who believed this story had to be told and guided me every step of the way.

31901067644940